GLOCK

CROWN PUBLISHERS / NEW YORK

THE RISE OF AMERICA'S GUN

CK

Paul M. Barrett

Library of Congress Cataloging-in-Publication Data
Barrett, Paul (Paul M.)
Glock : the rise of America's gun / Paul M. Barrett.—1st ed.
p. cm.
Includes bibliographical references.
1. Glock Gesellschaft—History. 2. Glock pistols—Hisotry. 3. Firearms
and crime—United States—History. 4. Firearms—United States—
Use in crime prevention—History. I. Title.
HD9744.P584G563 2012
338.7'683432509436—dc23   2011024141

ISBN 978-0-307-71993-5
eISBN 978-0-307-71994-2

PRINTED IN THE UNITED STATES OF AMERICA

Illustration by John Burgoyne
Jacket design by Whitney G. Cookman
Jacket photography © Mike Kemp/Rubberball/Getty Images

5   7   9   10   8   6

For Julie

Gaston Glock

Contents

GLOCK

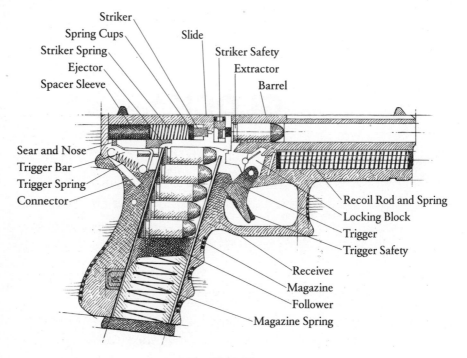

Striker

Spring Cups

Striker Spring

Ejector

Spacer Sleeve

Slide

Striker Safety

Extractor

Barrel

Sear and Nose

Trigger Bar

Trigger Spring

Connector

Recoil Rod and Spring

Locking Block

Trigger

Trigger Safety

Receiver

Magazine

Follower

Magazine Spring

The Glock 23

CHAPTER I

Shootout in Miami

It was nine forty-five a.m. on April 11, 1986, when Special Agents Benjamin Grogan and Gerald Dove spotted the two suspects driving a stolen black Chevrolet Monte Carlo on South Dixie Highway. The pair had been robbing banks and armored trucks in southern Dade County over the past four months. To catch them, Gordon McNeill, a supervisory special agent with the Miami field office of the Federal Bureau of Investigation, had set up a rolling stakeout. "They had killed two people; another woman was missing," McNeill said. "They had shot another guy four times. In my twenty-one years with the agency, I never felt more sure that when we found these guys, they would go down hard."

Moments later, other FBI units converged; soon, three unmarked sedans trailed the bank robbers. McNeill, closing from the opposite direction, spotted the black Monte Carlo at the head of the strange convoy. In the passenger seat, one suspect shoved a twenty-round magazine into a Ruger Mini-14 semi-automatic rifle. "Felony car stop!" McNeill shouted into his radio to the other units. "Let's do it!"

FBI vehicles corralled the Monte Carlo, ramming the fugitive automobile and forcing it into a large driveway. The three remaining government sedans skidded into surrounding positions. Two more FBI cars arrived across the street. In all, eight agents faced the two suspects.

Suddenly, one of the fugitives started shooting. FBI men scrambled for cover and returned fire. The occupants of the Monte Carlo seemed to be hit in the fusillade, but the government rounds weren't stopping them.

In the chaos, the federal agents struggled to reload their revolvers, jamming cartridges one after another into five- and six-shot Smith & Wessons. Three of the FBI agents were members of a special-tactics squad and carried fifteen-round S&W pistols. But none of the handgun fire seemed to slow the criminals. The gunman with the Ruger Mini-14 merely had to snap a new magazine into his rifle to have another twenty rounds instantly. One of his mags had forty rounds. His partner had a twelve-gauge shotgun with extended eight-round capacity. The bank robbers were armed for a small war.

Agent McNeill took a round in his right hand, shattering bone. Shredded flesh jammed the cylinder of his revolver, making it impossible to reload. He rose from a crouch to reach for a shotgun on the backseat of an FBI vehicle. As he did, a .223 rifle round pierced his neck. He fell, paralyzed. A fellow agent was severely wounded when he paused to reload his Smith & Wesson Chief's Special. "Everybody went down fighting," McNeill said. "We just ran into two kamikazes."

As law enforcement officials would later discover, the bank robbers, Michael Platt and William Matix, were no ordinary thugs. They had met in the 1970s at Fort Campbell, Kentucky. Matix served as a military policeman with the 101st Airborne. Platt received Special Forces training. Both were practiced marksmen. They operated a landscaping business and according to neighbors seemed like hardworking individuals. Neither one had a criminal record. But something had turned them into psychopaths.

Platt, demonstrating his deadly close-combat skills, worked the shoulder-fired Mini-14 with precision. Based on the M14 military rifle, the Mini-14 was popular with small-game hunters, target shooters, and, ironically, the police. Platt took full advantage of the semiautomatic weapon's large magazine and penetrating ammunition. Bobbing and weaving, he sneaked up on Grogan and Dove, the agents who had originally spotted the black Monte Carlo. "He's coming behind you!" another agent screamed. But the warning came too late. Platt fatally shot Grogan in the torso and Dove in the head.

The firefight had been going on for four minutes when Agent Edmundo Mireles, badly wounded, staggered toward Platt and Matix, who had piled into a bullet-ridden FBI Buick. A civilian witness described Mireles's stiff-legged gait as "stone walking." Holding a Smith & Wesson .357 Magnum at arm's length, he fired repeatedly at the two gunmen at point-blank range, killing them both. It was the bloodiest day in FBI history.

All told, the combatants fired 140 rounds. In addition to the deaths of Platt and Matix, two FBI agents were killed, three were permanently crippled, and two others were injured. GUN BATTLE "LOOKED LIKE OK CORRAL," the *Palm Beach Post* declared the next morning, quoting a shaken witness. But the legendary gunfight in 1881 in Tombstone, Arizona, had lasted only thirty seconds and involved just thirty shots, leaving three dead—one fewer than the modern-day battle in Miami.

/ / /

Lieutenant John H. Rutherford, the firing-range director with the Jacksonville Sheriff's Office, heard about the shootout later that day. "The bad guys," he recalled, "were starting to carry high-capacity weapons, unlike what they had carried in the past. . . . That was a scary, terrible thing to hear about," he said. "If the FBI is outgunned, something is wrong."

Scholars of law enforcement and small arms pored over the forensic records of the Miami Shootout, generating thousands of pages of reports. Police departments across the country held seminars on the gun battle. Gun magazines published dramatic reconstructions. NBC broadcast a made-for-TV movie called *In the Line of Fire: The FBI Murders.*

Later examination would reveal that, for all their bravery, the FBI agents prepared poorly for the violent encounter. At the time, though, and ever since, one idea about the significance of Miami eclipsed all others. The lawmen had been, in Lieutenant Rutherford's word, "outgunned." It was a perception widely shared by cops, politicians, and law-abiding firearm owners: The criminals were better armed than the forces of order. Nationwide, crime rates were rising. Drug gangs ruled inner-city neighborhoods. Guns had replaced knives in the hands of violent teenagers. The police, the FBI, and all who protected the peace were increasingly seen as being at a lethal disadvantage. The FBI helped shape this perception by emphasizing the seven revolvers its agents had used, deflecting attention from the three fifteen-round pistols and two twelve-gauge shotguns they also brought to the fight.

"Although the revolver served the FBI well for several decades, it became quite evident that major changes were critical to the well-being of our agents and American citizens," FBI Director William Sessions said in an agency bulletin after Miami. Revolvers held too little ammunition, and they were too difficult to reload in the heat of a gunfight. There were questions about their "stopping power": In Miami, the FBI fired some seventy rounds, and Platt and Matix received a total of eighteen bullet wounds. Yet the killers stayed alive long enough to inflict a terrible toll

In 1987, Jacksonville's Lieutenant Rutherford received the formal assignment to recommend a new handgun to replace the Smith & Wesson revolvers that his department issued. His counterparts in hundreds of local, state, and federal police agencies were given similar missions. "My job," Rutherford told me, "was to find a better gun."

CHAPTER 2

"Pistol of the Future"

After thirty years in manufacturing, Gaston Glock's industriousness had yielded a respectable social station and a comfortable life, without elevating him to the higher ranks of Austrian commerce. Still, he dreamed big.

Glock, the son of an Austrian railroad worker, managed an inconspicuous car radiator factory outside Vienna. In the garage next to his house in suburban Deutsch-Wagram, not far from the radiator plant, he operated a side business with his wife, Helga. Using a secondhand metal press made in Russia, they produced a modest volume of brass fittings for doors and windows. The garage metal shop expanded over time to make steel blades the durability and reasonable price of which so impressed Austria's Ministry of Defense that Glock obtained a contract to supply field knives and bayonets to the Austrian Army. The military work led to contacts at the ministry, where Glock became an occasional visitor, his eyes and ears open for new opportunity.

One day in February 1980, he overheard a hallway conversation between two colonels that jolted his imagination: The Army needed a new sidearm for officers, pilots, and drivers, to replace the antiquated World War II Walther P-38. Steyr, an Austrian arms maker since the mid-1800s, had offered to sell the military a modern pistol, but the gun fell short of the ministry's stringent specifications. Top generals were running out of patience.

Glock interrupted. Would it still be possible, he asked the officers, for another company—his company—to bid on the pistol contract?

The colonels laughed. In his garage, Gaston Glock made hinges, curtain rods, and knives. Now he thought he could design a handgun?

Reserved in manner, Glock, fifty, wasn't known for his sense of humor. He was a slender man of average height, with a receding hairline, sloping shoulders, and long arms. A recreational swimmer, he had a sinewy physique and unprepossessing looks. He spoke only as much as was necessary and dressed conservatively, a sweater beneath his dark suit coat. Glock had graduated from a technical institute and received training in mechanical engineering. He worked his way up in manufacturing from an entry-level position with a company that made hand drills. Designing firearms was something far beyond his experience.

Glock asked the colonels to describe the Army's requirements for a new handgun, which they did. "Mr. Glock, in his credulousness, said it shouldn't be difficult to make such an item," according to an official company account published years later. "To him, the handgun was simply another accoutrement that attached to a soldier's belt, similar to the knife he already produced." Or, as Gaston Glock himself put it in an interview: "That I knew nothing was my advantage."

Out of prudence and decorum, he sought an audience with the minister of defense. "I asked him if I was allowed to make a pistol for the Army," Glock recounted.

"He said, 'Yes, why not?'" The minister wanted Glock to

understand something, though: "'I'm not responsible for your costs, for your money. It's your problem.'"

"I said, 'OK.'"

Asked years later about his familiarity with weapons in 1980, he admitted it was slight: "I had very little training. I was just a few days in camps of the German Army" during the latter stages of World War II, he said during a deposition in November 1993 in a lawsuit in the United States. Born in 1929 in Vienna, Glock was conscripted by the Wehrmacht as a teenager. "I was very young in those days: 15, 16 years, but we had to undergo some sort of military training," he said. This instruction took place in "1944 and 1945," he explained with a notable lack of precision. How long had he served? "Only two, three days. That is all."

On other occasions, Glock tried even more strenuously to minimize his involvement with the German military, saying his training lasted for a single day, during which he feigned illness and was sent home. His attempt to play down his connection to the Wehrmacht seems unsurprising, if hardly admirable. Many Austrians of his generation, and the one that preceded it, did the same thing. More relevant to Glock's role as an arms designer was his assertion that his firearms background was exceedingly limited. "I saw rifle, pistol, hand grenade" in the German military, he said. "I was getting acquainted, when you pull a trigger that it makes boom."

As an adult, he didn't own guns. Soon after his fateful visit to the Defense Ministry in early 1980, he bought an Italian Beretta 92F, a Sig Sauer 220 from Switzerland, a Czech CZ 75, and a modern version of the German Walther P-38. All of these weapons were chambered for nine-millimeter ammunition, the standard in Europe.

He used the P-38 as his starting point. Developed in the 1920s to replace a World War I–era Luger design, the Walther was adopted by the German Army in 1938 and used by the Wehrmacht throughout World War II. Captured Walther pistols became prized trophies among Allied troops, who took them home in large numbers.

Glock brought the P-38 and other models to his home workshop in Deutsch-Wagram. He disassembled the guns, put them back together, and noted the contrasting methods used to make them. "I started intensive studies in such a manner that I visited the [Austrian] patent office for weeks," examining generations of handgun innovation, Glock recalled. "I bought and tested all modern pistols available at that time, and I tried to involve into conversation the best experts that I knew."

Gaston and Helga Glock owned a vacation home in Velden, a resort on a lake in southern Austria. One weekend in May 1980, Gaston invited several firearm specialists to join him there. Among those who attended were Colonel Friederich Dechant, a champion shooter who oversaw weapons procurement for the Austrian Army, and Siegfried Hubner, the author of technical books such as *Silencers for Hand Firearms.* Hubner had done research at the famous German gun manufacturers Mauser and Heckler & Koch.

"OK, gentlemen, now it is time to show me," Glock told his guests. "What would you want in a pistol of the future?"

/ / /

The discussion at Velden focused on pistols, rather than revolvers, and it is important to draw the distinction. Dating to the nineteenth-century marketing genius of Samuel Colt and the

mythology that came to surround his Peacemaker revolver—
"the gun that won the West"—Americans historically regarded revolvers with great affection. The Germans, the
Austrians, and the Swiss inclined toward the nine-millimeter
pistol designs of German arms designer Georg Luger. The
inner workings of the two types of handguns are quite different. A revolver, or "wheel gun," has a cylinder that typically
holds five or six rounds of ammunition. Pulling the trigger of a
double-action revolver turns the cylinder, cocks the hammer,
and then causes the gun to fire. In a pistol, also referred to as
a semiautomatic, ammunition is stored in a spring-loaded rectangular box, or magazine, which is inserted into the weapon's
grip. Spring pressure pushes rounds up from the magazine
into the chamber. Each time a pistol is fired, the spent shell is
ejected from the chamber and a new round moves up. Pistols
are more complicated mechanically, meaning that some models are susceptible to malfunction. On the other hand, their
larger ammunition capacity makes them more potent in a gunfight. Reloading a pistol with a fresh magazine is easier than
swiveling a revolver's cylinder outside of the frame and insert-
ing cartridges into the chambers.

Americans and Europeans traditionally also differ on ammunition. According to American custom, bullets—and the
weapons that fire them—are designated by diameter as measured in fractions of an inch (.38-caliber, .45-caliber, and the
like). European ammunition and firearms have been labeled
according to the metric system. A nine-millimeter round is
roughly the same diameter as its .38-caliber counterpart; a ten-
millimeter corresponds to a .40-caliber. In modern times, the
geographic differences in terminology have largely dissolved.

At the gathering in Velden, Colonel Dechant told Glock
that the Army desired a high-capacity pistol that held more

nine-millimeter rounds than the eight that the P-38 could accommodate, and weighed no more than eight hundred grams (twenty-eight ounces). The weapon should have a consistent and light trigger pull for fast, accurate firing. It should be streamlined and easy to holster. Dechant and Hubner recommended a frame width of no more than thirty millimeters (1.2 inches). Crucially, they said, the gun should have no more than forty parts—far fewer than the industry standard.

Glock asked his guests about grip-to-frame angle. He had nailed together two pieces of wood as a rough model. The experts experimented, pointing the model with their eyes open and closed. The consensus was that an ideal handgun should point "instinctively," so that an injured user could fire even if he couldn't see the gun's sights. The experts settled on an angle of twenty-two degrees, which Glock later reduced slightly.

Colonel Dechant admonished Glock that his pistol should be able to withstand extended contact with snow, ice, and mud. It should fire ten thousand rounds with no more than one failure per thousand. The figure 40,000 was recorded that evening, referring to the goal that the ideal pistol should have a long service life, of forty thousand rounds.

There was much discussion about safety. The P-38 and most other pistols had external levers that when engaged prevented the weapon from firing. Some soldiers and police officers carried their pistols "cocked and locked," meaning that the guns were ready to fire immediately upon disengagement of the safety. The problem with this common feature, Dechant said, was that an alarming number of soldiers and cops forgot whether their safeties were on or off. That led to confusion and accidental discharges.

"Those experts which I had consulted at the beginning of the development are people that had access to all the accident statistics, domestic and foreign statistics, which had examined how accidents happen and why they happen when a human being is in a stress situation and still able to operate or not operate a pistol," Glock recalled years later. "The experts said every [safety] lever is a potential source of mishandling or misoperation during the use of the pistol."

This counterintuitive insight—that safety devices can become hazards—rang true to Glock. He had carried the Walther P-38 in his pants pocket for two weeks. He discovered that he often couldn't remember whether he had the safety engaged. "If this level of doubt existed, manual safeties were indeed a hindrance to the quick operation of a handgun," the Glock company history noted.

At the evening's end, Glock had his guests sign and date one of the sheets of paper that memorialized their thoughts. He treated the occasion as if it would be remembered by history. At the time, Glock did not pay his guests for their ideas. After he retired from the Army as a major general, Dechant went to work for Glock in a salaried position.

Armed with expert insights, Glock began work on a prototype. He hired experienced technicians who labored long hours with him to implement the Army's demands. In the evenings, after dinner, he tested crude early versions in a basement firing range he built specially for this purpose. He shot alone, using only his left hand. If the gun blew up on him, he would still have his good right hand to do mechanical drawings.

"I learned to stay out of his way," said Glock's wife, Helga.

Some days, Glock attended police academy classes or took private shooting lessons. "My intention," he recalled, "was to learn as much as possible about general use of the pistol, not only combat situations, but also for police use and military use and all the aspects of pistol use."

Meanwhile, he and Helga continued running the second-hand metal press in the garage. They employed just a couple of laborers. Each morning, before he left for the radiator plant, Gaston set the controls of the ungainly Russian contraption: a coil of brass or steel fed into the stamping machine, depending on whether the Glocks were making door hinges or bayonets that day. When he came home for lunch, Gaston Glock would make any necessary adjustments. An employee loaded bins of product into a van, which Helga then drove to another shop for finishing. Mrs. Glock also had primary responsibility for raising their three children: Brigitte, a strong-willed firstborn; Gaston Jr., her introverted brother; and Robert, the doted-upon baby.

Some accounts claim that Glock developed his gun in just six months, or perhaps even three. Glock himself said the process lasted a year—still a startlingly short period of time for a novice firearm designer to produce a prototype. He filed for an Austrian patent on April 30, 1981. It was his seventeenth invention, so he called his gun the Glock 17. Coincidentally, his creation could store an impressive seventeen rounds in its magazine, with an eighteenth in the chamber, if the user so desired.

After another year of testing and improvement, Glock submitted four samples of the pistol to the Austrian Army on May 19, 1982. "I remember [the date], because I worked two years, day and night, to bring the sample to the Army on time," he said more than a decade later.

Two overarching concepts would set the Glock 17 apart. First, it was to be made largely out of light, resilient, injection-molded plastic, and second, it was designed without a preexisting factory.

By the 1980s, industrial plastic, often called polymer, was

remarkably strong and resistant to corrosion, a major problem with traditional steel guns. Glock had begun learning about the material when he bought an injection molding machine to make handles and sheaths for the military knives he produced in his garage. He had the wisdom and good luck to hire former employees of a bankrupt camera manufacturer who brought advanced injection-molding and plastic-design skills. One of these men, Reinhold Hirschheiter, continued for decades as Glock's right-hand man for production.

By fashioning the frame of his pistol from polymer, Glock foresaw savings on raw material and labor, as well as a weapon that had distinct ergonomic advantages over one cobbled together from blued steel and walnut. Earlier guns made from polymer frames—the American Remington Nylon 66 rifle and the German Heckler & Koch VP70 pistol—had engineering or design shortcomings; they never caught on widely. Steyr produced a successful plastic-stock rifle for soldiers and police, the AUG. But in the late 1970s and early 1980s, the Austrian manufacturer was struggling to figure out how to apply the technology to pistols, opening the door for Gaston Glock.

Glock imagined a thoroughly modern pistol factory, dominated by computerized workstations, and he conceived his gun to be made in this as yet nonexistent plant. "The important thing that gave him the big price advantage was he designed the pistol for complete production on CNC [computer-controlled] tools," said Wolfgang Riedl, a former Steyr executive who later joined the Glock team as marketing director.

/ / /

The task fell to Lieutenant Ingo Wieser, an aide to Colonel Dechant, to compare Glock's submission to that of five other manufacturers. Wieser, a twenty-five-year-old career soldier, had an unusually intimate view of the birthing of the Glock. Without contradicting any of the central elements of the story as told by Gaston Glock, and repeated over the years by his admirers, Wieser adds useful political context and a dose of skepticism to the heroic portrait of Glock.

Today, Wieser operates a security-consulting firm in Vienna and serves as a leading forensic adviser to the country's court system. He has an encyclopedic knowledge of modern pistol technology. In 1979, before Gaston Glock's opportunistic eavesdropping in the halls of the Defense Ministry, Wieser had supervised tests on potential replacement pistols. These trials found that Beretta offered the most effective model. But Steyr, the long-established Austrian arms maker, which was controlled by the Socialist-dominated government, objected fiercely that a foreign manufacturer should not receive the contract. In response, the defense minister told the Army that if Steyr did not win the competition, then another Austrian company had to be found. Otherwise, the military could end up accused of insufficient patriotism in its procurement. But there wasn't a suitable alternative company in Austria that already knew how to make handguns. "Mr. Glock was at the right place at the right time," Wieser told me.

Gaston Glock, through his production of knives, ammunition belts, and other accessories for the Army, had earned a reputation as a dutiful contractor. He had also forged strong ties to Socialist party officials. Colonel Dechant concluded that with meticulous guidance, Glock could be used as a means to build an Austrian pistol to the military's specifications and to head off a messy confrontation with Steyr.

Dechant brought Hubner into the project because of his vast knowledge about European pistols. Glock's role was to amalgamate ideas from Dechant and Hubner and borrow the millions of shillings needed to fabricate and test prototypes. This was not a small or unimportant function, Wieser told me. But in his view, Glock was more of a general contractor than a genius inventor. "Without Dechant and Hubner," Wieser said, "Glock would still be making curtain rings."

/ / /

Wieser did not try to conceal his envy of Gaston Glock's subsequent fame and wealth. As the Army's top handgun tester in the early 1980s, Wieser made many suggestions to improve the Glock prototype, but he received no pecuniary reward. No one celebrates his contribution to a revolutionary weapon. "Mr. Glock conveniently forgot about me," he said.

His bitterness notwithstanding, Wieser emphasized that he conducted a fair and objective competition that pitted the Glock against weapons from Heckler & Koch, Sig Sauer, Beretta, Austria's Steyr, and Fabrique Nationale of Belgium. Only the Steyr GB pistol held more rounds in its magazine—eighteen—than the Glock's seventeen. The Heckler & Koch P9S and the Sig Sauer P-220 each held nine; the Beretta 92F, fifteen.

With its plastic frame, the Glock was by far the lightest model, at 661 grams (23 ounces). The mostly metal H&K weighed 928 grams (33 ounces). The Steyr was the heaviest at 1,100 grams (39 ounces). Glock produced the simplest handgun, with only thirty-four components. That compared to fifty-three for the Sig. The Beretta, with seventy parts, and the H&K, with seventy-seven, had more than twice as many as the Glock.

All of the guns had slides made from steel; only the Glock's was machined from a solid rolled-steel bar, with no welding or riveting. The slide is the long rectangular component that sits atop the frame. The firing of a pistol causes the slide to move rearward against a strong spring, ejecting the spent cartridge. When the force of the gun's recoil is expended, the compressed spring pushes the slide forward to its original position. On its way, the slide scoops up a new cartridge from the top of the magazine and loads the round into the chamber, ready to fire. Because of the unfussy way Gaston Glock fabricated his slide, his pistol required fewer steps to manufacture, and there were fewer opportunities for error.

The Glock 17 was put through a preliminary firing run of ten thousand rounds. The Army set twenty stoppages as grounds for disqualification. The Glock malfunctioned just once. It was fired after exposure to heat, ice, sand, and mud. It was dropped from a height of two meters onto a steel plate without accidental discharge or damage to the frame. The other guns had been put through similar paces.

In the end, a comparison chart prepared by the Army ranked the submitted guns. The Belgian FN was "not regarded as [a] considerable competitor." The next-worst finisher, the hapless Steyr, was described as having an "extraordinary rate of misfires; heats up." The H&K, Sig Sauer, and Beretta fared better. The first-place finisher was the Glock 17.

On November 5, 1982, Gaston Glock received formal congratulations from the minister of defense. "Your pistol achieved 88.7 percent of the possible maximum points," the letter said. Glock's proposed injection-molding technique enabled his pistols to be supplied at a substantial discount from the next most expensive competitor. In 1983, the Ministry of Defense ordered twenty thousand Glock 17s.

The firearm industry suddenly had an ambitious newcomer.

All Glock needed, Riedl noted, were a factory and a workforce. "He only had a big garage where he produced the knives."

/ / /

"How was it that Gaston Glock was able to get it right?" the American firearm authority Patrick Sweeney asked in *The Gun Digest Book of the Glock* (2008). It is a question that handgun aficionados have debated for decades. Sweeney offered as sensible an answer as any, and one consistent with Glock's. "He got it right," Sweeney wrote, "because he hadn't done it before. One of the largest problems in getting a new design accepted by an established manufacturer is not just the 'not invented here' syndrome, but also the 'we don't have the tooling' syndrome. Why invent something new when you can simply modify what you have?"

Glock started with a blank sheet of paper. He listened to his military customers. He made adjustments they requested. As a result, he came up with something original—and, as it turned out, he did so at precisely the right moment.

Within just a few years, another market, far larger and richer than the Austrian defense sector, would be keen for "a pistol of the future." The Miami Shootout of 1986 helped foster this demand. American police officials wanted a new handgun, and Glock was there to offer a powerful alternative to the revolver. Across the United States, the preferences of local cops and county deputies have broad commercial consequences. The American civilian gun-buying population tends to gravitate toward what the professionals carry. For Glock, that translated into a bonanza. The Glock 17 gained profit-making momentum in the fashion of a classic American consumer fad—one that, rather than fade away, kept expanding year after year. Venerable rivals, chiefly Smith & Wesson, ignored Glock at first and then scoffed at him. Eventually, they began imitating the Austrian invader, flooding the market with knockoffs. The Americans, to this day, haven't caught up.

CHAPTER 3

"One Ugly and All-Business-Looking Piece of Self-Defense Hardware"

In the United States, guns are much more than a tool of law enforcement or an article of commerce. They are embedded in the country's history. By the time the Constitution was framed, a tradition of private firearm ownership was an aspect of daily life and American identity. Citizen-soldiers defeated the mighty British, beginning with the shot "heard round the world," fired by a Massachusetts farmer. The Second Amendment enshrined the principle of an armed populace. Folklore nurtured the gun tradition. "God may have created all men," according to a saying of the nineteenth-century West, "but Sam Colt made them equal."

To many Americans, over many generations, guns have represented freedom, individualism, and self-reliance. "No other country finds so much history, emotion, belief, vice, and virtue in so many guns," Henry Allen, an essayist, poet, and Pulitzer Prize–winning critic, has observed. Allen served as a Marine in Vietnam and shoots guns recreationally. "Snub-nose .38 revolvers," he continued, "stand for the world weary persistence of pulp-fiction detectives in the Depression. Single-action Army Colts are the attribute of the cowboy. A Parker double-barreled shotgun is your grandfather picking his way with a knowing elegance through the brush in search of quail. A .22 is the innocence of childhood—that spattering noise of the rifle range at Boy Scout camp, and afterward the smell of Hoppe's No. 9 cleaning solvent. The wood-sheathed M1 evinces the common-man determination that won World War II."

Guns have another, darker heritage in American life, of course, one related to disorder, crime, and murderous violence. Depression-era gangsters and 1960s urban bloodshed each led to legislation aimed at restricting gun sales and ownership. Cheap "Saturday Night Specials" flooded city streets in the 1970s and became emblems of steadily rising crime rates. In response, Clint Eastwood's Dirty Harry brandished his Smith & Wesson .44 Magnum.

The Glock, introduced in the 1980s, inherited all aspects of the American firearm heritage: It was seen as an instrument of law and security, but also menace, danger, and fear. It became the handgun of choice for cops and a favorite of some demented mass killers. Its black plastic-and-metal construction set it apart from everything else on the market, suggesting modernism and efficiency. The handgun is the weapon Americans really care about, and within a decade of arriving here, the Glock had become the ultimate American handgun.

/ / /

Hunters shoot deer with semiautomatic rifles, ducks with double-barreled shotguns. Aside from animal-rights activists, few people spend much time arguing about any of that. United States military involvement in Iraq and Afghanistan is controversial, but if American troops are going to be over there, who doesn't want them to have powerful machine guns? The firearm that plays in our fantasies and nightmares is the handgun.

The commonsense criminal uses a handgun because it is

concealable and disposable. The National Rifle Association's main cause is not the spreading of rifles; it is making sure that more people can legally carry handguns, ostensibly to protect themselves from armed thugs. Cops carry handguns too, because they are light and maneuverable.

Of the many makes on the US market, one stands apart: the Glock. Gun-control activists have denounced the Austrian pistol and tried to have it banned—attacks that only enhanced the Glock's glamour in the eyes of its fans. Today the Glock is on the hip of more American police officers than any other handgun. It is all over the television news and the Internet. When American soldiers hauled Saddam Hussein from his underground hideout in 2003, the deposed Iraqi ruler came to the surface with a Glock. New York Giants star wide receiver Plaxico Burress shot himself in the leg in 2009 with a Glock he had stuck in his waistband before heading to a Manhattan nightclub. Some of our most prolific psychopaths have favored the Glock, presumably because of its large ammunition capacity and lightning speed. Seung-Hui Cho, who murdered thirty-two people at Virginia Tech in 2007, used a Glock. So did Steven Kazmierczak when he shot twenty-one, killing five, at Northern Illinois University in 2008. Jared Loughner fired a Glock with a thirty-three-round magazine in his January 2011 attempt to assassinate Representative Gabrielle Giffords in Tucson, Arizona, an attack that resulted in six dead and thirteen injured, including Giffords, who survived after a nine-millimeter round passed entirely through her brain. The congresswoman herself, it turned out, owned a Glock.

Shapers of culture, low and high, have glommed on to the Austrian pistol. By the 1990s, no firearm brand turned up more often in the pugnacious lyrics and videos of hip-hop, the country's ascendant popular music. In their 1992 hit "Bitches

Ain't Shit," Dr. Dre and Snoop Dogg traded verses on women and romantic betrayal. "As we groove down the block / See my girl's house, Dre, pass the Glock," Snoop Dogg rapped. His girl turns out to be in the arms of another man, and the Glock becomes the means of Snoop's revenge.

On the big screen, Glocks turned up as early as 1990, in the hands of villains in the Bruce Willis action thriller *Die Hard 2*. Countless celluloid toughs followed suit. Think of all the snarling gangsters holding big, blunt pistols sideways, palm-down; most of those guns were Glocks, the ultimate badass weapon.

Referring to a Glock became a signal of cultural awareness. Aaron Sorkin, in his brilliant screenplay for *The Social Network*, the 2010 movie about the invention of Facebook, has one Harvard nerd verbally lash out at a classmate who publicly embarrassed them: "I'm gonna get a Glock 39, and I'm going to kill you."

Not "I'm gonna get a *gun*, and I'm going to kill you."

Say Glock to the mildest Quaker, and she will know you are talking about a tough handgun. Mention the brand to a firearm buff, and his eyes will light up. Glock is the Google of modern civilian handguns: the pioneer brand that defines its product category. Its boxy shape, black finish, and almost defiant lack of grace became the standard. The no-firearms symbol posted by the federal government at US airports incorporates the profile of—what else?—a Glock.

In the late-twentieth-century chapter of the long story of the gun in America, the Glock achieved the status of a literary character. Elmore Leonard, the crime novelist, gave the pistol a prominent role in *Freaky Deaky* (1988). Chris Mankowski, Leonard's suspended detective hero, confronts a hoodlum named Juicy Mouth: "Chris walked around to the front of the Cadillac. He raised the Glock in one hand and stood sideways—not the way Mel Gibson did it, two handed—Juicy looking right at him now, aimed at the fat top part of the seat next to the guy and began squeezing off shots." A few years later, in his epic satire *Infinite Jest,* David Foster Wallace imagined a deranged junior tennis star habitually carrying a Glock onto the court and threatening to kill himself if he loses: "Everybody watching the match agrees it is one ugly and all-business-looking piece of self-defense hardware."

How did it happen that in the most firearm-fixated country in the world, "Glock" came to *mean* "gun." How did a pistol produced by an obscure engineer in suburban Vienna, a man who spoke barely any English and had no familiarity with the American zeitgeist, become, in the space of a few years, an American icon? The answers reveal more than the history of one company or even the recent evolution of an entire industry. The progress of Herr Glock's gun illuminates the country's changing attitudes about law enforcement, self-sufficiency, and safety. It explains the strange, scary allure of the dull clicking sound the slide makes when a nine-millimeter communicates it is ready to fire the first round.

CHAPTER 4

"Plastic Perfection"

Karl Walter, gun-salesman-on-wheels, first learned about the Glock 17 from a report in the German weapons magazine *Deutsche Waffen Journal*. An Austrian transplanted to the United States, Walter had enjoyed precocious success selling specialized European firearms to American police departments and gun collectors. He closely followed industry developments back in Europe. When an unknown won a large contract to supply pistols to the Austrian Ministry of Defense, he was intrigued. How could this Gaston Glock have bested the old-line brands? Walter sniffed opportunity.

In the 1970s and early 1980s, Walter traveled the United States in a motor home customized as a rolling arsenal. He displayed his wares in locked, felt-lined showcases: Uzis, AK-47s, Steyr AUG bullpup assault rifles, you name it. Walter didn't sell ordinary firearms. He sold the heavy stuff—to police departments and retailers with special licenses allowing them to trade in fully automatic weapons. He drove a circuit from New England to the Middle Atlantic States, down to Miami, across to Dallas. For a certain breed of gun buyer, "it was a candy store," he recalled.

Undercover agents with the US Bureau of Alcohol, Tobacco and Firearms kept a wary eye on Walter. Occasionally, they tested him—would he sell a select-fire Uzi to a buyer who lacked the proper federal permit?

He refused the bait. But that did not save him from getting arrested once, in 1972, by the local police in Troy, New York. The Troy authorities accused the young man with the thick Austrian-German accent of illegally transporting weapons. Walter explained that he was a legitimate salesman just earning a living. The gun-trafficking charges were dropped—Walter, as usual, had all the necessary paperwork—but the police in Troy suggested that he make his way to the state border as swiftly as the speed limit permitted.

Walter first came to the United States in the mid-1960s as a high school exchange student. He enjoyed the sense of possibility in America. Back home in Austria, his father, a stern physician who served as a medical officer in the German Army during World War II, sent him to a parochial high school run by Benedictine monks. Frustrated by biblical Greek, young Karl switched to a public school but remained an indifferent student. He eventually obtained an engineering degree and, when he secured a US work visa, returned to the States in 1969 at the age of twenty-four. He got an entry-level engineering job in the auto industry in Detroit.

Some of his colleagues were target shooters, and Walter became interested in firearms as a hobby. "Guns have a mystique," he explained. "Young people are drawn to it. It's excitement. It's adventure. It's power." Before he became a US citizen, he couldn't legally own his own firearm (he borrowed from friends at the range), but in an odd twist of the law, he could mail $50 to Washington and get a federal firearm license allowing him to buy and sell guns as a business. Soon he was making more money moonlighting as a gun dealer than he was from his day job. He decided to get into firearms full-time.

His roots helped Walter develop a relationship with the Austrian manufacturer Steyr, whose rifles were popular with some American police departments. He established ties to the Belgian firm Fabrique Nationale and other European arms makers. Despite his success with Steyr's SSG sniper rifle and AUG assault weapon, Walter could not move a lot of the manufacturer's GB pistol, the same cumbersome model that the Austrian Ministry of Defense rejected as a replacement for the Walther P-38. "Steyr's handgun was far more complicated [than those of most rivals] and a pain in the ass to service," Walter told me.

Still, he saw a chance for gain in law enforcement handguns: "You know, I said, where there really is money to be made is to convert US police departments from revolvers to pistols." The nine-millimeter pistol had been standard in Europe since World War II. "I was astonished," Walter said, "that this modern country still hung around with revolvers, when the rest of the world had pistols, including the Soviet Union." To act on this idea, he needed a product better than the Steyr GB-80.

In spring 1984, Walter traveled on business in Germany and Austria with Peter G. Kokalis, a prominent American gun writer. Savvy small-arms marketers forge close ties to gun magazines (and now websites) in a symbiotic relationship that benefits all concerned. Kokalis, then the technical editor of *Soldier of Fortune*, could help Walter's clients by writing about their products. That burnished Walter's reputation as a middleman. *Soldier of Fortune*, meanwhile, sold advertisements to the gun and ammunition manufacturers.

Browsing at a Vienna gun shop, Walter and Kokalis came across a Glock 17. This was the pistol Walter had a notion of trying to sell in the United States. "Jeez, that's ugly" was his reflexive reaction. The squared-off plastic Glock lacked the steel frame and polished wooden grips of a classic American revolver. Its black matte finish seemed homely. "But still, I was extremely curious why the Austrian Army bought it," Walter told me. "There had to be more to it than what meets the eye initially."

He suggested to Kokalis that they pay a visit to the Glock homestead in Deutsch-Wagram, fifteen kilometers from central Vienna. Walter's Austrian-inflected German eased the telephone introduction, and a meeting was set.

Gaston Glock received the visitors from America with an awkward shyness. His English was slight. Walter was struck by how unsophisticated and provincial his host seemed. Glock smiled but even in German demonstrated little facility with small talk. Helga, his gracious wife, served coffee.

Walter explained that he represented Steyr in the United States. Perhaps he could do the same for Glock.

Glock responded tentatively. He had not given much thought to America.

Walter, trying to stimulate conversation, asked his host to explain the mechanics of his pistol. Suddenly Glock grew more animated. The gun maker took apart a Glock 17, showing how its parts were housed in stand-alone subgroups: easy to remove and replace, without the skill of a trained armorer. There was no safety or decocking lever to confuse the user. The Glock 17 couldn't fire if dropped or jarred, Glock said. Its "Safe Action" system required a user to depress a small device built right into the trigger—a "trigger safety."

Walter and Kokalis had never seen such a feature. They were impressed that the Glock 17 had so few components. Walter concluded after just twenty minutes that he could persuade American police departments to consider replacing their revolvers with the innovative Austrian pistol. "This is *kinder-spiel*," he thought, child's play.

"This pistol will sell," Walter told Glock. "But it must be sold." He meant, in a self-serving way, that the Glock 17 required a wizard marketer who could explain to the American law enforcement market and civilian retailers why a gun that looked so, well, strange deserved a chance.

Gaston Glock seemed intrigued but also overwhelmed. He knew little about the United States and its tastes in guns. He was still building his new single-story factory on a compound adjacent to his home. (He had persuaded the town of Deutsch-Wagram to sell him the land for practically nothing, based on the prospect of his creating jobs and generating taxes.) He had hired about three dozen workers, many of them Turkish immigrants, but he lacked a business plan beyond the contract with the Austrian Ministry of Defense.

The possibilities were extraordinary: The armies of Norway and Sweden had shown interest. The North Atlantic Treaty Organization was considering adopting the Glock 17 as an approved sidearm for member countries. Elite presidential guard units from Syria, Jordan, and the Philippines were inquiring, as were antiterrorist squads in Austria, Germany, and Canada. Yet Glock seemed uncertain how to proceed, especially with finance and marketing.

Walter had a suggestion: The entrepreneur should give Kokalis and *Soldier of Fortune* a scoop on publicizing the Glock 17 in the United States. Word of mouth would spread in gun circles. By the time Gaston Glock had expanded his manufacturing capacity, America would be hungry for the new pistol.

Yes, Glock said, the plan made perfect sense. In a celebratory mood, he invited his guests to try firing his creation on the range in the cellar.

Kokalis remained dubious. Five thousand miles was a long way to travel to shoot another nine-millimeter pistol. Then he lined up the Glock 17's front sight between the U-shaped rear sights, and he pulled the trigger.

///

PLASTIC PERFECTION, announced the headline in the October 1984 issue of *Soldier of Fortune*. The title alluded to Glock's assertive marketing slogan: "Glock Perfection," which came stamped on the company's products, along with a logo of Gaston Glock's design that highlighted an oversized sans serif "G." The Glock pistol, Kokalis wrote, "represents an entirely new era in small arms technology."

"In our pop culture," the article continued, "'plastic' has come to mean vacuous or devoid of substance. Yet plastic is a salient feature of the Glock design. Not only the frame, but the trigger and magazine as well are made of this material. The proof of the pudding, in this instance, is in the firing. And the Glock 17 does that quite well, thank you." With erudition and no small measure of zeal, Kokalis argued that the Glock's design set it apart from everything else on the market. It was lighter, thinner, and almost gentle to shoot: "The plastic frame's elastic qualities absorb a significant portion of the counter recoiling forces during firing."

Gaston Glock's "only condescension to conventionality," Kokalis observed, was the method of operation he adopted for his handgun. Glock borrowed his basic mechanics from John Moses Browning, the greatest gun designer of the late nineteenth and early twentieth centuries. Born in Ogden, Utah, in

1855, Browning was the son of a Mormon pioneer and gunsmith. The younger Browning developed legendary shotguns and rifles for the manufacturer Winchester. His semiautomatic pistols included the .45-caliber 1911 manufactured by Colt and used by the American military during the world wars and for decades afterward. Browning died in Belgium in 1926 while working on a smaller nine-millimeter model.

Under the Browning recoil-operated system, as interpreted by Gaston Glock, the barrel of the pistol is locked up in the slide by a single lug that recesses forward of the ejection port (through which spent cartridges are expelled). The barrel moves back slightly with the slide as the bullet leaves the barrel, and the gas pressure created by the explosion of the gunpowder drops back to a safe level. At that point, the barrel separates from the slide and drops downward. The slide continues to move back until the force of the recoil is expended. A spring then pushes the slide forward, and it grabs the next round from the top of the magazine on its return to battery.

Kokalis marveled at how the Glock's wide outer trigger couldn't be depressed unless the smaller trigger safety was pressed first. This arrangement should prevent accidental discharge by, for example, contact with a holster, he explained. "There is no manual thumb safety and no hammer."

The trigger operates in two stages, he noted. The first stage has a very light pull of only 2.2 pounds and a travel distance of a quarter inch. During the initial stage, three things happen: the firing pin is cocked, a separate internal safety that prevents the firing pin from moving forward is released, and the previously blocked trigger bar is released. The second stage of trigger operation requires five pounds of pressure that cause the release of the cocked firing pin. The firing pin strikes the primer, which is the part of an ammunition cartridge that ignites the powder charge. Pressure from rapidly expanding gas propels the bullet through the 4.5-inch barrel and out of the gun.

"The pistol points instinctively, and despite its large magazine capacity, the grip sits well in normal-sized hands," Kokalis wrote. Many expert shooters obsess about the angle formed between the grip of a gun and the barrel, as well as the height of the barrel above the top of the user's hand. Glock fans applaud what they consider the pistol's "natural" pointing angle, meaning that when they aim the gun, the experience feels similar to aiming an imaginary weapon formed by an extended index finger and lifted thumb. The Glock's barrel sits relatively low, closer to the hand than the barrels of comparable handguns. That also improves what some shooters call "pointability." The grip angle and the low bore combine with the flex of the polymer frame to diminish the recoil the shooter feels, which makes the Glock more controllable and accurate. The steel slide striking the plastic frame produces less jarring force and vibration than the metal-on-metal impact of other pistols. The Glock's lack of sharp metallic edges means fewer shooting-hand abrasions and greater ease in holstering.

"With a clean, constant trigger system, hit probability is quite high. The Safe Action trigger mechanism should pose no problem to even the rankest amateur," Kokalis wrote. "Other pistol manufacturers have much to fear from the tiny village of Deutsch-Wagram."

CHAPTER 5

"Hijacker's Special"

More than six hours of talks between US Secretary of State George Shultz and Soviet Foreign Minister Andrei Gromyko in Vienna in May 1985 produced little progress on nuclear arms control, Central America, or other points of Cold War contention. Accompanying Shultz on his visit to Austria was his usual retinue of aides and bodyguards. The diplomats brought back the standard communiqués on frank and constructive dialogue. The US Secret Service agents, however, returned with more unusual gifts from their Austrian counterparts: three high-capacity black polymer pistols. It was the Glock's first official foray westward. The Austrian-made handguns fascinated American officials but would come to trouble them as well.

The Secret Service kept one of the pistols for closer examination; the agency passed the other two along to the US Department of Defense. The Pentagon, as it turned out, was already well aware of the Glock 17. Alerted by NATO to Gaston Glock's emergence as a gun maker, American defense procurement officials had invited him to compete in trials in 1984 to select a new sidearm for US soldiers. Glock had declined, saying he couldn't build the required thirty-five test samples to meet American specifications and deadlines. But he also objected to the Pentagon's insistence that rights to manufacture the winning gun design would be open to competitive bidding; Glock intended to collect all profit from the production of his gun himself. (Beretta, the Italian manufacturer, won the Pentagon competition with the model the Austrian Army had passed over in favor of the Glock.)

Another branch of the Pentagon had the Glock 17 on its radar as well. Noel Koch, the Defense Department's civilian chief of counterterrorism, had learned about the Austrian pistol from counterparts in West German security. The Germans had given Koch a sample gun to take home, but he kept his prize confidential at first. As sometimes happens in the murky world of the military and intelligence services, supposedly allied arms of the US government contradicted each other. While Pentagon procurement officials had made friendly overtures to Gaston Glock, Koch saw the Austrian pistol in a different light—as a potential tool for terrorists. "I was worried about aviation security—could we stop a mostly plastic gun at the airport?" he told me.

Koch wasn't alone in his fears. Israeli intelligence operatives had found out that, not long before Shultz's visit to Vienna, Syrian ruler Hafez Al-Assad had ordered Glock 17s for his presidential guard. Gaston Glock prepared a special shipment of pistols for Assad with ornamental Arabic inscriptions inlaid in gold. Israel, which monitored Assad's every move, passed word to Washington about the transaction. The Reagan administration viewed Assad as a Soviet ally, a mortal enemy of Israel, and an instigator of international terrorism. The Syrian president's interest in the new firearm reinforced Noel Koch's unease about Gaston Glock and his gun.

Koch's apprehension was compounded when the Israelis

told their American intelligence contacts that emissaries from another terrorist financier, Libyan dictator Muammar al-Gaddafi, had visited the Glock plant in Deutsch-Wagram. The Libyans, whose activities in Europe Israeli spies closely followed, looked over the merchandise but hadn't made a purchase—at least not directly from Glock.

Israel had its facts essentially correct, according to Karl Walter and his fellow Glock employee Wolfgang Riedl. In separate interviews, they admitted that Assad was an early Glock customer, and Gaddafi, or someone in his inner circle, showed, at the very least, intense curiosity about the pistol. Walter and Riedl insisted that Glock never sold guns to Libya.

Nonethless, Koch had ample reason to be alarmed. The unpredictable Gaddafi remained an active threat to Americans. In December 1985, he reportedly provided logistical aid to Palestinian terrorists who carried out murderous mass attacks on travelers at airports in both Rome and Vienna. Koch, an experienced national security hand who had served as an intelligence operative with a covert Army unit in Vietnam, decided to conduct some personal research into whether the Glock 17's plastic construction would allow hijackers to sneak it onto planes.

In late 1985, Koch stripped the Glock he received from the West Germans and bundled the components into a duffel bag. He disguised the gun's main spring by wrapping it around a pair of metal-framed glasses. He separated the magazine from the frame and slide and emptied the ammunition into a small plastic pouch. He then put the duffel bag through the X-ray machine at Washington National Airport. Alarmingly, no one noticed.

Reverberations from this experiment would be loud and

long. Koch, for one, was determined to stop the Glock from entering the United States. "We didn't need another thing to worry about," he said.

///

Unaware of the growing consternation over the Glock 17 at the Pentagon, Gaston Glock, Karl Walter, and Wolfgang Riedl were trying to establish a market for the gun in America. Walter recommended that the manufacturer locate an outpost near Atlanta. Georgia was a gun-friendly state, and the city's large international airport allowed for efficient shipping. The three settled on the quiet suburb of Smyrna.

Riedl felt that the European market alone for handguns was too small. Military and law enforcement orders, by their nature, were unpredictable and subject to political whims. The American commercial market, with its tens of millions of civilian gun enthusiasts, was the mother lode. "I thought if I can get two percent or three percent of the US commercial market, that's much more than the commercial markets of fifty other countries," Riedl said.

The son of a three-star general in the Austrian Army, the well-connected Riedl had first heard of Gaston Glock several years earlier from his father-in-law, who was also a senior army officer. "There is an interesting guy," his father-in-law had mentioned. "He never in his life designed a field knife, and he delivered the best-quality samples among all the industry participating, and all those guys have been in the knife industry for hundreds of years." Then this "interesting guy" came back and sold a newly designed handgun to the Ministry of Defense. Riedl's father-in-law introduced him to Gaston Glock, and a week later, the pistol inventor offered Riedl a job.

An engineer by training, Riedl had a comfortable position at the time as an executive at Steyr, a conglomerate that manufactured not only weapons, but tanks, trucks, and bicycles. Government-controlled, Steyr was stodgy, and the road to promotion into senior management was long. "I was interested to work for a small company, but one with potential," Riedl explained to me. "From what Mr. Glock showed me, I thought the company had potential."

Gaston Glock was rightly proud of the gun he had designed, but he was devoid of management or finance skills, and fearful of revealing his weaknesses. Glock complained when workers spoke to one another on the job, claiming that if they had time to talk, they weren't staying busy enough—an approach sure to breed needless resentment. Glock was so nervous about dealing with Viennese bankers that he instructed Riedl to do all the talking at meetings they attended together. "This created a strange impression of a mute business owner," Riedl said. "Mr. Glock seemed to outsiders as naïve or aloof, a little odd. In private, within the company, he made all the decisions, but in public, at this time, he was awkward."

In November 1985, Glock signed the legal papers that established Glock, Inc., as a Georgia corporation. He wired money from Austria to a new company account in Atlanta, and Walter found a small suburban warehouse-and-office complex in Smyrna. Riedl flew to the States to plot a pricing strategy with Walter. They worked in Walter's basement, with Walter's wife, Pam, serving ham sandwiches and coffee.

The pair settled on a commercial wholesale price for the Glock 17 of $360 and a recommended retail price of $560. These levels undercut comparable American and European brands, yet assumed generous potential profits. According to Riedl, Glock's gross margins exceeded an astounding 65 percent—the manufacturer pocketed $240 on each gun sold. By comparison, manufacturer margins on pistols at companies such as Smith & Wesson and Beretta ranged from 5 percent to 20 percent, according to people in the industry. The Glock's simpler design and the computerized manufacturing methods allowed for larger profits.

Gaston Glock at first urged his marketing men to try a lower price to boost demand even further. Walter strongly disagreed. "If you sell it for cheap, you will have the image of a cheap gun," he told Glock. "Quality will always bring you more money." Glock deferred to Walter's experience in the American market. It was a crucial early decision, one that eventually made Gaston Glock a very rich man.

Riedl drafted an initial sales plan. Under the plan, the company's gun operation would break even in its first year if it sold 8,500 units. By comparison, S&W and Beretta each sold hundreds of thousands of guns annually. For Glock, the sale of knives, bayonets, and other products, such as machine-gun belts and plastic fragmentation grenades, to the Austrian military provided a revenue cushion for its fledgling firearm business.

That December, Riedl and Walter traveled to Denver for the annual trade show of the National Association of Sporting Goods Wholesalers. Industry rumors had piqued interest in their gun, even though it wasn't widely available yet in the United States. The Austrians themselves had only a handful of pistols to display. They borrowed exhibition space from one of the wholesalers with whom Walter was friendly.

The response was overwhelming. On the very first day of the event, Riedl and Walter logged orders for 20,400 guns—far more than Riedl's target for the entire first year. It would take months to manufacture and ship that many pistols to the

United States. "We couldn't get enough out the door," said Walter—the sort of predicament any small company would love to have.

/ / /

To celebrate their triumphant debut in Denver, Riedl and Walter invited sales representatives to join them that night for free drinks at the bar of a Holiday Inn. The men from Glock arrived in navy blue business suits and ties, as they had dressed for the trade show. The Americans, to their dismay, turned up in cowboy hats, denim jeans, and pointy Western boots. "A little embarrassing," Riedl admitted.

The next morning, he and Walter rushed to a Western outfitter to buy Stetsons and the rest of the frontier costume. Feeling prepared, they invited their new colleagues back to the Holiday Inn bar on the second night of the wholesalers' show. This time, the Austrians came attired like John Wayne in *Stagecoach*. Once again, however, they were confounded—the Americans had switched to business suits.

It turned out that the previous evening had been a special Western Night at the Holiday Inn—which was why everyone had dressed like a cowpoke. "We had something to learn about the United States," Riedl said.

A few weeks later, the Glock team received another lesson in business, American style. During a retailers' trade show in Dallas, an FBI agent with whom Walter was acquainted asked the salesman what he thought about that morning's column by Jack Anderson in the *Washington Post* about Gaddafi buying Glocks to distribute to terrorists.

Walter assumed the gossip was some kind of strange joke. A couple of days later, when he returned to his still-bare office in

Smyrna, he discovered that the FBI man had not been kidding. "Sure enough," Walter said, "the shit hit the fan."

Jack Anderson, in the sunset of a long muckraking career, thrived on scandal. Factual accuracy was not his strength. But when he broke a story, other journalists often followed, fixing the mistakes as they went. His syndicated column ran in the *Post* and scores of other major newspapers. On January 15, 1986, Anderson's headline declared: GADDAFI BUYING AUSTRIAN PLASTIC PISTOLS. Cowritten with his assistant and leg man, Dale Van Atta, the column reported that "Gaddafi is in the process of buying more than 100 plastic handguns that would be difficult for airport security forces to detect." An unnamed "top" US official told Anderson and Van Atta: " 'This is crazy. To let a madman like Gaddafi have access to such a pistol! Once it is in his hands, he'll give it to terrorists throughout the Middle East.' " The official was none other than Noel Koch, the Pentagon's counterterrorism chief.

"The handgun in question is the Glock 17, a 9mm pistol invented and manufactured by Gaston Glock in the village of Deutsch-Wagram, just outside Vienna," the column continued. "It is accurate, reliable, and made almost entirely of hardened plastic. Only the barrel, slide, and one spring are metal. Dismantled, it is frighteningly easy to smuggle past airport security." Cloaking Koch's identity, the column described his experiment at Washington National: "One Pentagon security expert decided to demonstrate just how easy it would be to sneak a Glock 17 aboard an airliner."

The Anderson column created havoc in the Glock world. Everyone who had anything to do with the sale of firearms was desperate to know about the Glock 17. Politicians and activists who opposed widespread ownership of guns, as well as those who favored it, formulated instant opinions on why the violent

Libyan pariah might be so fascinated by the plastic pistol. The phones at Glock, Inc., in Smyrna did not stop ringing. "We were inundated," Walter said. "Not only media, anti-gun people, hostile people, but law enforcement, too."

"The amazing thing was that nobody had even heard of Glock before the Anderson column," recalled Richard Feldman, a lawyer then working as a political operative for the National Rifle Association. "'Glock? What's that? . . . I've got to see one of those.'"

The media-political echo chamber amplified the excitement. The *New York Times* published an editorial on February 9 headlined HIJACKER'S SPECIAL? that summarized the alarmist Anderson column. Mario Biaggi, the dean of the New York City delegation in the US House of Representatives, announced that he would introduce legislation to restrict non-metal firearms. In a February 26 press release, the liberal Democrat's office described how he had confirmed the danger the Glock posed by having one of his aides carry a disassembled pistol into the Capitol: "When dismantled, the frame and magazine of the weapon, which are made of plastic, went undetected by the metal detector, and the barrel created a deceiving image on the X-ray screen."

The next day, *USA Today* devoted its entire editorial page to plastic handguns. The paper's editors argued that firearms like the Glock ought to be outlawed. A large cartoon showed a gun store advertising the Glock with a poster: HIJACKER SPECIAL! PLASTIC GUNS: BEAT THE METAL DETECTORS! In the drawing, an obsequious salesman asks a grinning Gaddafi how many Glocks he wants. The Libyan ruler, rubbing his hands together with evil glee, answers: "5,000, please!"

Two weeks later, Jack Anderson came back with a second syndicated column, recounting the Biaggi staff episode on

Capitol Hill. Josh Sugarmann, communications director of the National Coalition to Ban Handguns, a Washington lobbying group, published an opinion piece in the *Los Angeles Times* that relied heavily on the Anderson columns and was entitled PROGRESS GIVES US GREAT NEW HANDGUN—HIJACKER SPECIAL. Sugarmann, who would go on to start his own anti-gun organization, recalled digging up everything he could find about the Glock. The fawning reviews in the American firearm press got his attention. Glock "did a good job of creating an image for itself as being outside the gun industry," Sugarmann told me. "That was a key selling point for them: 'You guys have been building your guns in Quonset huts and brick factories. We're from the future, and we are here to give you a new gun.'"

As the furor over the Glock built—congressional hearings were scheduled for May—several pertinent facts were obscured. The National Airport test that inspired the initial Anderson column had actually involved two handguns, not just the Glock. The Pentagon's Noel Koch arranged to smuggle a fully assembled Heckler & Koch pistol through the security checkpoint, along with the Austrian handgun. He taped the German-made H&K, also a nine-millimeter model, to the bottom of a leather briefcase. Made entirely of metal, the H&K weighed more than the Glock and presumably should have been even easier to pick up, since it wasn't stripped to its component parts. That neither gun was noticed indicated that the weakness at National Airport was one of ineffective detection machinery, possibly combined with inattentive security personnel. The "plastic pistol" wasn't any more of a hijacking threat than an ordinary firearm.

Also strangely absent from the debate was that both the US Bureau of Alcohol, Tobacco and Firearms and the Federal

Aviation Administration had scrutinized the Glock 17 in late 1985 and determined that it did not pose a special threat. "As a result of these tests, it was determined that when put through an airport X-ray screening system, the outline was readily identifiable as a pistol," the FAA's director of civil aviation security, Billie H. Vincent, said in a document dated March 21, 1986. Despite the approval of these two federal agencies, major media outlets repeated and augmented the alarmist Anderson columns. "Easily concealable handguns like the Glock," *Time* reported on April 14, 1986, "along with hard-to-detect components for putty-like explosives that are also readily available, give air pirates an edge that officials are finding increasingly difficult to counter."

///

The National Rifle Association leapt to Glock's defense, publishing supportive articles in its in-house magazine and on the opinion pages of major newspapers. Feldman, the NRA operative, was dispatched to a meeting of the US Conference of Mayors in San Juan, Puerto Rico, to hand out X-ray-machine images demonstrating that the Glock 17 could be readily identified. Unimpressed, the mayors passed a resolution calling for a ban on the manufacture and importation of plastic handguns.

In New York, Representative Biaggi's hometown, the police department banned the Glock by name, based on its reputation as a terrorist weapon. Several states, including Maryland, South Carolina, and Hawaii, would follow suit, using a variety of regulations and laws to restrict the Austrian weapon. "It felt like there was real momentum against this one pistol, and the opposing sides in the gun-control debate were gearing up bigtime," Feldman recalled. "Hijacking was a big concern, and here was one pistol that supposedly the terrorists loved—or that's what the media and some politicians said. Was this going to kill the Glock in the crib?"

/ / /

Into this turmoil stepped the Subcommittee on Crime of the US House of Representatives. Chaired by William Hughes, a Democrat from New Jersey, the panel held hearings that began in May 1986 and continued sporadically over the following year, ostensibly to review the Biaggi bill and other legislation that would make plastic guns illegal.

The subcommittee convened in the wake of a bitter and much broader clash in Congress over gun control that did not involve the Glock. The NRA and its allies got the best of that bigger fight, winning passage of the Firearm Owners Protection Act of 1986, which loosened restrictions on gun sales and reined in the authority of the Bureau of Alcohol, Tobacco and Firearms. President Ronald Reagan signed the law in May, the same month as the House hearings on "plastic pistols." Anti-gun activists saw the Glock controversy as an opportunity to push back in a protracted war they weren't prepared to surrender.

Hughes, a stalwart of the gun-control movement, had led a successful drive for his side's main amendment of the Firearm Owners Protection Act, the NRA's one disappointment with the otherwise gun-friendly law. The Hughes amendment banned the manufacture or sale of new fully automatic machine guns for civilian ownership (possessing and transferring older machine guns remained legal, with special permission). The New Jersey congressman seemed like a natural to lead an investigation of the Glock. To his credit, Hughes did not exacerbate the "hijacker special" hysteria. Setting a calm tone, he said by way of introduction: "This subcommittee, indeed this Congress, cannot solve the problem of terrorism, but we can and must take steps to protect ourselves against terrorist acts. A new threat that seems to be emerging is firearms made of materials which can escape detection in X-ray machines, or which can be smuggled through metal detectors."

The star witness to appear before the subcommittee was Gaston Glock himself. Up front, Hughes alluded to "controversy over the Glock 17," but he dampened that in two ways. First, he sounded quite friendly to the gun's namesake. "We are very pleased," Hughes said, "that Mr. Gaston Glock, the inventor of the Glock 17 handgun, has come today from Austria to testify about this famous gun." More generally, Hughes played down any immediate danger created by Glock pistols by stressing that "the development of non-metal firearms that will be even less traceable, and detectable, will soon be upon us." This view was reasonable enough, given that during this period, various tinkerers and entrepreneurs were experimenting with all-plastic gun designs. None of them, however, reached the marketplace.

Unlike Hughes, some of the other participants in the House hearing weren't terribly scrupulous in distinguishing between the theoretical possibility of an all-plastic gun and the reality of the Glock 17. Biaggi, attending the session not as a member of the subcommittee but as a witness, saw an opportunity for political theater. A twenty-year member of Congress, he was still famous for having been a hero during his pre-political days as a New York City cop. Biaggi condemned "the plastic handgun" as "the latest tool of terrorist technology." He offered no illustrations of terrorists using plastic guns, but he singled out the Glock 17 as "the weapon that aroused my concern" because "it is mostly plastic. I say that the Glock 17 is far more difficult to detect than any conventional weapon."

Federal security officials who testified following Biaggi clearly tried to avoid offending anyone, but just as clearly refused to concede that the Glock, or any other firearm then available, posed a significant detection problem. "While the Glock 17 pistol uses a considerable amount of plastic in its construction," said Edward M. Owen Jr., chief of firearm technology at BATF, "the pistol contains more metal by weight than many other handguns constructed entirely of metal." Owen and Billie Vincent of the FAA tiptoed around the personnel problem: that air travelers were—and are—protected by low-paid, barely trained human screeners doing boring, repetitive work.

When it was their turn at the witness table, Karl Walter and Gaston Glock put on an awkward performance. Glock spoke haltingly, using Walter as an interpreter. Yet, in an odd way, the two were disarming.

Until Walter led off the Glock presentation, no one at the hearing had raised the Libyan connection alleged by Anderson and Van Atta. A well-coached corporate executive would have left the issue alone. Walter instead plunged in: "The truth is Glock has at no time . . . offered directly or indirectly, or negotiated about, or concluded any deal, to or with Libya, Libyan agents, or representatives or other entities representing Libya."

His tortured assertion may have been technically accurate. The Libyans who, according to Walter's own account to me, had visited the Glock plant in Deutsch-Wagram supposedly did not discuss an actual sale. But they had not traveled to the Vienna suburb for the Wiener schnitzel. Walter's decision to make this just-barely-true denial of the Anderson charges seems tendentious at best. Strangely, Hughes and other members of the subcommittee showed no interest in pursuing whether Gaddafi had sent his personal shoppers to the Austrian gun factory.

Walter tackled the question of detection in a more sensible way. He produced an X-ray image of a disassembled Glock 17, inside an attaché case, with other items such as pens and pencils. The reproduction in the hearing transcript reveals that the pieces of the pistol were recognizable, at least if the viewer knew what to look for. Walter stressed that the company had addressed this concern from the outset: "Austrian security authorities confirmed the clear detectability of the pistol in tests at the Vienna International Airport in 1982."

When Gaston Glock had his turn as a witness, he offered no opening statement and answered questions with Walter's laborious assistance. Little was accomplished. Hughes inquired into methods for disassembling a Glock, which led its maker to offer pronouncements that sounded alternately like sales pitches and filibusters, none of them particularly coherent. "This is an advantage for every weapon which you can easily [break down] for cleaning purposes," Glock said, "because even during peacetime, training with weapons is required."

The businessman never faced any real pressure from Hughes or other members of the panel. Instead, he gave a tedious tutorial on the pistol's design and its relatively few component parts. "Our important thing is," he said, "because of these components, less parts can break, and therefore, the weapon will last longer." Not exactly a blinding insight. The Austrian ran out the clock and avoided serious trouble.

/ / /

The appearance before the House panel was only one stop in an impressive circuit the Glock executives traveled through the halls of Washington. Without benefit of expensive lobby-ists or legal counsel, Glock's tiny executive group responded to the Anderson column by paying courtesy calls on the BATF, the FAA, the separate training academies of the Secret Service and the FBI, the US Capitol Police, and the National Rifle Association. Walter, Riedl, and Glock also secured multiple meetings at the Pentagon. They even visited Noel Koch, the self-appointed scourge of the Glock. The encounter in Koch's office quickly deteriorated when Glock began lecturing the American. "You're trying to destroy my company," Glock said.

"I don't have anything against your company," Koch responded. "I just want to keep your gun out of my country."

"We didn't like each other," Koch recalled later. "He was a sour, self-righteous SOB. He was not a great representative for his product, I'll tell you that."

For his part, Glock demonstrated impressive chutzpah, scolding a senior American security official when the Austrian was selling his handgun to the likes of Assad and hosting Libyan operatives at the plant in Deutsch-Wagram. But Glock's risky indignation paid off. In another meeting, Defense Department officials said that despite Koch's instigation of the Anderson column, the American security establishment had no objection to the Glock 17. The Austrians thanked their hosts and asked that they issue a corrective public statement. The Americans refused, but they made a conciliatory counterproposal. They arranged for the Austrians to meet with weapons experts from a variety of elite military units that had the authority to choose their own small arms.

///

The House Crime Subcommittee would hold three more days of hearings spread over more than a year, keeping Glock in the headlines. Considering all the melodrama that preceded it, passage of legislation in May 1988 to ban the manufacture, import, or sale of undetectable plastic firearms seemed a ho-hum afterthought. As a practical matter, the law had no effect on the Glock 17, which was deemed detectable. Since no other manufacturer has tried to market an all-plastic invisible gun, the statute, at best, stands as a prohibition of a bad idea that never became a reality. Viewed more skeptically, the congressional fuss seems like a waste of legislative time and energy.

But the intense public attention devoted to the Glock did have an impact on the gun and its manufacturer. Within months of the original Anderson column in January 1986, questions about the pistol's unusual design and materials become a major selling point.

Civilian orders continued to pour in, as thousands of gun buyers decided to see what all the commotion was about. Karl Walter also tallied more than one thousand requests for free samples from law enforcement agencies in 1986 alone. Some came from small municipal police departments; others, from large state prisons and international airport-security offices. The US Capitol Police obtained a Glock and passed it along to the Federal Law Enforcement Training Center in Glynco, Georgia. Soon Walter was holding seminars with representatives from the Customs Service, the Border Patrol, the Marshals Service, the Bureau of Prisons, and the Drug Enforcement Administration. All of them wanted Glock 17s for closer study and tryouts on the range. Nine out of ten of the recipients eventually sent a check, saying they would like to keep the test guns.

At the Pentagon, Noel Koch eventually dropped his campaign against the Glock. He even bought one for his private gun collection. "Actually, it shoots very nicely," he told me. "With a full clip, it's nicely balanced and comes back on point easily." He expressed an amused insouciance about the tumult he had initiated: It was but one more Washington war story.

/ / /

Shipments arrived from Deutsch-Wagram every weekend at the Atlanta airport. The first batch of eight hundred was delivered in January 1986, before Walter had managed to get an alarm system installed at the Smyrna facility. He slept in the plant that night, accompanied only by his loyal Samoyed, Tasso. Walter hired his wife, Pam, to help him repackage the guns, record their serial numbers, and send them out to wholesalers via United Parcel Service. As the business expanded, he brought on more employees. The Glock's success illustrated that in the gun industry, all publicity is good publicity, and high-profile enmity from anti-gun forces is the best publicity of all.

Marty Arnstein, an American wholesaler who placed an early order for Glocks, congratulated Wolfgang Riedl on the plastic pistol controversy. "You just got $5 million worth of advertising for free," Arnstein said.

CHAPTER 6

"Super Gun"

While the FBI was quick to blame inadequate firepower for its losses in the Miami Shootout, the nation's premier law enforcement agency moved cautiously to replace its Smith & Wesson revolvers. A lumbering bureaucracy in the best of times, the FBI was traumatized by the bloodshed of April 1986 and embarrassed at how the confrontation spun out of control. Its choice of a new handgun would take years.

The Feds' hesitation, however, did not slow others. A patrolman in Colby, Kansas, read an article about Glock in the spring of 1986 and suggested that the small town order a couple of the exotic-sounding weapons. With a full-time force of only twelve officers, Colby made the very first formal US police acquisition of Glocks. Karl Walter instituted what would become a permanent Glock policy of offering cops a big discount from the wholesale price of $360 per pistol; Colby paid $300 apiece. "Officers found them unconventional, but really liked their performance," recalled Randall Jones, now the chief of the Colby PD. His department switched over exclusively to Glocks and carries them to this day.

Curtiss Spanos, a firearm trainer with the larger Howard County Police Department in Maryland, began carrying a Glock 17 in mid-1986. In December, he and a fellow officer encountered two armed robbery suspects. "There would be two dead officers if I didn't have the nine-millimeter gun," Spanos told the *Washington Post*. The hero cop explained that during a thirty-minute chase and gunfight, he was able to return fire rapidly with the seventeen-round Glock as the suspects reloaded several times. "I fired a total of 16 rounds," Spanos said. "I couldn't have done that with a revolver."

Several months after municipal cops from Miami responded to distress calls about the brutal FBI shootout, the Miami PD became the first big-city department to inquire about a force-wide purchase from Glock. A six-month pilot program yielded positive reviews. Miami city commissioner J. L. Plummer called the Glock 17 "reliable, accurate, and very fine." Beretta protested that it had not been given an adequate opportunity to compete for the Miami contract, but the Italian manufacturer's complaint was brushed aside. The Miami PD ordered eleven hundred of the Austrian pistols.

Dallas, San Francisco, and Toronto quickly followed Miami's lead. In St. Paul, Minnesota, John Nord, the deputy chief, was alarmed that twice in early 1987, officers involved in shootings emptied six-shot revolvers while criminal suspects kept firing. Those incidents, combined with the Miami PD's decision to go with Glock, inspired St. Paul and neighboring Minneapolis to switch. "It's the wave of the future," said Minneapolis chief Tony Bouza.

/ / /

In 1987, Miami's crime scourge was spreading north. "The crack cocaine wars were hitting Jacksonville," recalled John Rutherford. The police felt threatened. Rutherford headed firearm training for the Jacksonville Sheriff's Office, which was responsible for the growing city and surrounding Duval County. His range served all police and correctional officers in northeast Florida. Rutherford's boss, the sheriff, ordered him to conduct a study of whether to change over to semiautomatic pistols and, if the answer was yes, which one. Thirty-five years old at the time, Rutherford was a rising star in the department, the son of a Navy man, and a graduate of Florida State University. The assignment became a major test.

Rutherford had hunted as a boy and liked guns. He kept a framed copy of the Second Amendment on his office wall and taught his two children to shoot. He carried a handgun at all times, on and off duty—even to church on Sunday, which annoyed his wife. Rutherford's view was that if some armed nut decided to take out his frustrations on the congregation, he wanted to be prepared.

As of 1987, he had little experience with semiautomatic pistols. He knew only revolvers. So he had the department hire an outside consultant to help sort through the many options on the market. He chose Emanuel Kapelsohn, a well-known firearm trainer who called his advisory business Peregrine Corp., after the Peregrine falcon, a sharp-eyed bird of prey.

Gun manufacturers from all over the world sent the sheriff's office their latest models, a dozen in all. Rutherford and a brain trust of fellow officers with firearm expertise gathered to examine the candidate guns. "We're taking these guns out and looking at them," Rutherford recalled. "'Ooh, Beretta 92F. Isn't that pretty? Sig Sauer! You know everybody loves Sig.' Then, I pull out this black box and pop the thing open, and here's this Glock. I'm like, 'What the heck is this?' I'm tapping it on the table. It's plastic! What the hell? And there's no hammer on this thing. I literally said, 'We don't want any crap like this,' and I slung it over onto the couch, didn't even put it back in the mix with the other guns."

Kapelsohn noticed the lonely Glock. "You need to give it a chance," he said.

His words carried weight. Kapelsohn, who came from New Jersey, had a national reputation and heavy connections at the NRA. His credentials were unusual in the weapons-training business: He held a BA in English literature from Yale and a law degree from Harvard. He had worked at a New York firm as a civil litigator for corporate clients; on the side, he drew on a lifetime love of guns to become a noted shooting instructor. Eventually he decided to turn his sideline into a full-time job. He earned gun-instructor certification from the FBI and studied with some of the best-known handgun authorities in the country, including the legendary Jeff Cooper, who ran a school in Arizona. The 1988 treatise *Police Defensive Handgun Use and Encounter Tactics* named Kapelsohn one of the five top trainers in the United States. He also testified as a paid expert for both plaintiffs and defendants in lawsuits over allegedly wrongful shootings.

Kapelsohn's suggestion that the Austrian pistol be taken seriously proved prescient. Within a few days, "we were fighting over who was going to get the Glock," Rutherford said. "It's just like shooting a revolver, and that's what everybody liked about it. You pull it out, you pull the trigger, and you put it away. That was the beauty of it."

Revolvers typically don't have external safeties. As Kapelsohn explained to Rutherford, training a cop—or a civilian—to switch to a standard semiautomatic pistol requires intensive drills on deactivating the safety lever before firing. Many officers forget whether the safety is on or off. Some standard pistols, including the Beretta, remain cocked after being fired, with the hammer poised to fall again. To be safe, the user has to "decock" the gun manually before replacing it in u holster. Between operating the safety and decocking, there is a lot of opportunity to make mistakes.

The Glock 17, Kapelsohn said, presented none of these challenges. There is no external safety lever or decocking mechanism. As Rutherford recalled the lesson: "The safety in a Glock was the exact same as the safety in a revolver: trigger travel, trigger weight. You have to overcome both for the gun to go off, and that's where the safety is at."

Rutherford and his colleagues in Jacksonville had a nostalgic affection for the standard-issue Smith & Wesson .38. Some of them liked the look of the large .45-caliber S&W Model 645 pistol, the American company's nominee in the Jacksonville shoot-off. "But the problem was, several of us had gone out on target [with the S&W 645] with the safety on," Rutherford said. "That's chilling. We just had a two-week class on using these guns, knowing about decocking and the safety and all that. . . . Here we are going out on target with the safety on."

The Glock had another advantage: a light, steady trigger pull. The Smith & Wesson .38-caliber guns in use in Jacksonville had a heavy pull of twelve to fourteen pounds—standard for revolvers. Shooters who train regularly can achieve accuracy with a heavy trigger. But only a small minority of cops practice diligently. "There's this myth out there that all police officers are gun enthusiasts, and they train like crazy and shoot all the time," said Rutherford. A dirty little secret of law enforcement is that many cops don't take range time seriously. And even in high-crime cities, the vast majority of officers go years, or even an entire career, without getting into a gunfight. The average officer is a mediocre shot, or worse.

With a Glock, poor marksmen become adequate; moderately skilled shooters begin grouping rounds in small bunches near dead center of their target. The pistol's gentle five pound trigger action doesn't require the sort of muscular squeeze that can cause the user to jerk the gun off target.

The Smith & Wesson Model 645 and other semiautomatic pistols at the time had an inconsistent trigger pull that didn't solve the accuracy problem. On most semiautos other than the Glock, the first squeeze was comparable to that of a revolver: around twelve pounds. This initial heavy pull both cocked the gun and fired it. The momentum of the recoil and rearward movement of the slide automatically recocked the pistol for the second and subsequent shots. Succeeding shots required a much lighter, shorter trigger pull because the hammer was already in a cocked position. As a result, a less-than-expert shooter was prone to fire low on the first heavy squeeze of the trigger, and then high on the second, much lighter pull. With training and practice, these tendencies can be overcome, but few police officers receive sufficient preparation. The Glock requires training too, of course, but its soft, consistent trigger action and modest recoil make it "the easiest semiautomatic to transition to," Rutherford said.

When word got out that Rutherford was leaning toward the Glock, some of his superiors warned him that could be risky. "Now, John," he recalled one senior officer telling him, "you know the sheriff and the undersheriff, they really like that Smith & Wesson 645." Smith & Wesson was what the Jacksonville Sheriff's Office had always known. It was the American cop's brand.

But Rutherford was adamant. He had worked for months on his report, he said. "Now you want me to change it to something else that I know is not the best gun?" During a two-hour presentation to the sheriff, he stressed the Glock's accuracy and safety advantages, as he saw them. He explained that the Austrian pistol was much easier to maintain because it had only thirty-four parts; the Smith & Wesson 645 had more than one hundred. "You can take fifty [Glocks] apart and put fifty guns back together after mixing up all the parts, and they all shoot," he said. As beloved as the brand had been, Smith & Wesson had allowed its manufacturing quality to slip, Rutherford told his superiors. The story was similar to that of the American auto industry; gun makers in the United States had lost ground to foreign competitors more diligent about engineering and quality control. That is how Toyota sneaked up on General Motors. Out of a shipment of forty new Smith & Wesson revolvers, three or four would malfunction right out of the box. "The damned things wouldn't even fire," Rutherford said. This was something the sheriff hadn't known. In the Firearm Training Division, Rutherford said, "we were a little miffed at Smith & Wesson by that time."

A decision came quickly: "We're buying Glocks," the sheriff said.

An order went to Smyrna for nine hundred pistols to arm the Jacksonville force. Over the next six months, more than one hundred police agencies around the country requested copies of Rutherford's ninety-page report on Glock. And Rutherford received a promotion to captain.

Not that the pistol conversion went flawlessly. Shortly after Jacksonville began issuing the Glock 17, a deputy mistakenly shot and killed a teenager he was trying to arrest on suspicion of stealing a pickup truck. An investigation revealed that the officer had drawn his gun and had his finger on the trigger, as he attempted to cuff the juvenile suspect. The deputy should have holstered his gun, especially since the Glock required much less force to fire. "This was a horrific accident, but a training issue, not the fault of the gun," Rutherford said.

He similarly did not blame the Glock for several incidents early on when deputies' pistols jammed. After consultation with the manufacturer, Rutherford concluded that the ammunition the department was using didn't feed properly from the Glock's magazine. After a switch to Winchester rounds recommended by Glock, the jamming ceased. "That gun does not jam with proper ammo," Rutherford said. Still, serious questions about Glocks discharging accidentally and having finicky appetites in ammunition would recur in other jurisdictions as the handgun's popularity spread.

Rutherford's allegiance never wavered. Twenty-two years later, the Jacksonville Sheriff's Office, which he now presides over as the popularly elected sheriff, has seventeen hundred officers. It still arms them with Glock pistols.

/ / /

Emanuel Kapelsohn's recommendation of the Glock wasn't happenstance. In mid-1986, Karl Walter began putting some of the country's most admired shooting instructors on contract to spread the word about the Austrian pistol. This melding of training and marketing, motivated by a keen sense of customer needs, became a Glock hallmark. Kapelsohn was one of the specialists Walter hired.

In some cities, the Glock gun instructors were paid by the local authorities; that's the way it worked in Jacksonville, where the sheriff's office hired Kapelsohn. In other situations, usually after a department indicated it would make a purchase, Glock dispatched Kapelsohn or another trainer as part of the procurement deal—a freebie for the new customer.

Strictly speaking, Kapelsohn's role as an expert hired by the Jacksonville Sheriff's Office had a built-in conflict of interest. During the plastic pistol debate before Congress, he testified in Washington with notable eloquence on Glock's behalf. Nevertheless, he insisted he "did not have an axe to grind" and endorsed Glock on the merits.

After the Jacksonville Sheriff's Office placed their order for the Glocks, the company sent Kapelsohn back to north Florida to provide transitional training on the company's dime. "Karl Walter had the genius at that time to take the training programs on the road," Kapelsohn said. "You had to go to the Smith & Wesson Academy [in Springfield, Massachusetts] if you were going to use the Smith & Wesson. If your agency was going to adopt the Glock, [Walter] would send some training your way." Many times, instructors from neighboring agencies attended these sessions out of curiosity, or Glock would sponsor an open-house seminar for all federal, state, and municipal trainers in a given region. "The effect of it was to get Glocks in the hands of instructors all over the country," Kapelsohn explained. "This was just a brilliant way to sell this gun."

Making customers' encounters with Glock memorable was one of Karl Walter's talents. He showed up to close big deals, zooming into town from Smyrna in a Porsche roadster stocked with boxes of Austrian pistols and free ammunition. (He switched to the sports car from the RV once he became a full-time Glock employee.) Walter also made a habit of inviting police customers and wholesale distributors for all-expenses-paid visits to the Glock facility outside of Atlanta. The cops were treated to steak dinners at a downtown restaurant, expensive liquor, and imported cigars.

On occasion, a visiting Gaston Glock put in an appearance. "He looked very European, smoked like a chimney," one law enforcement official recalled. "He knew his stuff. You could not ask him anything he couldn't tell you about that gun." Glock enjoyed showing off the Glock 18, a fully automatic version of the pistol. Depressing the trigger of the Glock 18 unleashes a stream of bullets in the fashion of a machine gun. It can hold a capacious thirty-three-round magazine that sticks out of the gun's grip and empties in a matter of seconds. Unless the user is familiar with the Glock 18, its enormous recoil results in the barrel jumping upward. Many an embarrassed police officer inadvertently peppered the ceiling of the company shooting range with rounds. Unavailable on the civilian market, the Glock 18 is designed for police SWAT squads and military special-ops units. Rolling it out for visitors to Smyrna remains a Glock marketing practice.

Using imaginative financing and trade-in arrangements allowed Walter to sign up police departments on tight budgets. In Marietta, Georgia, he won over Police Chief Charles Simmons in 1988 by promising to arm his hundred-person force without any money changing hands. The Marietta PD simply exchanged 126 old handguns for 100 new Glock 17s. The *Atlanta Journal-Constitution* published an article about the transaction, noting that the Glock "would be an easy gun to switch to since officers train quickly with it and gain better accuracy than with the present revolver."

Such publicity introduced the brand to a wider audience at no cost to Glock. The deals worked financially because of the company's startlingly low manufacturing costs, which Glock was able to push down even further—to less than $100 a unit—as its production volume grew. When it did trade-ins, Glock sold the used police handguns to wholesalers, who refurbished them for sale at firearm shops and weekend gun shows. Overhauled police weapons became a staple on the used-gun market throughout the United States, and trade-ins emerged as an important aspect of the Glock modus operandi.

As the company's reputation and revenue grew, Walter began hiring full-time employees from the agencies that bought his guns. These revolving-door recruits became some of his most effective evangelists. The New York State Police, a 4,500-person force, initiated its move to semiautomatic pistols in 1988. The veteran sergeant in charge of the review process, Frank DiNuzzo, was known throughout the Northeast as a firearm trainer and author of instructional manuals. At first inclined toward Smith & Wesson, DiNuzzo ultimately recommended the Glock for reasons similar to Rutherford's in Jacksonville. Glock sweetened the deal by arranging for a $1,246,000 credit when the agency traded in 4,550 old handguns. New York received 4,310 new Austrian pistols for an additional payment of only $40,000. The used police guns were later resold by a Massachusetts gun wholesaler. After DiNuzzo retired from the department in 1990, Walter hired him as Glock's first full-time in-house trainer. Retirees from the US Drug Enforcement Administration, the Detroit PD, and the special-operations Navy SEALs went to work for the company as well.

/ / /

New York City had, and has, the biggest police force in the United States, with thirty-five thousand officers—more than twice the size of the FBI. Other departments take cues from the NYPD, and no municipality sees its officers depicted more often in movies or on television. At the same time, New York City is not a gun-friendly jurisdiction. It has strict local gun-control laws. And while the state troopers based upstate in

Albany were receptive to Glock, the leadership of the NYPD imposed a brand-specific ban on the Austrian gun in early 1986, based on the terrorism fears fanned by Jack Anderson.

None of this stopped Walter, who had sold Steyr sniper rifles to the NYPD during his pre-Glock days. In May 1986, a contingent of New York police trainers invited him to make an unofficial presentation at the department's range at Rodman's Neck. To Walter's surprise, twenty firearm instructors showed up; he had brought only a handful of sample pistols. Not to worry, his hosts told him. Several had privately obtained Glock 17s and retrieved them from their lockers.

Walter took this as a promising sign: Some of New York's top in-house firearm trainers were curious enough about what he was selling to spend their own money on the gun, and in the process violate the ban on possessing a Glock within city limits. That summer, with the prohibition still in place, the Emergency Services Unit of the NYPD, what other cities called SWAT, quietly ordered seventy Glock pistols—another hopeful development. Walter continued to press for a broader hearing in New York.

In June 1986, the limitations of the six-shot revolver were convincingly illustrated in a gunfight in Far Rockaway, Queens. Rookie NYPD officer Scott Gadell and his partner chased a gunman who opened fire on them. Gadell leaped for cover behind a stoop and shot back, emptying his .38-caliber Smith & Wesson. As he tried to reload, the gunman stepped forward and fired a fatal shot into the left side of Gadell's forehead, just above the ear. The gunman fired a total of nine shots from a nine-millimeter semiautomatic. "Every cop knows about Scott," a fellow officer later said. "He's an example of a cop who did everything he was supposed to but ended up dying because of second-rate equipment."

Then, in September 1988, the Associated Press landed a scoop that ricocheted around the city's media and beyond: New York Police Commissioner Benjamin Ward was carrying a Glock 17 beneath his suit jacket! The *New York Post* teased the story on its front page and ran this punning all-caps headline:

TOP COP WARDS OFF BAN ON SUPER GUN

"Police Commissioner Benjamin Ward is licensed to carry a controversial plastic super-pistol that is banned in New York City," the *Post* reported. "Ward can carry a state-of-the-art nine-millimeter Glock pistol, according to a copy of a renewal of Ward's carry license, dated July 6."

Caught flat-footed, the NYPD told the *Post* that "the Glock issued to Ward was 'part of a controlled test.'" Since the department wasn't very responsive, the newspaper sought others to describe the "super gun." One was Dr. David Mohler, an orthopedic cancer specialist at Sloan-Kettering who said he had owned a Glock in California but had been discouraged from bringing it with him to New York because of the licensing ban. "The Glock," Mohler told the paper, "is one of the best combat pistols you can find."

"'Super gun,' can you imagine?" Karl Walter would muse more than two decades later. Shaking his head, he chuckled. "You can't buy that kind of attention, not for $50 million, not for $100 million."

A day after the Ward disclosure, the NYPD ended the Glock ban. A deputy police commissioner explained that research had demonstrated that the gun "could not be defined as an undetectable weapon, and in fact can be detected with today's present technology in the security field."

"From that moment on, everything started to roll," Walter

said. Soon hundreds of NYPD narcotics detectives, organized crime investigators, and other specialized units were carrying Glocks. Today the brand is one of three that New York authorizes, and about twenty thousand of the city's officers carry a Glock.

/ / /

Gaston Glock was not the first firearm designer to promote a handgun to Americans in uniform as a means of developing a lucrative market. "The first was Samuel Colt," Karl Walter noted. Nor is there any evidence that Gaston Glock was consciously inspired by the mid-nineteenth-century impresario of the revolver. But the strategy that the Glock-Walter team pursued 140 years later uncannily resembled that of Sam Colt. The similarities illuminate lasting themes in the American gun business.

Born in Hartford, Connecticut, in 1814, Colt was a mechanically inclined boy who grew bored working in his father's textile mill. At fifteen, he shipped out as an apprentice seaman, and, according to most biographies, it was on this youthful voyage that he got the idea for his version of a repeating firearm the cylinder of which revolved, wheel-like, around the barrel. Some accounts say the design came to him while he fixated on the operation of the ship captain's wheel; others, that he got the idea while focused on the capstan used to raise anchor. More prosaically, according to historian Chuck Wills, young Colt may have seen early flintlock revolvers in India, where they were used by British troops. "By the time he returned to the US, he had carved a working model out of wood."

Colt hired two experienced gunsmiths to advise him on the details and fabricate experimental models. Like Glock, he required the assistance of specialists. Revolvers had been in use for decades. Colt's advance was to link the cylinder to the firing mechanism, eliminating the need to manually rotate the cylinder. The user pulled back the hammer, which caused the cylinder to turn and lined up the chamber containing the ammunition with the barrel. To fire, the shooter then simply pulled the trigger.

Colt's guns became known as powerful, reliable, and durable, a reputation much like the Glock's later on. After several years of difficulty getting his business off the ground, Colt had a series of breakthroughs winning endorsements from prominent lawmen and military officers, foreshadowing the path Karl Walter followed with the Glock. One of Colt's earliest champions was Captain Samuel Walker of the Texas Rangers. In 1844, newspapers reported that Walker and fifteen of his mounted men, armed with Colts, fought off some eighty Comanche Indians. "People throughout Texas are anxious to procure your pistols," Walker wrote to the gun maker in the sort of testimonial that Colt reproduced in illustrated pamphlets. (In the 1800s, "pistol" and "revolver" were used interchangeably.) Two years later, Walker, by then an officer in the Army, collaborated with Colt to develop a .41-caliber model. The US government ordered one thousand of the "Walker Colts" for use in the Mexican-American War, allowing Sam Colt to get his company aloft. Colt built one of the most advanced factories of the era, a facility in Hartford that was the first in the firearm field to take full advantage of mass-production techniques, such as the manufacture of interchangeable parts.

It was only in the 1850s that urban police departments in

the United States began to allow officers to carry handguns, especially following the riots that accompanied the economic panic of 1857. Eager to serve this new market, Colt came out with the New Model Police Revolver, one of the last new products his factory made before its founder's death in 1862. The Police Revolver was an inexpensive, lightweight six-shooter with a three-and-a-half-inch barrel, making it easy to conceal. "What speaks most of Colt's character is his hyperactive brand of opportunism," biographer William Hosley observed.

A pioneer of mass advertising, Colt used high-quality brochure art to promote his products as symbols of frontier adventure and technological advancement. Seeking credibility, he wrangled celebrity endorsements from the likes of General Sam Houston, the former president of the Republic of Texas. Colt relentlessly pursued public contracts, regardless of the profit margin. "Government patronage," he once said, "is an advertisement, if nothing else." Colt spent lavishly to entertain celebrated military officers and politicians, buying cigars by the thousands and running up enormous bills for liquor and entertainment.

While rivals invoked tradition, Colt made his easy-to-remember single-syllable name (not unlike "Glock") a synonym for "new." In 1854, he said: "A musket is an old established thing; it is a thing that has been the rule for ages, but this pistol is newly created." He stirred consumer interest by continually introducing slightly altered models with patriotic-sounding names. One of his most successful revolvers was the six-shot .36-caliber Navy, so called not because it was made for the US Navy, but because it had naval scenery engraved on its barrel. And, of course, the name "Navy" sounded valiant. As with several other designs, Colt also produced a smaller, more easily concealed Pocket Navy Revolver. Eleven years after he died, the factory in Hartford introduced the .44 Colt Army Model, which was sold to the military and spawned several popular civilian variants. This won the legendary single-action sidearm—still made in replica today—that became known as the "Peacemaker."

In many ways, Gaston Glock became the Sam Colt of the twentieth century. It is an assertion that might offend some American handgun historians and revolver loyalists. But it is no exaggeration to say that a pair of Austrians—a reticent engineer and his ambitious salesman—set about to remake the handgun business in the United States.

CHAPTER 7

Going Hollywood

From his company headquarters in the downtown SoHo neighborhood of Manhattan, Rick Washburn supplied movies and television shows with guns, knives, bombs, machetes, stilettos, ninja throwing discs—any instrument needed for theatrical violence. His company, Weapons Specialists Ltd., also stocked swords, daggers, spears, and shields for the opera and ballet. Washburn kept his collection behind triple-locked doors in a basement vault invisible to the boutique shoppers strolling by on Greene Street.

A native of Arkansas, Washburn came to New York in the 1970s to be an actor. He landed some minor roles: a hit man in *The Cotton Club* in 1984, an FBI agent in *Mississippi Burning* in 1988, and a hit man, again, in *Billy Bathgate* in 1991. As a boy growing up in the country, he had learned a lot about guns. He offered advice on the set to directors who didn't know a revolver from a semiautomatic pistol. Sometimes his kibitzing was resented; often it was appreciated. He began charging for gun consulting and discovered he could make a much better living in the prop business than from performing. Washburn trained actors, as well, on how to handle firearms realistically. He worked with everyone from Martin Scorsese to Arnold Schwarzenegger.

Karl Walter first went to work on persuading Washburn of the Glock's merits in 1986. "He ran the Glock spiel on me," Washburn recalled with a laugh. "He was like, 'Did you know that it has half the parts of a regular gun? Did you know it won't jam when a regular gun will jam? Did you know we've dropped these things out of helicopters and then picked them up and shot them?'"

At first, like many handgun aficionados, Washburn was skeptical. A devotee of the .45-caliber Colt 1911, he considered the Glock homely. "I was one of those people who believed, you know what, this thing is going to be a flash in the pan. . . . Maybe it'll be popular in Europe, not here." Fellow Colt chauvinists derided the plastic Glock as "handgun Tupperware." At Walter's insistence, Washburn finally took a Glock 17 to an indoor shooting range on the far West Side of Manhattan, one of the few places a civilian with a permit can fire a gun legally in the city. "There I am—*bang! bang! bang!*—just popping those targets like it was going out of style," he recalled. "I found it to be handy, easy to shoot, didn't jam. I was hitting targets on a regular basis with it. Suddenly I realized, as a tool, as a carry gun, as a military sidearm, this thing would be hard to beat." In Arkansas, he explained, "we used to have what we called our 'truck gun'—that old gun that you threw in the back of the truck, so if you saw a rabbit or a squirrel, you had something to shoot. It stayed in the back of the truck, and it got beat up. It shot OK, but it looked like hell. It wasn't the gun you hung up on the wall or showed to your friends. Glocks were kind of like that to me: a truck gun."

Until there were more Glocks in circulation, Washburn hesitated putting one in an actor's hand. But as a proponent of the Second Amendment right to keep and bear arms, he resented that New York banned the Glock by name. "It was a typical elitist attitude," he explained. "You know, you can't trust the regular people." In 1988, he had an opportunity to strike back. A friend of his ran a firm that helped New Yorkers navigate the procedures for obtaining handgun permits from the NYPD. Curious about which public officials had permits, Washburn's pal requested the records under the state freedom-of-information law. To his surprise, the city supplied the names and the types of weapons each official was licensed to own. Police Commissioner Benjamin Ward was on the list, and his permit noted the Glock 17. Washburn and his buddy decided the rest of the world should know about Ward's secret Glock. The prop man picked up the phone and called the Associated Press—and that is how word got out about the "super gun."

/ / /

As NYPD officers began carrying Glocks, Washburn felt it was time to give the Austrian gun entertainment-industry exposure. He was providing prop weapons for a television show on CBS called *The Equalizer,* which concerned a fictional former CIA operative who helped ordinary people deal (often violently) with hoodlums, drug dealers, rapists, and other unsavory sorts. The vigilante character made his services available via a cryptic newspaper ad: "Got a problem? Odds against you? Call the Equalizer." As befit a suave secret agent, the Equalizer carried a small Walther PPK stainless steel pistol. But late in the series' prime-time run, courtesy of Rick Washburn, walk-on characters began appearing with Glocks. "Once the [New York] Police Department started using them," he said, "we started putting them on cops, and particularly detectives."

Washburn liked helping the Austrian company; he realized

he also could benefit financially from having an up-and-coming gun maker favorably inclined to supply him with pistols on reasonable terms. Washburn sensed a groundswell of interest in Gaston Glock's invention: "You had people buying Glocks, using Glocks, checking Glocks out just because they were pissed off, just because of the notoriety." In the United States, he observed, "the people who are most against firearms usually end up being the best salesmen for firearms."

/ / /

Only the automobile rivals the gun as a Hollywood prop. Wheels and firepower—representing adventurousness and machismo—are seen by many shapers of popular culture as essential American characteristics. Karl Walter wasn't a deep-thinking media analyst, but he knew that "people buy what they see on television and in the movie theater."

Colt revolvers had a surge of popularity among American gun owners in the 1950s and 1960s as a result of being featured in cowboy movies and TV shows. The elegant Walther PPK gained cachet as James Bond's favorite pistol. Smith & Wesson received a huge marketing boost when Clint Eastwood appeared as Inspector Harold "Dirty Harry" Callahan in 1971 carrying his signature S&W Model 29 .44 Magnum. The movie "had a major impact on the sale of our .44 Magnums and our products," said former S&W company historian Roy Jinks. Pointing the enormous revolver at one criminal suspect, the Callahan character uttered one of the classic tough-guy speeches in cinema history: "I know what you're thinking: 'Did he fire six shots or only five?' But to tell you the truth, in all this excitement, I've kinda lost track myself. But being this is a .44 Magnum, the most powerful handgun in the world, and would blow your head clean off, you've got to ask yourself one question: 'Do I feel lucky?' Well, do ya, punk?"

Walter wanted the Glock to have its Dirty Harry moment.

"Product placement" first became a common marketing technique in the 1980s, as manufacturers paid to have their brand of soda, clothing, or car written into scripts. But the gun industry never had to pay for this kind of recognition. Screenwriters and directors needed no financial incentive to weave firearms into their plots. Gun companies, though, can make it easier or more difficult to cast their weapons. From its inception, Glock gave every consideration to prop men who could influence the process. Walter provided pistols to Washburn at huge discounts and, when Washburn ordered guns for rush delivery, let him cut in line ahead of other customers.

Colt and Smith & Wesson, by contrast, insisted that Washburn pay full price for their wares. Sometimes there were long delays in shipping from the American companies. The US marketing people at the German manufacturer Heckler & Koch, the Swiss Sig Sauer, and the Italian Beretta were even more recalcitrant, to the point that they seemed to Washburn almost indifferent as to whether their brands received theatrical exposure. Most gun makers tried to negotiate approval of how their products would be used. Cops and good guys were OK; criminals, not. Walter expressed a preference for Glocks being on the side of the law, but he didn't enforce the rule strictly. Dirty Harry, after all, was no Boy Scout, and he sold a ton of .44 Magnums. According to Washburn, "People don't care if a bad guy or a good guy uses your gun." The key, he said, is to get noticed.

In the late 1980s, Michael Papac, an up-and-coming weapons master in the Los Angeles area who specialized in action movies, worked on the *Lethal Weapon* films with Mel Gibson and Danny Glover and *Predator* with Arnold Schwarzenegger. "You were starting to hear about Glock, this plastic gun," Papac recalled. "There were stories about how you couldn't see it on an X-ray. People didn't know what they were talking about, but they were talking. Eventually you knew it would end up in a movie." Then Papac landed the assignment to provide weaponry for the sequel to Bruce Willis's slam-bang hit *Die Hard*. In *Die Hard 2: Die Harder*, which was released July 4, 1990, Willis reprised his role as John McClane, a hard-bitten and resourceful Los Angeles police lieutenant. This time, McClane faced off against a band of mercenaries involved with Latin American drug trafficking, who take over a major US airport. The villains threaten to cause the crash of incoming planes, including one containing McClane's wife.

The script for *Die Hard 2* called for the mercenary terrorists to carry Glocks—the big-screen debut for the Austrian pistol. "Those were the first Glocks I owned; they were new to Hollywood," said Papac. In the movie, the McClane character, who was armed with a Beretta 92FS, expressed surprise that his foes possessed the latest in handgun technology. At one point, he yelled to an airport police captain: "That punk pulled a Glock 7 on me! You know what that is? It's a porcelain gun made in Germany. It doesn't show up on your airport X-ray machines, and it costs more than you make here in a month!"

The Glock had its Dirty Harry moment. It didn't matter that every single trait Willis/McClane ticked off about the pistol was incorrect: There never was a model called the Glock 7. The gun was made in Austria, not Germany. It did show up on airport X-ray machines, and the Glock didn't cost more than what a police captain made in a month. "Everything Bruce Willis said about the Glock was made up," Papac said. "You can tell them the truth on the set, but that doesn't mean the director is going to change the script. They didn't listen to me."

Despite all of the errors—or, more likely, because of them the Bruce Willis *Die Hard 2* soliloquy on the Glock became an instant favorite of American gun enthusiasts. "Lots of people, whether they know about cars or World War II or the layout of New York, love to pick at errors in movies or television," noted Richard Feldman, the former NRA operative. "Gun people are the worst. They love to go on and on about mistakes about guns in the movies. It makes us feel smart and special: we know guns, and those stupid liberals in Hollywood don't know anything." The faulty *Die Hard 2* references to Glock "just got everyone talking again about this gun," Feldman said. "You had Jack Anderson, and Congress, and now, Bruce Willis—everyone's making things up about Glock. And gun owners, they want to defend the 'porcelain gun' or the 'plastic pistol' or the 'hijacker special,' or whatever the media are calling it. What fabulous publicity!"

Hollywood, in its growing love affair with the Glock, would go on to put the gun into countless movies in the 1990s, and screenwriters improved their technical accuracy, if not necessarily their literary sophistication. In *U.S. Marshals* (1998), Tommy Lee Jones, as US Deputy Marshal Sam Gerard, lectured Robert Downey Jr., who played a State Department security agent carrying a stainless-steel Taurus PT945. Holding the Taurus aloft with obvious disdain, Jones snapped, "Get yourself a Glock and lose that nickel-plated sissy pistol."

Arnold Schwarzenegger, an Austrian native, took pride in his home country's famous export and requested it by name for his movie roles, according to Washburn. Gaston Glock gave the actor a pair of complimentary pistols as a gift and showed off a framed photograph of the two men shaking hands. But

Glock couldn't persuade Schwarzenegger to endorse the brand publicly in the United States. Washburn calls Schwarzenegger "a closet gun guy, like a lot of Hollywood people." But the former champion bodybuilder more than made up for this reticence with his characters' on-screen pronouncements. In *End of Days* (1999), a supernatural thriller in which Schwarzenegger battles the Devil, he responds irritably to a priest's lecture on religious devotion, "Between your faith and my Glock nine-millimeter, I take my Glock."

/ / /

What set Glock apart from other handguns in the realm of pop culture was that it so quickly acquired a reputation as the firearm of both the cop and the outlaw. The former association had roots in reality; police officers from Colby, Kansas, to New York City had migrated to the Austrian pistol. The television police-and-prosecutor procedural *Law & Order*, which began its prime-time run on NBC in 1990, evolved into what some called one long Glock advertisement. Filmed in New York and outfitted by Rick Washburn, the show had its detectives and beat cops over the years move en masse from Smith & Wesson revolvers to Glock semiautomatics.

Glock's link to the world of criminals was, at first, more fantasy than fact. The Glock has an intimidating profile. It does not look like the gun of a hero, in the fashion of the Colt Peacemaker in westerns. It had been introduced to the American public by its critics as a hijacker weapon (however tendentiously). *Die Hard 2* portrayed it in the hands of paramilitary maniacs. But more important in terms of popular culture, the Glock was embraced by leading stars of hip-hop.

All sorts of major apparel, liquor, and jewelry brands took

advantage of rap's rapid rise to popularity, not just in the inner city but in predominantly white suburbs across the country. Big consumer-product companies sponsored concerts, bought advertising in music magazines, and used performers as spokesmen. "While virtually every other industry maneuvers to exploit hip-hop's commercial influence, gun manufacturers have been saved the work," Rodrigo Bascunan and Christian Pearce wrote in their rap history, *Enter the Babylon System: Unpacking Gun Culture from Samuel Colt to 50 Cent.* "Guns are a part of life, death, and status in the same neighborhoods that hip-hop grew up in. It only makes sense that firearm brands would come to pervade rap music."

"Gangsta rappers" peppered their lyrics with references to firearms and gunplay. The gun represented manhood; it was brandished in response to punk street rivals and perceived challenges from the police. Some MCs adopted stage names alluding to favorite brands: AK-47, Beretta 9, Mac 10, Mikhail Kalashnikuv, Smif-n-Wessun, and Young Uzi. But no model was more popular than the Glock. The rhyming potential alone—"pop," "drop," "cop," and, of course, "cock"—made it a lyricist's dream. Rappers Glock 9 and Glokk borrowed versions of the Austrian name as their professional identities. Song titles incorporated the brand: "Mask and da Glock" by Three 6 Mafia, "Hand on the Glock" by Cypress Hill, "Ain't No Glock" by TRU. The repertoire of rap works that refer to Glock is so voluminous in no small part because one of the most influential performers of the early 1990s, Tupac Shakur, featured the brand in "Soulja's Story" on his 1991 debut solo record, *2Pacalypse Now.* "I chose droppin' the cop, I got me a Glock," Shakur rapped, "and a Glock for the niggas on my block."

Apart from accelerating Shakur's career, the album sparked a national debate in 1992 when a Texas state trooper was killed by a teenager who allegedly listened to *2Pacalypse Now*. Vice President Dan Quayle denounced the record and demanded that it be withdrawn from stores. Chuckling all the way to the bank, executives at Shakur's studio, Interscope, refused. Shakur, whose mother, a former Black Panther, named him for a Peruvian revolutionary, defended his work, claiming it reflected the inescapable violence of poor urban black existence. Critics argued that he glorified such carnage. In the darkly poetic culmination of a life marked by real bloodshed, Shakur died in 1996, at the age of twenty-five, after he was shot four times by a drive-by triggerman in Las Vegas. The handgun used to kill the rapper was a .40-caliber Glock.

Shakur had firsthand experience with guns. For most rappers, Glock was just a weapon that rhymed. "Most people who talk about a Glock, they can't tell you a model number or how many shots it holds. They've never fired it, they've never felt spent shells hit them and burn their forearm, they've never done any of that shit," said Paris, an Oakland-based rapper. "Most people whose knuckles are draggin' in the streets aren't making records."

Little of what the urban crime rappers sang about actually involved Glocks. Rick Washburn points to *Juice*, a 1992 film about down-and-out inner-city black life. It starred Shakur as Bishop, a young man who sought respect and credibility—"juice"—by means of firepower. Washburn was asked to arm the movie's street figures. He went to the NYPD and asked what guns the police were taking from young black men at crime scenes. "The rappers would have you think it was Glock this, Glock that," Washburn said. "That's not the truth, at least not stickup guys and drug gangs in the ghetto. They used cheap revolvers and cheap American-made pistols, like they had since the 1960s and 1970s." Glock, fast becoming the "it" gun in Hollywood, had a tough-sounding name that rhymed easily. It had acquired cachet. But in the early 1990s, it wasn't common yet on the streets.

/ / /

Worlds away from the one Tupac Shakur inhabited, Karl Walter was stoking demand for Glock with other promotional methods. Glock, Inc., the US unit of Gaston Glock's company, was growing rapidly, adding salaried employees and signing up independent regional sales representatives who worked on commission. Walter retained an Atlanta advertising firm called Indelible Inc. to generate stark, simply worded display ads, mostly for gun magazines. "Set your sights on the handgun of the future. It's here. . . ." declared one early ad, a full-page, text-only spread in the *Shotgun News*. "The Glock 17 'Safe Action' 9mm semi-automatic pistol," it continued. "Unprecedented performance and reliability. Revolutionary concept and design. Unsurpassed shooting comfort and durability."

American handgun makers offered many diverse models, in the fashion of the Detroit car companies. Gaston Glock saw that as competing with himself and resisted the temptation. The fully automatic Glock 18 was a rarity sold to SWAT units. The Glock 19, a compact nine-millimeter pistol that held fifteen rounds, was marketed to detectives for concealed carry and as a more manageable alternative for women police officers with smaller hands. But the original Glock 17 remained the company's mainstay.

In 1988 Glock, Inc., had moved to larger quarters on

Highlands Parkway in Smyrna that included firing ranges and classrooms to accommodate training programs. The expanded facility became a gathering place, almost a clubhouse, for visiting cops and federal agents. Deputy marshals transporting prisoners through Atlanta would stop by to chat or squeeze off a few rounds on the Glock range. DEA, Customs, and Border Patrol agents on their way to or from Georgia's Federal Law Enforcement Training Center did the same. Instructors from the London Metropolitan Police and law enforcement agencies from Australia, Canada, Venezuela, and Colombia made appearances as well. The regional wholesalers that distributed Glocks and the independent sales agencies that visited retail gun shops on behalf of the company were required to send personnel to Smyrna for a four-day course on the use and maintenance of the unusual handgun.

After a businesslike curriculum that began on Monday morning, by Thursday evening the group of cops, salespeople, and Glock employees was ready to unwind. Karl Walter hosted lavish dinners in Atlanta restaurants followed by visits to the Gold Club, the city's best-known venue for exotic dancing and allied entertainment. Thursdays became known as "Glock Night" at the Gold Club. The group from Smyrna—as many as twenty-five or thirty men—was assigned its own VIP room on the enormous strip joint's second floor, above the main pole-dancing stage. Guests could watch the action below from a wraparound balcony or retreat to the roped-off VIP lounge for a lap dance. Loud electronic music pounded; strobe lights pulsed. Professional athletes from the NBA and NFL ambled by. In shadowy corners, cocaine could be had. Full-on sex wasn't on the official menu, but behind closed doors, who knew what transpired?

The girls, the liquor, the brushes with celebrity—to Glock

it was all part of doing business. "For a lot of guys coming in from out of town, this was the best time they were going to have all year, or maybe in their entire life," said one former police official. "You go to Smyrna, get laid at the best strip club in town, drink champagne, you're not going to forget the experience when it comes time to choose between Glock and Smith & Wesson."

Walter emphasized that he never paid for anyone's drugs or hookers. If there was illegal activity, he didn't know about it. As far as he was concerned, there were always plenty of cops at the Gold Club whose job it was to arrest any lawbreakers.

In the late summer of 1989, Walter had another marketing brainstorm. He convened a meeting for more than fifty independent regional sales reps and their managers. As Thursday evening approached, he gave the group a special assignment for their night out at the Gold Club: "What I thought was we should pick the best-looking, the best candidate, among the three hundred girls, to promote the product at the SHOT Show."

The Shooting, Hunting, Outdoor Trade (SHOT) Show is the US gun-and-ammunition industry's main conference of the year, often held in Las Vegas. In January 1990, Glock planned to unveil a new model, the Glock 20, a larger pistol that fired ten-millimeter rounds. Walter's idea was that the company should export some of the Gold Club sparkle to the SHOT Show. This wasn't entirely out of character for the firearms convention; it wasn't unusual for gun or ammo makers to decorate their booths with provocatively attired young ladies. Hiring a professional stripper, Walter hoped, might turn heads.

The audition that evening lasted until midnight. The Glock

delegation settled on a performer in her early twenties: Sharon Dillon, a blond, full-breasted, and strikingly tall young woman. When Walter asked Dillon if she would be willing to promote Glock in Las Vegas, she agreed. Next, he asked permission of the management of the Gold Club; the club was in no position to displease one of its steadiest corporate customers.

Walter told Dillon that she would have to go through a standard Glock four-day training. "We didn't want to send someone stupid to the show," he said. So the buxom stripper attended a program alongside personnel from the Defense Department and several federal agencies and police departments. Dillon's presence in the Glock classes and on the company firing range caused a significant stir, to be sure. "The guys came in and asked, 'Who is this girl?'" Walter recounted. He didn't want to tell federal agents and police SWAT specialists they were training with an erotic dancer. So he didn't. "I can't tell you," Walter said. "They all thought she was with the CIA."

"To everyone's surprise, she was the top shooter in this class and was the only one who finished all written tests 100 percent," Walter recalled. "She was . . . no dummy."

To heighten anticipation and draw maximum attention to the new Glock 20 ten-millimeter pistol, Walter had Dillon pose for a photographer and created an enormous billboard on the highway from the Las Vegas airport to the downtown Strip, featuring her comely image. Convention attendees were greeted by Dillon's dazzling smile and head-turning figure, with the slogan: "THE HOTTEST '10' IN TOWN. See the new Glock 10mm at the Shot Show (booth 1200)."

At the show, the aisles all around the Glock booth were jammed. Retailers and wholesalers jostled to get a peek at Dillon in her tight-fitting blouse. The Gold Club star posed for pictures with attendees and signed eight-by-ten glossy photographs; by general acclamation, she helped make Glock the hit of the SHOT Show. "A lot of guys from mom and pop gun shops had their ears pulled by the mom," recalled Dean Speir, a federally licensed firearm dealer from Long Island who wrote for gun periodicals. "You're talking real excitement—sex and guns. . . . The Glock reps must have taken a thousand orders the first day."

Some distributors got carried away. "People came up and said, 'Karl, I'll give you a $1 million order right now if I can go to bed with her,'" Walter recounted. Glock discouraged any extracurricular contact. But, then again, it was Las Vegas, and Walter didn't tuck her in at night.

At the awards ceremony marking the end of the SHOT Show, Dillon was called to the stage and given a plaque honoring her as "Best All-Around Model." Covering the event, *Shooting Industry* magazine reported: "After seeing Glock's Sharon Dillon, it is easy to see why dealers were anxious to get 'Glocked.'" Most would agree that hiring Dillon had been a stroke of genius.

In the wake of the show, the Gold Club became an even more integral element of Glock marketing and a symbol of the brand. Glock fashioned itself as the hot handgun, the sexy pistol. Gold Club girls received black Glock T-shirts and were urged to wear them at the club and elsewhere in Atlanta. When the company began using corporate jets for marketing trips, Gold Club girls sometimes went along for the ride. And for major events like the SHOT Show or the International Chiefs of Police convention, Sharon Dillon continued to accompany the Glock team. Glock parties at such events eclipsed the staid cocktail hours sponsored by rival companies. In the evenings at trade shows, Walter brought Dillon to Glock-hosted dinners. "All of a sudden, the president of Sigarms stops by," he recalled. "The president of Smith & Wesson, he sits down. . . . Everybody around the table trying to be with this beautiful woman. The information you can pick up in this conversation is priceless. I learned their thinking. Through their thought process, you learned how they're going to run the company." Glock, Inc., was on a tear.

CHAPTER 8

The Mark of Cain

I will never forget how it felt to hold a loaded gun for the first time and lift it and fire it, the scare of its animate kick up the bone of your arm, you are empowered there is no question about it, it is an investiture, like knighthood, and even though you didn't invent it or design it or tool it the credit is yours because it is in your hand, you don't even have to know how it works, the credit is all yours, with the slightest squeeze of your finger a hole appears in a piece of paper sixty feet away, and how can you not be impressed with yourself, how can you not love this coiled and sprung causation, I was awed, I was thrilled, the thing is guns come alive when you fire them, they move, I hadn't realized that.

—BILLY BATHGATE, FROM
BILLY BATHGATE: A NOVEL BY E. L. DOCTOROW

Sell a handgun to a civilian, Karl Walter understood, and you have sold one handgun. Sell a handgun to the police, as Colt had proved a hundred years before, and you sell handguns to an entire village.

John Davis, the owner of a financial-services firm in a small town west of Jacksonville, Florida, was a walking example of that adage. Davis didn't know much about Glocks when he traveled to Miami in 1986 to attend a personal-defense seminar. Even years later, he could recall with reverence the talk given at the multi-day class by Sergeant Paul Palank, the chief firearm instructor at the Miami PD. Such civilian courses, common around the country, combine lectures with practical instruction at a firing range. They are one way that knowledge about firearms passes from law enforcers to the public.

At the time, Palank was helping lead Miami's testing of the Glock as a replacement for Smith & Wesson revolvers. He recounted the FBI's harrowing Miami Shootout and how it illustrated that revolvers were inadequate for police and civilians alike. Davis took to heart the lesson that the cops were "outgunned." Palank did not raise—and probably did not know about—statistics that suggested a more complicated reality. Violent crime rates were rising in the 1980s, but studies in New York and elsewhere showed that the average police gunfight involved officers firing only two or three times each. In other words, six-shot revolvers still provided sufficient firepower for the typical violent encounter. Moreover, the number of US law enforcement officers killed annually on the job was falling. In 1973, police fatalities hit an all-time high of 268. By a decade later, the figure had dropped to 191; by 1993, it was down to 157. The real lesson of the Miami Shootout was that the FBI was poorly prepared. The agents on stakeout failed to equip themselves with military-style rifles at their disposal, and most of them neglected to wear armored vests. The FBI—and experts like Palank—played down these disheartening facts to promote a less damning story about revolvers having lost the day through no fault of the valiant federal agents.

Unsurprisingly, civilians such as Davis readily accepted what they were told. After hearing Palank's talk, Davis went home "and ordered several Glock pistols to try out."

/ / /

A chaplain and religious historian by training, Davis works in a one-story office building he owns on the main commercial street of his north-central Florida town. Every day he puts on a white shirt, striped tie, and business suit—and tucks a handgun in his belt holster. His decision to carry a firearm presents challenges in the Florida humidity. He explained that a finish called Tenifer makes the Glock's steel slide largely impervious to rust and even to the corrosive effects of sweat and salt water. Perspiration is not a threat to the gun's plastic frame. Davis's wife and adult son, who work in the family business, also carry handguns, usually Glocks.

The Davis men are statistically typical American gun owners: white, Protestant, politically right-leaning, and middle class. The elder Davis serves as a GOP committeeman, sings in his church choir, and meets some afternoons with friends at the local gun store. He lifted weights competitively as an undergraduate at Florida State University and, in his early sixties, resembles nothing so much as a 170-pound, five-foot-nine tree trunk. Sporting a bristly gray flattop, he doesn't speak so much as rumble, in a thick north Florida dialect.

Davis and his wife, Mary, a wispy, high-voiced woman of roughly the same age, met at the Reformed Theological Seminary in Jackson, Mississippi, where John enrolled after Florida State to prepare for his intended career as a hospital or prison chaplain. Mary completed her undergraduate English degree at a small religious college in Jackson. "I didn't know what I wanted to do with my life," she said. Then she corrected herself: "I wanted to get married and raise a Christian family." A minister she knew recommended that she attend the seminary to look for a husband. She did, and she found one. They married and moved to Florida so John could take a job as chaplain of a center for troubled children. He later switched careers, going into business for himself.

The Davises compete together in a monthly tournament sponsored by the International Defensive Pistol Association. John loaned me his twenty-two-year-old Glock 17 for the competition. He believes that all adults should carry guns as an exercise of civic responsibility. "An armed society is a polite society," he said, echoing a popular NRA aphorism originally coined by the science-fiction writer Robert Heinlein.

/ / /

In an essay called "America as a Gun Culture," historian Richard Hofstadter traced our distinctive regard for firearms to the anti-militarism of eighteenth-century British Whig politicians. For those English thinkers, the ultimate civic vice was a standing army of the sort the American Revolutionaries resented and eventually shot at. Virtue was embodied by the rugged yeomen admired by Thomas Jefferson, who included in his first draft of the Virginia constitution that "no freeman shall ever be debarred the use of arms."

"What began as a necessity of agriculture and the frontier took hold as a sport and as an ingredient in the American imagination," Hofstadter observed. "For millions of American boys, learning to shoot and above all graduating from toy guns and receiving the first real rifle of their own were milestones of life, veritable rites of passage that certified their arrival at manhood."

For Christmas when he was sixteen years old John Davis's grandparents gave him a .45-caliber pistol that had been in the family for decades. "That was something special," he recalled. "That was my self-defense pistol for a long time." He practiced at an old sawmill, shooting targets he propped up in front of piles of wood dust that served as a backstop. Davis spoke about the pleasure over the years of "working" with guns, "feeding" various models different brands of ammunition to see which ones they would "digest" the best. In his description, firearms are alive.

/ / /

On several occasions, Davis said, he was "really, really glad I had a firearm with me." Before he was married, for example, he was sitting late at night on a deserted beach in Pensacola with a girlfriend; three men approached, menacingly. "They had come up using the dune as a screen," he recounted. "I happened to have that little firearm. Never even pointed at them. As soon as I produced the gun, they were just like ghosts. They just melted away."

A self-described orthodox Presbyterian, Davis believes that "this self-defense stuff has to be driven by principles that are not just from the inside of men. . . . There is a God in Heaven who has not just put everything in place and backed off and left it like a wound-up grandfather clock to tick. He has told men in the Scriptures how they are to live. Those principles that are enscripturated are there for us to bring out and apply for life." He illustrated his point with the Sixth Commandment: "Thou shall not kill." Liberals, he argued, interpret the divine rule too broadly, as a ban on all killing. Many conservatives understand the proscription as applying only to murder. Davis sees the issue slightly differently. "If you are not to slay, if you are not to arbitrarily take human life," he said, "then the opposite side is you must protect human life, which is part of the basis for self-defense."

/ / /

Mary Davis says firearms make her feel safer. Like her husband, she has a Florida concealed-carry permit, and she usually is armed with a nine-millimeter Glock when she leaves the house.

Has she ever had to use a weapon to defend herself?

No, she said. But it does give her reassurance. One time when she accompanied John to a business conference in Houston, she and a tour bus full of other wives ended up in a tough inner-city neighborhood. The driver seemed lost, and it was getting dark. "I was glad to have that gun," she said. "I didn't know what could happen in a neighborhood like that."

"You have a right to peace of mind," her husband said. "Wrong neighborhood of a strange city—you [can] get in trouble quick."

"I don't ever want to shoot someone," Mary added, "but I don't want to be a victim."

Mary told a story about the sometimes heavy responsibility of carrying a firearm. Years ago, she attended a family wedding in Texas. She hitched a ride with a relative to the celebration, but planned to return to Florida by plane. She had her Glock with her. You can't carry a handgun onto a plane, of course, although airlines do allow guns to be transported with checked luggage. But Mary didn't want to bother checking her bag, so she gave the weapon to a male relative who was driving home. The gun was loaded.

"I was not as responsible as I should have been," Mary said, her head bowed in confession.

The relative stayed overnight with his son in a motel on the car trip home. When the father and boy got to their room, the man took the Glock from his bag, saw that there was a magazine in the grip, and decided, understandably, to unload the gun.

"But he was beyond his level of competency," said John, who is a stickler for firearm safety.

The man pushed the magazine-eject button and slid the mag out. But before doing that, he made a cardinal mistake. He pulled the slide back to look in the firing chamber. He didn't see a round in the chamber and released the slide. When a semiautomatic pistol's slide is released in that fashion, it scoops up a cartridge from the spring-loaded magazine and places it in the chamber. Basic safety procedure is to remove the magazine first, *then* rack the slide to check if the chamber is empty.

For whatever reason, the man pointed the gun, which he thought was empty, in the direction of the motel room bed and pulled the trigger.

"That Glock did what a Glock is supposed to do," John said. *"Bam!"*

The bullet ricocheted off the bed frame. A fragment of the round hit the man's young son in the leg, shattering bone. The injury was severe, requiring extended hospitalization. The police investigated, but no charges were filed. The boy recovered over a period of months. The Glock was returned to Mary in the end. No one blamed her—but she couldn't forgive herself:

"I will never be able to forget it. That boy won't forget it. His father won't forget it."

"You were not irresponsible," John insisted. After a minute of awkward silence, he sighed and put a hand on his wife's shoulder. "That marks you," he said, not specifying who was marked. "It marks you like Cain. There are consequences."

Mary's experience had not caused her to rethink the prudence or propriety of carrying guns.* That very night the three of us attended a lecture on Second Amendment rights, followed by blueberry pie at the Davises' home. I joined John and Mary on other occasions at shooting ranges in Florida; she certainly never seemed timid on the firing line. She claimed the accident with the Glock made her more careful, the way a car crash might make a driver more careful.

---

* Later, she had powerful misgivings about revealing this episode. The accident remains a source of emotional pain within the extended family. I agreed to use Davis, rather than their real name, and to refrain from identifying their hometown in Florida. The rest of their story is unchanged, and they are the only people in this book referred to by pseudonym.

CHAPTER 9

"Copy the Motherfucker"

By 1990, the predicament at Smith & Wesson headquarters over what to do about the ascendance of Glock had gone from worrisome to alarming.

Smith & Wesson built its storied reputation on revolvers. Horace Smith, an employee at the federal armory at Springfield, Massachusetts, and Daniel Wesson, an apprentice to his older brother, a leading New England gunsmith, had joined forces in the early 1850s to make a repeating rifle that could fire metallic cartridges. Smith and Wesson were part of a long-standing New England tradition. The government armory in Springfield had its roots in the Revolutionary War and spawned a gun industry in Massachusetts and Connecticut that went through cycles of boom and bust for more than two centuries. If Sam Colt was the most colorful character in what became known as Gun Valley, Smith and Wesson were sturdy rivals.

As with Colt, success at first eluded Smith and Wesson. Eventually they found a source of steady revenue by supplying the Union Army during the Civil War. Like the Colt, Smith & Wesson's guns also found their way into some famous frontier holsters. Jesse James, "Wild Bill" Hickok, and members of the Younger gang carried S&W. By the 1930s, police departments

around the United States were increasingly arming their pa-
trolmen with Smith & Wesson .38s, and the company grew
into the world's predominant manufacturer of handguns. Its
most famous designs included the powerful .357 Magnum and
.44 Magnum revolvers, as well as the first American-made
nine-millimeter pistol.

Constructed after World War II, the S&W plant in Springfield is an art deco fortress designed to withstand aerial bomb-
ing. In 1990, the company employed two thousand people and
was a mainstay of the western Massachusetts economy. Prepared for a Soviet military invasion that never occurred, Smith
& Wesson didn't anticipate commercial incursions from Brazil,
Switzerland, Italy, and, most threateningly, from Austria.

Foreign handgun makers looked toward the United States
in the 1980s and saw a domestic industry in disarray. The dol-
lar value of firearm sales was falling as economic hardship
devastated the farm belt, oil-producing states, and other gun-
friendly parts of the country. Fear in the insurance industry
of product-liability litigation had made corporate policies far
more expensive for firearm makers, even though few verdicts
of any size had been imposed on gun companies. Similar anxiety hit mass retailers like JCPenney, which phased out gun
sales, citing litigation risks, low margins, and criticism from
gun-control activists. Smith & Wesson and Colt had another
set of problems: aging plants, expensive workforces, and a failure to introduce new models that piqued the interest of consumers, law enforcement, or the military. Colt fumbled away
several lucrative Pentagon contracts. Smith & Wesson, which
had endured a series of destabilizing ownership changes, suffered an embarrassing falloff in the quality of its revolvers.

Sensing S&W's vulnerability, Brazilian firearm manufacturer

Forjas Taurus, which at one time was affiliated with S&W, expanded distribution in the United States of its moderately priced handguns. Beretta made its move in 1984, when the US Army invited bids for a nine-millimeter semiautomatic to replace the heavier, higher-caliber Colt .45. European allies in the North Atlantic Treaty Organization preferred the smaller nine-millimeter, which accommodated more rounds in its magazine. The Pentagon decided to follow suit on the theory that, in combat, the ability to fire more bullets quickly outweighed the advantage of ammunition that punched larger holes in an enemy. The Army demanded that delivery start within six to nine months after a contract award. Neither Colt nor Smith & Wesson could meet the tight schedule. Italy's Beretta and Switzerland's Sig Sauer said they could. After spirited bidding—colored by the Reagan administration's desire to reward Italy for its willingness to host nuclear-tipped missiles—Beretta won a five-year contract for more than three hundred thousand pistols. Sig, although frustrated in the Army competition, carved out the high end of the US pistol market, selling guns in the $700-to-$800 range (and later won an American military contract to supply compact pistols).

But of course far more threatening to US gun makers than Beretta, Sig, or Taurus was Glock, the Austrian upstart. Glock was aimed directly at Smith & Wesson's stronghold: the police.

While Gaston Glock hadn't been prepared in 1984 to respond to the Pentagon's solicitation of bids for a new pistol, his company benefited indirectly from the military's switch to the nine-millimeter. The change gave added credibility to a caliber previously little appreciated in the United States, and to pistols over revolvers in general. Police chiefs concluded that if the high-capacity nine-millimeter met Pentagon specifications, it was suitable for fighting urban violence. And the fact that Glocks were less expensive, lighter, simpler, and more durable than Berettas or Sigs gave them a significant competitive edge in the marketplace.

Astute observers of American gun commerce noted with dismay that foreigners were moving in on the firearm business, up to then arguably the most American of any industry. *BusinessWeek* magazine published a piece in May 1986 entitled "US Gunmakers: The Casualties Pile Up—Depressed Sales, Costly Insurance, and Foreign Competition Keep Claiming Victims." Henry Allen, the gun-owning essayist and former Marine, wrote in March 1990: "What America needs are better guns." He noted that the Secret Service was equipping agents with Israeli-made Uzis; the M-16s originally made for the Pentagon by Colt were being manufactured by a Belgian company. The Washington police were converting to the Glock. "It's bad enough that we invented the VCR and can't manufacture it, or that the Mercedes is the top-prestige sedan in the land of Cadillac," Allen lamented. "But guns! The gun is to America what the sword is to Japan—a tool that shaped our geography, politics, and psyche."

/ / /

Sherry Collins, a former copywriter for the marketing department of an insurance company, stepped unknowingly into the American firearm debacle. In the mid-1980s, a corporate headhunter recruited her for the post of head of public relations and advertising at Smith & Wesson. She had next to no experience with guns; as a woman, she was a rarity in the executive ranks in the firearm business. "I just admitted to everybody that I didn't know squat, but I wanted to learn," she said. Collins spent her first month being tutored on how to assemble and disassemble revolvers.

Slim, brassy, and not averse to an after-work drink, Collins was a fallen-away English literature graduate student in her thirties. She smoked enthusiastically and slung profanity with the guys. She also wrote clever ad copy.

When she arrived at the monolithic Springfield facility, she found that "Smith wasn't that concerned about Glock, as far as inroads into the law enforcement area. They were convinced at that time that the police were going to be very slow to switch to semiautos, because of their reputation for unreliability. What they failed to factor in was the Glock goes 'bang' every time."

In fact, Smith & Wesson executives were obsessed with the wrong foreign challenger. In 1965, the Wesson family had sold S&W to a conglomerate called Bangor Punta Allegra Sugar Co. Five years later, Bangor Punta bought a controlling stake of Forjas Taurus in Brazil. The two gun companies operated as affiliates, sharing equipment and technology, with Taurus focusing on sales in Latin America. But in 1977, Brazilian owners bought the Bangor Punta stake in Taurus, splitting it from Smith & Wesson and making it a potential rival for sales in the United States. According to Collins, some of her superiors at S&W feared that they would lose the American revolver market to the less-well-known Brazilian competitor. The S&W executives were obsessed by the fact that Taurus had retained American technology and plant equipment. In the early 1980s, Taurus established a unit in Miami and offered buyers a lifetime repair guarantee. Smith & Wesson countered by enlarging its array of revolvers in a marketplace already overflowing with similar models. Meanwhile, S&W barely noticed the major shift to pistols.

"Glock was out there," Collins recalled. But "the word in the industry was, 'The gun's uglier than a sack full of assholes.' Who'd want it? It's plastic."

/ / /

An incident at the 1990 SHOT Show, the same year in which Glock's Sharon Dillon starred at the gun industry convention, illustrated how the Austrian company outmaneuvered its American competition on substance as well as sex appeal.

With bureaucratic sluggishness, the FBI had been deliberating for several years over which pistol and ammunition would replace the six-shot Smith & Wesson. The agency at first decided to leapfrog existing gun models and ammo to equip its forces with a hard-hitting ten-millimeter pistol. "The Ten" would be a real "man-stopper," FBI ballistics experts believed. Word of this inclination, which seeped out from Washington in 1988 and 1989, stimulated gun and ammunition makers to go large. Glock had readied the ten-millimeter Glock 20 for introduction at the SHOT Show, under the assumption that the FBI's choice would influence tastes in wider law enforcement and commercial circles. By then, however, the FBI had discovered that conventional ten-millimeter ammunition—fired from a pistol about the same size as the traditional Colt .45 model that the military was phasing out—produced too much recoil for many agents to shoot accurately. The agency was beginning to recruit female personnel, and the women had even more trouble with the ten-millimeter. As an alternative, S&W collaborated with Winchester to design a new, shorter cartridge of the same bore diameter, which could be fired from a slightly altered version of the nine-millimeter pistol. To distinguish the new product, and give the FBI its own distinctive load, the manufacturers called the ammunition the ".40 S&W." (Forty-caliber rounds are the same diameter as ten-millimeter rounds.)

Glock, with its ten-millimeter, seemed to have missed a subtle twist in handgun tastes. Obviously, Smith & Wesson would come out with a pistol to match the .40 S&W ammunition. With the FBI's imprimatur, that combination would become the hot new handgun—or that, at least, was what everyone in the industry assumed.

Gaston Glock traveled from Vienna to Las Vegas to attend the SHOT Show that year. American wholesalers and retailers, to whom Karl Walter, the company's top executive in the United States, introduced Glock, treated the Austrian engineer with respect bordering on awe. He was the hero of the plastic pistol controversy, the champion of greater police firepower.

For all his stature at the SHOT Show company booth, however, Gaston Glock wasn't yet known on sight by most executives and marketing men in the American gun industry. He could stroll the exhibition floor without being noticed. Walter had told him about the .40 S&W round. Glock decided to take a look for himself. He walked over to the Smith & Wesson display area, scooped up samples of the .40 ammo, and put them in his pocket. Later he took measurements and made an important discovery. "Mr. Glock realized," said Walter, "that with only very minor changes to the Glock 17, we could introduce a pistol to fire .40-caliber rounds, and we could steal this opportunity from Smith & Wesson."

Before S&W could get its distribution wheels turning and put a .40 model on gun store shelves, Glock began shipping its own version: the .40-caliber Glock 22. By mid-1990, the new Glock pistol, which, to the layman's eye, appeared virtually identical to the original Glock 17, was headed toward being a big hit in its own right.

"Oh, my God, what an embarrassment," recalled Smith & Wesson's Sherry Collins. "We're beaten to market on the gun for our own ammo, the round we've made especially for the FBI. And some Austrian gets there first!" Swirling a midday cocktail, Collins added: "The technical industry term for that kind of experience is 'getting your ass kicked.'"

///

Panic rippled through Smith & Wesson. Tomkins, a British conglomerate, had bought the company in 1987 and brought in a new chief executive officer to shake things up. The former head of United Technologies' Pratt & Whitney Engine Division, Steve Melvin knew little about firearms. Collins, also new to the industry, was one of the few S&W executives working for Melvin who openly acknowledged the reality of the company's decline. When Henry Allen, who worked as a feature writer for the *Washington Post,* called her in early 1990 to discuss the deterioration of American gun quality, she decided to plead guilty and promise that S&W would do better in the future. "Smith & Wesson admits its quality control became a laughingstock, even among writers for American gun magazines, who tend to be shills for the gun companies," Allen wrote. "'We are aware of that, and we feel we have corrected those problems,'" Collins told him.

While Smith & Wesson already made pistols, in addition to its better-known revolvers, its steel semiautos were mechanically complicated, prone to malfunction, and, as a result, not very successful in the marketplace. As more police agencies indicated they would switch from S&W .38 revolvers to Glocks, Melvin pressed his engineers to come up with a fresh pistol design that would keep these departments in the Smith & Wesson fold. The engineers whined about how the whole pistol trend was overblown. They insisted the plastic gun was a fad.

Melvin disagreed. Not only was Glock taking over the new market for nine-millimeters, but if the .40-caliber caught on, S&W would fall even further behind. In early 1991, the CEO gathered his top engineers and marketing executives around a conference table at the Springfield factory. He demanded to know what prototypes were in the works. What polymer pistol could S&W offer to compete with the Glock 17, the new Glock 22, and their respective compact variants?

The engineers fiddled with their Styrofoam cups, making excuses. Plastic, they repeated, would never catch on in the United States. They clearly resented being lectured by Melvin, a guy who made airplane engines.

Melvin lost his temper. He had brought a Glock 17 with him to the meeting; he took out the (unloaded) pistol and slammed it on the conference table. "If you can't come up with a better handgun than the Glock," Melvin shouted, *"then copy the motherfucker!"*

"And they did," Sherry Collins recalled.

Melvin's tantrum became the subject of gossip throughout the industry—an emblem of the American industry allowing a foreigner to beat and embarrass it. Reluctantly, the S&W engineers produced a polymer pistol. The company called it the Sigma, but it was a blatant knockoff of the Glock 17. Moreover, it was generally considered less reliable than the Austrian original. Introduced in 1994, the Sigma reinforced the growing impression that Smith & Wesson had lost whatever mojo it had left.

"I remember the first Sigma I saw," said Rick Washburn, the New York–based theatrical prop master and gun trainer. "I called the Smith & Wesson people and said, 'You guys, what do you think Glock's going to say about this?'"

His S&W contact argued that the Sigma was different from the Glock—an improvement.

Washburn didn't buy it. "I went, 'Ah, I've taken your gun apart. I've taken the Glock apart. Yeah, the trigger is a little bit different. But, I'm sorry, I think you guys got some problems.'" Handgun experts made fun of the Sigma, calling it "the Swock" or "the Glock & Wesson."

Within a few months, Glock filed suit against Smith & Wesson, alleging that the American company infringed on Glock patents and deliberately caused confusion among consumers by marketing an almost identical gun. "These patents are my personal property," Gaston Glock said in a company newsletter at the time. "If someone stole my wallet or stole my car, I would call the police. The situation here is no different, except that I can't call the police. So I must rely on the courts."

Smith & Wesson claimed the suit was "totally without merit," but three years later, it agreed confidentially to settle the matter out of court. S&W made a multimillion-dollar payment to Glock and altered the Sigma design slightly. But by then, the Sigma was a commercial afterthought. It never posed a real competitive threat to Glock.

///

The successful patent suit against Smith & Wesson constituted a dazzling industry debut for Glock's young in-house lawyer, a gregarious former prosecutor named Paul Jannuzzo. Despite the risk of offending American gun owners by taking a legendary rival to court, Jannuzzo pushed for aggressive legal action. The approach paid off handsomely, and there was little, if any, backlash from gun buyers. For an attorney in his mid-thirties who liked guns and shooting, the Glock general counsel's job turned out to be a dream come true.

Jannuzzo, the son of a middle-class Catholic family, had majored in political science at Pennsylvania's Villanova University. He attended mass on Sunday, often after a boisterous Saturday night of partying. Charming when he wanted to be, Jannuzzo had an explosive temper, especially when he had been drinking.

After college, he enrolled at the newly opened Vermont Law School, where he befriended an irreverent and equally loquacious classmate named Richard Feldman. The two shared a bawdy sense of humor and both joined an informal law student shooting club. Jannuzzo had been taught about guns as a child and enjoyed plinking bottles and cans in the Vermont woods. He subscribed to the NRA's view—that guns per se were not a problem; it was guns in the hands of the wrong people that threatened society. He decided to become a prosecutor and put the bad guys in jail.

Armed with a J.D., Jannuzzo passed the bar in New Jersey and became an assistant district attorney. He enjoyed the work and helped with a major death penalty case. After learning his way around the courtroom for several years, he moved on to the more lucrative private practice of law in 1985. At a small firm in Red Bank, he handled criminal defense assignments and represented companies in product liability cases. Some of his clients were gun retailers who had been sued when firearms they sold were later misused.

Jannuzzo became an active member of the New Jersey

Coalition of Sportsmen, the local NRA affiliate, where his path crossed again with that of his law school friend Feldman, who was a regional organizer for the NRA in the Northeast. Feldman recruited Jannuzzo to testify against gun-control laws before the New Jersey legislature. "Paul was a very effective witness," Feldman recalled. "Here's the young ex-prosecutor telling the politicians that New Jersey's version of the assault weapons ban is just symbolism."

Feldman was so impressed by Jannuzzo's performance that he asked him to address a pro-gun rally on the State House steps in Trenton in 1990. Jannuzzo obliged, appearing before a rambunctious, casually dressed collection of hunters and hand-gun owners. The attorney wore his usual dark suit and conservative tie, as well as horn-rimmed eyeglasses that made him look more like a law professor than a rabble-rousing Second Amendment activist. For several years afterward, the NRA used a video of the event in its advertising.

By 1991, Karl Walter realized that Glock, Inc.'s, increasing litigation burden required a full-time staff lawyer. He called Feldman, who was an acquaintance, and asked if he knew any attorneys who were "not assholes." Feldman suggested Jannuzzo. "I guess it didn't totally escape my attention that it wouldn't be bad to have my friend working inside Glock, the up-and-coming manufacturer in the industry," Feldman told me. "Was I looking out for my own interests? Sure. But Paul really was perfect for the job."

Jannuzzo became Glock's in-house attorney and, over time, its main spokesman, as well. Sharply worded sound bites came naturally to the ex-prosecutor. Responding to an Associated Press report on liability lawsuits against Glock, he said: "Nike gets sued by people who have twisted ankles. It doesn't matter if you make tennis rackets or pistols, you get lawsuits." That may be true, and it is certainly glib, but of course sneakers are rarely implicated in life-threatening injuries. Jannuzzo was not above bending logic to make his point.

Within the company, he became a popular figure, admired for his ability to impress Gaston Glock without being pretentious. Most of the American employees in Smyrna were intimidated by the German-speaking Austrian and his entourage. Jannuzzo, a quick study, picked up enough German to figure out what the Austrian executives were saying. But rather than hoard this information to his own advantage, he used it to try to reassure his American colleagues. Out of the Austrians' presence, Jannuzzo would roll his eyes or wink when explaining how to "manage up" in the company. "I'm not embarrassed to say I loved the man," said Ed Pitt, a gunsmith employed by Glock. "He was a straight shooter."

A fall 1992 newsletter sent to members of the Glock Shooting Sports Foundation, a company-sponsored group that held competitions, featured a profile of Jannuzzo, describing him as an exemplary employee. Jannuzzo arrived earlier and stayed later than anyone else at the Smyrna corporate offices. The circular added: "The most common remarks heard about Paul are: 'He's always up. You never see him angry.' 'I value his opinion and advice.' 'A great sense of humor.' And, more often than not, 'He's a lawyer, but I like him anyway!' "

///

Sherry Collins had helped promote a .38-caliber revolver at Smith & Wesson marketed to women as "The Ladysmith," for which she became well known in industry circles. But to her, Smith & Wesson seemed lost, despite the affection she still felt for the company. She left S&W in late 1991 to edit a gun-industry magazine.

In 1994, Glock, Inc., offered her a job as head of public rela-tions in the United States. Collins, like Jannuzzo, thought the foreign label had a unique advantage: "Glock owners have a kind of brand loyalty that's incredible, because they were pari-ahs in a way. You know, you own 'the hideous plastic gun.'" So she agreed to move to Smyrna.

CHAPTER 10

Massacre in Killeen

About eighty people were crowded into Luby's café in Killeen, Texas, eating lunch on October 16, 1991, when George Hennard, a thirty-five-year-old former merchant marine, crashed his pickup truck through the plate-glass front of the restaurant. Some customers, thinking the vehicle was out of control, moved to help the injured. Then Hennard began shooting.

"He was firing at anyone he could shoot," said Luby's patron Sam Wink. He "had tons of ammo on him." Another witness described him shooting "as fast as he could pull the trigger." When he emptied one seventeen-round magazine in his Glock 17, he inserted a fresh one. Some witnesses said Hennard spoke to his victims as he approached them. "Was it worth it?" he asked before pulling the trigger of the Glock.

Hennard's fellow residents in Belton, Texas, would describe him as a strange man. On occasion, he came out of his house screaming. He had sent neighbor Jane Bugg a rambling letter about "treacherous female vipers . . . who tried to destroy me and my family." Bugg gave the letter to police, but they did not investigate.

On the day of the attack, Texas state law enforcement officials happened to be leading a class for local police officers in Killeen. The coincidence probably saved a number of lives. Cops arrived less than ten minutes after Hennard started shooting. They found the café floor covered with glass, blood, and spent ammunition. The police opened fire and wounded Hennard, who retreated into a hallway leading to the restaurant's restrooms. Trapped, he shot himself fatally in the head. But by then, he had killed twenty-two people and injured many more. At the time, it was the worst mass shooting in United States history.

An investigation revealed that Hennard had purchased the Glock legally. It was swiftly traced by its serial number to the company plant in Smyrna, which told the police that the gun had been sold to a distributor in Sparks, Nevada. The distributor transferred it, legally, to Mike's Gun House, a federal firearms license holder in Henderson, Nevada. Mike's sold the Glock to Hennard, who at the time was staying in Henderson with his mother. Hennard provided the salesclerk with all of the information requested on the registration form required in Clark County, Nevada, a jurisdiction that had relatively stringent rules governing gun purchases. The Las Vegas Metropolitan Police Department ran a criminal background check on Hennard, but it turned up only a 1981 misdemeanor arrest for marijuana possession in El Paso. A felony conviction would have disqualified him from owning the weapon; the misdemeanor dope arrest did not.

/ / /

On the day Hennard made history in Killeen, the US House of Representatives was debating proposals to tighten national rules about gun ownership. House members gathered in the Capitol to consider a major anti-crime bill, a version of which the Senate had passed in July. Republicans and Democrats were waging a raucous political contest to claim the title of toughest crime busters.

House Republicans added provisions to the bill that would broaden the kinds of cases eligible for the death penalty and give prosecutors more leeway to use illegally obtained evidence. The most heated debate focused on provisions in the anti-crime bill that banned guns classified as "assault weapons" and put restrictions on high-capacity magazines. As drafted, the legislation limited magazines to no more than seven rounds, fewer than half the number in the magazine of a Glock 17.

Several hours into the debate, news broke about the Killeen killings. Lawmakers seized on the horrific reports to score rhetorical points. George W. Gekas, a Pennsylvania Republican, said the Luby's massacre showed that more crimes deserved capital punishment. Most Democrats drew a different lesson: that semiautomatic weapons and large magazines should be curbed. "Twenty-two people died," said Charles Schumer of New York, then a House member. "Maybe they didn't have to." The Glock 17 wasn't one of the weapons on the list of thirteen guns to be banned, but the seventeen-round magazines Hennard used would be outlawed if the proposed legislation passed.

The clash over high-capacity weapons intensified the next day. Harold Volkmer of Missouri, a conservative Democrat in the camp of the National Rifle Association, put forward amendments that would do away with the bans on assault weapons and large-capacity magazines. James Sensenbrenner, a Wisconsin Republican, derided the notion that a seven-round limit would have made a difference in Killeen. "The killer was in the cafeteria for over ten minutes," he said. "He had plenty of time to change clips, and apparently he did."

Ed Feighan, an Ohio Democrat and one of his party's more

vociferous anti-gun proponents, rose to oppose the Volkmer amendments. "I would have thought that yesterday in Killeen, Texas, this body had run out of time for posturing on this crime bill, or pandering to one of the most powerful special-interest groups in the country," Feighan said. Weapons commonly used for hunting would not be affected by the legislation, he argued. Rather, the firearms at issue were the AK-47 and its military-style brethren. "And we are talking about seventeen-round magazine clips on guns like the Glock nine-millimeter that was used yesterday afternoon to kill twenty-two innocent Americans." John Conyers, a Michigan Democrat, also lashed out at the Austrian pistol: "Innocent people lost their lives to a gunman whose import Glock 17 was a death machine which fed bullet after murderous bullet in the firing chamber."

Amid all the speechifying, few lawmakers wavered in their views. One who did, setting gun-control hearts racing, was Representative Chet Edwards. The Killeen massacre took place in his home district. A Democrat of moderate-to-conservative views, Edwards said the killings had caused him to rethink his long-standing opposition to tough gun control. "For me the old arguments ring hollow," Edwards said. "It's a human story now, a human tragedy, and I just simply have to vote to put some limit on assault weapons that could be used by drug king-pins and crazed killers to murder innocent victims." He added that if the magazine limit were already law, "the killer could not have had seventeen bullets in each clip, and we could have perhaps saved lives."

"It was not the pistol that caused those deaths," countered Volkmer. He deplored the bloodshed but said the proposed curbs would not have prevented it. "If it was not a pistol," he said, "it could easily have been a rifle; if not a rifle, a shotgun; if not a shotgun, a can of gasoline."

President George H. W. Bush expressed himself similarly in a television interview broadcast during the debate. Two years earlier, in a move that enraged the NRA, Bush had used an executive order to stop the importation of certain semiautomatic assault weapons. He had done so at the urging of his anti-drug czar, William Bennett. The administration suffered politically, and Bush now tried to mend fences with pro-gun forces. "Obviously, when you see somebody go berserk and get a weapon and go in and murder people, of course it troubles me," the president said. "But what I don't happen to have the answer to is can you legislate that behavior away. . . . I don't believe there is one federal law that is going to rule against aberrant behavior of that nature."

At the end of the debate, the House voted 247–177 against limiting assault weapons and magazine capacity.

/ / /

In Smyrna, Karl Walter held a news conference the day after the shooting, expressing sorrow for the victims and their families. But he waved off suggestions that the Glock's design exacerbated the carnage in Killeen. You can't blame an inanimate object for the actions of a madman, he said. In fact, what happened at Luby's illustrated why there should be *fewer* restrictions on handgun use. If more Americans had legal access to Glocks, he argued, the murders in Texas could have been kept to a minimum. "If there had been one armed person there," he said, "it would have stopped."

Walter was not prone to self-doubt. The Glock was a phenomenal commercial success. He took offense that anyone would criticize it. Beginning with production for the United States of 25,000 pistols in 1985 and 1986, Glock had more than tripled that figure in 1989. In 1990, Glock shipped 120,000 hand-guns to the States. Several thousand law enforcement agencies across the country had purchased Glock 17s, putting a serious dent in Smith & Wesson's near monopoly on the police handgun market.

And as a result of the company's low costs, Gaston Glock was enjoying extraordinary profits. In the space of a few years, he had become a multimillionaire, and his lifestyle shifted ac-cordingly. The once-frugal engineer acquired a yacht and a BMW Series 7 sedan. His company bought gleaming execu-tive jets—one for the United States, one for Austria. Glock, who held a pilot's license, flew the aircraft himself, with a pro-fessional copilot. He enjoyed the airplane pilot's relative isola-tion, explaining: "There are fewer crazy people in the air."

In Velden, Glock built a more spacious vacation villa and spent lavishly at two-star Michelin restaurants, glitzy night-clubs, and high-end casinos. He did not try to join high society in Vienna, however. He did not become a patron of the arts or hobnob with diplomats or international bankers. If he dined out in Austria's worldly capital, he did not create a sensation among other patrons. The newspapers did not report on his comings and goings.

Glock also retained his middle-class affection for bargains. When in Atlanta, he took extended trips to Home Depot for discount plastic bathroom fixtures, which he shipped back to Velden. He outfitted the bedrooms of his five-story villa with inexpensive mattresses bought in bulk at a Georgia shopping mall. While Glock traveled first class to and from Europe, he diligently kept the giveaway airline toiletries and hoarded per-fumed soap from the fancy hotels he patronized.

Glock was the sort of boss who monitored closely the com-pany's expenses, including what he paid his top executives. He was very aware that Karl Walter was profiting handsomely. In addition to a salary, Walter's contract with Glock provided that he would receive a small percentage of the company's US revenue. To his surprise, and Gaston Glock's, that commission had ballooned to hundreds of thousands of dollars a year—not bad for an immigrant gun salesman who once trundled from town to town selling rifles from an RV. With the likelihood that Walter's total compensation would soon hit seven figures, jealous grumbling began to be heard among less-well-remunerated Glock aides back in Austria. "Some who had Mr. Glock's ear," Wolfgang Riedl recalled, "asked whether Karl was getting too big for his pants."

/ / /

Despite the setback in the House of Representatives, gun-control advocates and the media kept the spotlight focused on Glock. "The Glock 17," the New York Times reported, "is popular with drug dealers and at one time was banned by the New York City Police Department, which feared that terrorists could sneak it through airport metal detectors." But the Times offered no evidence that drug dealers preferred Glocks. The paper did note that the NYPD "recently bought 1,000 of the pistols," which were also being used "by the Federal Bureau of Investigation, Customs agents, the Secret Service, and more than 4,000 other federal, state, and local law enforcement agencies, including the New York State Police."

Contrary to the Times' assertion about the Glock's popularity with criminals, federal traces of guns recovered from crime scenes showed that compared to its rivals, the Glock was not a weapon of choice on the street. In June 1992, the

US Bureau of Alcohol, Tobacco and Firearms reported the top eighteen models of the nearly fifty-seven thousand handguns seized by law enforcement and traced during 1990 and 1991. The Glock 17 ranked last, meaning it was recovered the least often at crime scenes. The most common crime gun, according to the ATF, was the .38-caliber Smith & Wesson revolver, almost certainly because it had been on the market for generations, and millions of the guns circulated on the legitimate used market and on the black market. Filling out the top five, in descending order, were: a cheap and unreliable .25-caliber pistol made by Raven Arms; an inexpensive Davis Industries .380 (like the Raven, a type of handgun often referred to as a Saturday Night Special); the nine-millimeter Smith & Wesson Model 3904 semiautomatic, with an eight-round capacity; and the heavy-duty Colt .45, another model that had been sold for many decades. For all of its notoriety, the Glock was less popular with criminals than the older S&W and Colt or the junky Raven and Davis.

These statistics did little to blunt the fulminating of editorialists who condemned the Glock's lethal force. "It is one in a class of weapons known as 'assassin's guns,'" the *Houston Chronicle* stated. The paper quoted Bernard Horn, state legislative director for the Washington-based nonprofit Handgun Control Inc., as saying that the Austrian pistol, equipped with its large magazine, was one reason police were "outgunned." Civilians, Horn said, "have no business with magazines this size."

Despite what Handgun Control and newspaper editorial boards might have assumed, continuing attacks on the Glock only seemed to enhance its image in the eyes of potential buyers. Whenever gun-control advocates announce that citizens should not have access to a certain handgun, firearm enthusiasts are prone to take a closer look. "This kind of media reporting does not hurt sales," Karl Walter asserted.

///

The Killeen killings actually inspired some people to consider buying a gun for the first time. Two months after the massacre, the *Dallas Morning News* published a feature on the post-Killeen gun boomlet in middle-class north Texas. The Bullet Trap, a gun shop in suburban Plano, told the paper it had seen an increase in registration for its gun-safety courses and a related uptick in handgun sales. Pete Waldroop, a twenty-three-year-old computer engineer, said he had never considered owning a gun. Then "I saw the Killeen thing and thought I ought to know more." He paid $59 to take a beginner's class at the Bullet Trap, where he tried out several models in the store's indoor range. A few days later, after some more practice, Waldroop returned to the Bullet Trap and paid $459.95 for a Glock 17. He kept the pistol in a briefcase beside his bed.

Suzanna Gratia Hupp, too, became a pro-gun activist as a result of Killeen. A chiropractor, she was eating lunch at Luby's with her parents when Hennard crashed through the restaurant's glass front. After Hennard started shooting, Suzanna and her seventy-one-year-old father flipped their table to provide cover. She reached into her purse for the .38 Smith & Wesson Chief's Special she usually carried. After groping around for a few seconds, she realized that on that day, of all days, she had left the revolver in her car. Suzanna's father, a World War II vet who didn't own a firearm, charged at Hennard. The gunman shot him fatally in the chest. And when Suzanna's mother tried to comfort her dying husband, Hennard killed her, too. Suzanna survived, and in the wake of the tragedy, she became an advocate for relaxing laws on when and where civilians may carry concealed handguns.

In testimony before legislatures in Texas and other states, she spoke of her painful regret at leaving her revolver in her parked automobile at Luby's. "My state has gun-control laws," she told lawmakers in Missouri in March 1992. "It did not keep Hennard from coming in and killing everybody." Elected to the Texas House of Representatives, Hupp became a nationally known gun-rights activist who appeared on television programs such as the *CBS Evening News* and ABC's *World News Tonight*. The NRA gave her a life membership and its Women's Freedom Award. Texas changed its gun-permit statute in 1995 to make it easier for residents to carry concealed handguns.

CHAPTER 11

Lawyers, Guns, and Money

Richard Feldman learned about Killeen during a telephone conversation with a friend who owned a gun store and had seen a television bulletin about the massacre. The police had identified the killer's gun as a Glock. Feldman flipped on CNN with one hand and hit the speed-dial on his desk phone with the other, calling his old law school buddy Paul Jannuzzo. He suspected Glock's general counsel might appreciate some public relations advice.

Jannuzzo, speaking from his office in Smyrna, confirmed the dire nature of the situation. "Richie, the phone lines are already lighting up: reporters, TV. How should we respond?" Jannuzzo didn't have any experience with a media frenzy of this magnitude.

Feldman's history with Glock went back almost to the company's arrival in the United States. Like other NRA staff members, he had defended Glock against gun controllers' attacks in 1986. Five years later, he took a new job as executive director of a fledgling gun industry organization called the American Shooting Sports Council. Killeen was the first crisis on his watch running the trade group.

"Make sure to say that this was a terrible tragedy," Feldman said. "Whatever you do, Paul, do not say 'no comment.'" It was Feldman who insisted that Glock hold a press conference, even as members of Congress were castigating the Glock in Washington "Empathize with the victims and the community of Killeen," Feldman advised. "Obviously the killer was another crazy. Be sure to stress it was the criminal, not the gun. Tell the press how many police and law-enforcement agencies are now armed with Glocks."

Jannuzzo passed this advice along to Karl Walter, as well. Together they followed Feldman's script, and, for the most part, it worked. The media emphasized the Glock 17 as the murder weapon but also pointed out how popular it was with cops. Democrats in the House of Representatives kicked the Glock around during the floor debate, but pro-gun forces in the House prevailed by a wide margin. Though he knew gun-control proponents in Washington would not give up, Feldman considered the immediate legislative response to Killeen at least an interim victory. "Richie," Jannuzzo recalled, "always had a good feel for how things would play in the media."

/ / /

In the Northeast, Feldman had become Glock's top defender at the NRA in the 1980s. When Sheriff Eugene Dooley of suburban Suffolk County, New York, banned the gun by name, following the lead of the NYPD, a local Long Island gun dealer and shooting enthusiast named Dean Speir appealed to the association. It was Feldman whom the NRA dispatched to speak with Sheriff Dooley. When polite persuasion didn't work, Feldman delivered a blunter message: "Let Speir and other dealers transfer Glocks to licensed individuals, or we'll take you to court and pull your pants down."

Within the month, Sheriff Dooley folded, and Glocks were

legal on all of Long Island. "Richie Feldman got it done," Speir recalled.

Feldman did his job as a gun lobbyist with a zeal the NRA famously inspires in its employees and members. Over the years, though, he grew to resent the organization's top officials. NRA management, Feldman concluded, cared just as much, if not more, about getting members to make financial contributions as it did about protecting gun owners' rights. "That was one reason that we were all pleased when the anti-gun groups and their media and congressional allies made so many embarrassing technical errors in the protracted 'plastic gun' controversy," Feldman wrote in his spirited memoir, *Ricochet: Confessions of a Gun Lobbyist.* The NRA used the controversy, he continued, "to spread the incipient fear that the gun grabbers were not just after the Glock 17. Once they used their bogus information to outlaw Glocks (a well-made and expensive pistol), all handguns—revolvers and semiautos alike— would be threatened. Emergency alerts flooded the nation from the [NRA's] Institute for Legislative Action, and contributions to fight this potential 'unprecedented' gun grab poured back into the NRA's mailroom."

The NRA's leaders, Feldman realized, "don't really want us to educate people on this issue. The association wants to use it as a club to beat the antigunners." The NRA "had no interest in compromise. It would have been relatively easy to demonstrate to the public that the Glock pistol was no more dangerous than any other weapon. But educating the public—either through elected officials or the media—was not the association's paramount goal. Its overriding aim was preserving its dominant position as protectors and guardians of the faith, a sort of Knights Templar extraordinaire, of the Second Amendment."

Opinions like that did not endear him to the NRA's inner circle. They were weighed with suspicion against the victories he won for the gun lobby. Feldman, for example, had orchestrated an imaginative media campaign on behalf of Bernard Goetz, the New York "Subway Vigilante" who shot four black young men armed with sharpened screwdrivers after they threatened him. Acquitted of serious felonies, Goetz was convicted of a single firearm charge for which he served just eight months in jail. But for every pro-gun public relations triumph, Feldman had two run-ins with his NRA bosses. Forced off the full-time NRA payroll in the late 1980s, he continued to work from time to time as a paid consultant for the organization, finding other employment defending the interests of gun manufacturers and firearm owners.

Part of what made Feldman a bad fit within the NRA was his upbringing in a politically moderate middle-class Jewish family on Long Island. He understood that many patriotic Americans—like his parents—felt little affinity for hunting or guns. As a young man, Feldman supported strong gun control. His views began to shift after college, when he took a job as a deputy tax collector and auxiliary police officer in Cambridge, Massachusetts. The city issued him a .38 Smith & Wesson for making his rounds. He met store owners and other working-class people who kept guns to protect themselves. Feldman decided that their down-to-earth desire for self-defense seemed reasonable.

The American Shooting Sports Council, or ASSC, was a quirky trade group—a rump caucus of firearm wholesalers, retailers, and importers uneasy about the NRA. Its members worried that the NRA's take-no-prisoners strategy didn't always promote their best interests. The ASSC advised against incessantly provoking paranoia among gun owners and urged its members to avoid the "annual crises so dear to the NRA." When Feldman was hired to run the group in 1991, he set up an office in Atlanta, near Glock, Inc., and far from the NRA's Washington stronghold.

Eager for the membership of any company that would pay dues, Feldman presided over a decidedly mixed constituency. In addition to some of the country's largest gun-distribution and retail businesses, the ASSC included Intratec, manufacturer of the TEC-9 made famous by crime lords on *Miami Vice,* and Action Arms, importer of the feared Israeli Uzi. Feldman didn't discriminate. He also catered to well-established foreign manufacturers, including Heckler & Koch of Germany and Sig Sauer of Switzerland, whose executives were more committed to expansion in the United States than to Second Amendment absolutism. For much the same reason, Smith & Wesson signed on, as did Glock. The latter two, focused as they were on selling to the police, saw a political advantage in crafting a more moderate image.

One point of contention was the availability of federal firearm sales licenses. The NRA ceaselessly fought to make the licenses as widely available as possible. The more people who retailed guns, in the NRA's view, the more people would buy and own guns—and potentially join the NRA. Feldman, in contrast, argued that the gun industry should try to restrict the number of licenses to include only businesses that owned brick-and-mortar storefronts, paid taxes, and charged full retail prices. Some at-home dealers skimped on recordkeeping and sold to criminals. But that wasn't Feldman's or his constituents' main concern. For purely competitive reasons, the better-established gun dealers who helped pay Feldman's salary sought to eliminate less formal operators.

He called his group "the kinder, gentler gun lobby," a clever slogan that helped win favorable press coverage. As a rule, he avoided the NRA's demonization of the "liberal media" and the federal Bureau of Alcohol, Tobacco and Firearms. He didn't suggest that government agents dressed in black were plotting to confiscate firearms as part of some larger conspiracy to impose United Nations sovereignty on the United States. Feldman established a reputation as a less extreme voice for business interests, in contrast to the NRA's bullhorn for continual culture war.

/ / /

When Bill Clinton was elected president in November 1992, along with Democratic majorities in both houses of Congress, federal gun-control proposals that had been dead on arrival under Republican administrations suddenly became viable. Sensational shooting incidents continued to inject emotion into the firearm debate: In August 1992, FBI agents and deputy US marshals faced off against a family of gun-trafficking white extremists at Ruby Ridge, Idaho. In February 1993, federal forces began a violent months-long siege of the heavily armed Branch Davidian compound near Waco, Texas. And in July 1993, a client with a grudge against his former attorneys shot up their tony San Francisco firm, Pettit & Martin.

These events, and the perception that ordinary violent gun crime continued to increase, helped seal the success of the federal Brady Bill, named for James Brady, the White House press secretary grievously injured by gunfire in the 1981 attempt to assassinate President Ronald Reagan. Signed by Clinton in November 1993, the law imposed a five-day waiting period and background check for all handgun purchases (thirty-two states until then lacked background check requirements). The Brady Bill obliged the federal government within five years to replace the waiting period with a computerized "instant check" system overseen by the FBI.

NRA purists declared Brady a dire threat to individual liberty, tantamount to the repeal of the Second Amendment. Feldman took a calmer position. He bemoaned the temporary waiting period but embraced the instant-check system, which would apply to all firearms, handguns and long guns. A quick records check should only inconvenience criminals and nuts, Feldman argued. It would not seriously interfere with lawful sales. To mollify the NRA, he cried some crocodile tears in public about a section of the law that increased firearm sales license fees, but, in fact, Feldman's retailer members quietly applauded the change. The higher fees helped reduce the ranks of kitchen-table dealers.

While the NRA raised millions of dollars ranting against the Brady Bill, Feldman advised his trade group members to remain composed. The political turmoil was actually boosting business, he noted, and would continue to do so. The inauguration of Bill Clinton in January 1993—apart from any particular piece of legislation—had set off anxiety in gun-buying circles. Passage of the Brady law only fanned the flames. "'There is a tremendous amount of fear buying,'" Feldman told *Newsday* later that year. "Part of that fear," the Long Island paper added, "is of looming restrictions on handgun sales." Glock in particular profited from fear buying, because the Austrian pistol was already perceived as a favorite target of gun controllers. John Reid, owner of Reid's Gun Shop in Auburn, Maine, told the Associated Press that he couldn't keep Glock 17s on the shelf. He put out word to suppliers that he would buy as many as they could provide. "I had a distributor call me," Reid said. "He had a dozen [Glocks], and I bought all twelve."

The threat of new restrictions, Feldman lectured his allies, often becomes a selling point, whether or not the curbs ever become law. Keep your eye on the ball, he told Jannuzzo and other gun company executives. Focus on the next fight and how you can benefit from it. Don't come off as fanatics. Leave that to the NRA.

///

Democrats' determination to curb so-called assault weapons and large ammunition magazines did not diminish. Tasting victory on the Brady background check, gun-control advocates revived their push for restricting the military-style weapons. The Glock found itself swept into this drive because of its jumbo magazine—the one that so impressed police departments. But once again, as Feldman predicted, legislative efforts to curb the potent pistol had the opposite result.

The assault weapon, a loose translation of *Sturmgewehr,* a German World War II rifle, had moved to the center of the gun-control debate after an attack on an elementary school playground in Stockton, California, in January 1989. Patrick Purdy, a twenty-six-year-old drifter obsessed with foreigners, targeted a group of children, some of them of Asian descent. Using a Chinese-made knockoff of the Soviet AK-47 Kalashnikov, fitted with an enormous seventy-five-round drum magazine, he killed five children and wounded twenty-nine others and a teacher before fatally shooting himself in the head.

The Stockton massacre sparked outrage over the easy availability of the AK-47 and other rifles that accommodated large magazines. Like the later AK-47 and the American M-16 carried by GIs in Vietnam, the original *Sturmgewehr* had a switch that allowed it to fire in either semiautomatic mode or as a fully automatic machine gun. Set for semiautomatic functioning, a rifle fires one round with each pull of the trigger, essentially the way a semiautomatic pistol works. In fully automatic mode, a rifle fires a stream of bullets, as long as the trigger is depressed. US law prohibits civilians from owning or transferring fully automatic machine guns without obtaining a special federal license. However, some semiautomatic-only rifles cosmetically resemble machine guns; as a result, the two categories are often confused. Exacerbating the muddle, both types of firearm are commonly referred to as assault weapons.

Hollywood has reinforced the confusion with images of terrorists and drug gangsters blazing away with fully automatic AK-47s. In real life, military-style rifles have been used only in a handful of high-profile crimes, including the Stockton massacre. But Patrick Purdy's knockoff AK-47 was a semiautomatic rifle, not a machine gun. Criminal gang members in the United States, especially drug traffickers, have been apprehended with semiautomatic rifles, but only on the rarest of occasions have they had fully automatic machine guns. The fact is, handguns are easier to conceal than rifles, and thus are far more popular among street thugs.

Experienced gun-control advocates understand these nuances. Nevertheless, they sometimes succumb to distortion in hopes of stoking public anxiety. Shortly after the Stockton killings, Josh Sugarmann, the former spokesman for the National Coalition to Ban Handguns, published a strategy paper called *Assault Weapons: Analysis, New Research, and Legislation*. As the head of a new organization called the Violence Policy

Center, he favored outlawing handguns across the board. But he also recognized that this goal was politically impossible. So he decided to push for a "ban" that had a better chance of passing Congress. "Many who support the individual's right to own a handgun have second thoughts when the issue comes down to assault weapons," he observed in his paper. "Assault weapons are often viewed the same way as machine guns and 'plastic' firearms—a weapon that poses such a grave risk that it's worth compromising a perceived constitutional right." The "menacing looks" of assault weapons, he added, "coupled with the public's confusion over fully-automatic machine guns versus semi-automatic assault weapons—anything that looks like a machine gun is assumed to be a machine gun—can only increase the chance of public support for restrictions on these weapons."

There are legitimate arguments against assault weapons that do not rely on this kind of rhetorical mystification. The one that is intuitively appealing to many people—the seemingly reasonable question of why any civilian needs an AK-47—is ultimately not very logical, however.

Few liberal gun skeptics would suggest banning standard big-game hunting rifles—say, the familiar Remington that is used to shoot deer or elk. But what is the appeal of a weapon associated with the Cold War Soviets and terrorists? Why, gun-control advocates ask, do civilians need a variant of the military rifles carried by American troops? The answer relates to aesthetics and psychology.

Military-style rifles, whether of Russian or American design, do not use particularly powerful ammunition, at least compared to the .30-06 rounds preferred by many hunters. The AK-47, as it happens, is not very accurate, either. Still, some gun buffs get a kick out of using weapons derived from military models. (The military look and black finish of the Glock have appeal for the same reason.) This may be objectionable to gun skeptics, who associate a Remington with killing deer and an AK-47 with killing people, but the aversion relates more to symbolism than lethality. Today's traditional hunting rifles originated as military weapons issued to soldiers during the world wars; there is a long-established custom of civilian gun owners adopting former military arms.

The stronger argument against semiautomatic assault weapons is that they usually accommodate large magazines. Recall that Purdy had attached a seventy-five-round drum to his knockoff AK-47. More commonly, semiautomatic rifles and some pistols accept magazines holding fifteen, twenty, or thirty rounds. Although there are gun competitions geared to high-capacity firearms, no hunter or target shooter *needs* thirty rounds in a magazine to pursue his or her sport. And it's not obvious why a civilian handgun owner requires seventeen rounds in the magazine of a Glock pistol. Ten bullets, with the opportunity to reload swiftly, provide adequate firepower for most self-defense emergencies.

Gun skeptics who want to push measures that actually might slow a crazed killer should focus on ammunition capacity, not the superficial appearance of firearms. Even then, they will face a tough fight. Once Glock persuaded police departments that they needed big magazines, civilian buyers found the feature attractive too. The NRA's muscular version of the Second Amendment—keep your hands off my guns!—tends to meld with the more generalized American instinct that anything worth doing is worth overdoing.

/ / /

In the wake of the Stockton massacre, California enacted a state law prohibiting the AK-47 and fifty-five other types of rifles labeled assault weapons. Several other states later passed similar restrictions. The NRA and its allies in Congress were able to resist assault weapons legislation at the federal level until the summer of 1994, when President Clinton signed the national ban into law.

Some in the gun industry were distraught. "We're finished," Ron Whitaker, the chief executive of Colt, told other ASSC board members. The AR-15, a civilian semiautomatic-only version of the military M-16, was one of Colt's most lucrative products.

But the fine print of the federal legislation left plenty of room to maneuver, Feldman pointed out. The law banned nineteen weapons by brand and model, as well as any other semiautomatic rifle that could accept a detachable magazine and had at least two military-style features, such as a flash suppressor, protruding pistol grip, or bayonet mount. The law also prohibited magazines holding more than ten rounds of ammo, regardless of the kind of firearm. It was that last provision that affected growing sales of the Glock.

As tough as the law sounded, the ban was laughably easy to evade in practice. By renaming their guns and modifying them cosmetically—removing the superfluous bayonet mount, for example—a manufacturer could transform a banned assault weapon into a perfectly legal "sporting" rifle. The ban had another, even bigger loophole: It grandfathered all weapons lawfully in existence at the time of enactment in September 1994. That meant that any gun or magazine manufactured by the day the law took effect could be legally sold, and resold, later on.

Nearly a year before passage, Feldman had given ASSC manufacturers a very clear directive: "Make as many guns and high-capacity magazines as you possibly can," he told them. "Put your plants on three shifts, seven days a week. You won't get stuck with unused product." The political controversy and the perception of a finite supply would pump up demand and prices.

At Glock, Paul Jannuzzo fully backed his friend's advice, as did Karl Walter. Gaston Glock ordered production in Austria into high gear. Before the deadline, the company stockpiled inventory. "We're getting five thousand guns and eight thousand to nine thousand magazines a week from Austria," a Glock representative in the US, Dick Wiggins, told the *Minneapolis Star-Tribune* in May 1994. Consumers were buying everything Glock could produce. "We're tens of thousands of orders behind," Wiggins said. "Our pistols are scarcer than hen's teeth."

The actual enactment of the ban on assault weapons and high-capacity magazines spurred yet another round of shopping frenzy. "People who own guns that use magazines holding more than ten rounds—including the Glock 9mm popular with police—are buying extra magazines as fast as they can," *USA Today* reported. "'We were cleaned out of magazines in the space of a few hours,' says Mike Saporito of RSR Wholesale Guns of Winter Park, Fla., which supplies thousands of retail shops. 'Sales have gone through the roof.'"

Tales from gun counters from California to Maryland confirmed the trend. "People bought everything they could get their hands on in every store in town: ammo, handguns, semiautomatics," said Nancy Nell, owner of a gun shop in West Valley City, Utah. Chris Encinas, a twenty-five-year-old resident of Van Nuys, California, bought a Glock 22 with a fifteen-round magazine that May, hoping to beat the shortages

and rising prices he expected would follow the passage of legislation. "I'm trying to rush it," he told the *Los Angeles Times*. "If
we didn't have the ban, I wouldn't have to, but it's better that I
buy it today." He paid $510 for his .40-caliber Glock. By 1995,
the same weapon, grandfathered under the law, would retail
for 50 percent more.

Even as the company scrambled to ship pistols, Glock built
up an enormous surplus of grandfathered "pre-ban" magazines, which gradually filtered out to the public, as the retail
price of a Glock seventeen-round magazine rose—from less
than $20, to $30, to $50 and higher, after the ten-round limi-
tation became law. Jannuzzo and other Glock executives each
personally bought large crates of high-cap magazines at insider
prices and gradually sold them as prices soared.

"If the purpose of the assault weapons ban was to reduce
the number of these guns [and large magazines] on the street,"
Feldman noted, "the bill had exactly the opposite effect." He
recalled driving in the early fall of 1994 to the Glock facility
in suburban Smyrna for a meeting with Jannuzzo. Passing a
large sporting goods store called Adventure Outdoors, Feldman saw two long lines snaking down the block. He stopped
to investigate. One was a customer line: people waiting to buy
grandfathered guns and Glock magazines. The other line was
for volunteers signing up to work for Bob Barr, an outspoken
pro–Second Amendment Republican challenger running for
Congress. Barr had put a campaign table near the gun store.

At their tête-à-tête, Jannuzzo took out cigars and declared:
"Our business has never been better. Mr. Glock is going to be
very pleased."

CHAPTER 12

"Ka-Boom"

In the United States, a company manufacturing a handheld product that launches metal projectiles at high velocity eventually will encounter lawsuits. Whatever one thinks of plaintiffs' lawyers or the large corporations they sue, the prevalence of legal skirmishing is as much a fact of American life as the pervasiveness of automobiles, fast food, and firearms. Glock was no exception.

The company's internal legal files offer an unusual window on how Glock, Inc., dealt with the challenges posed by the plaintiffs' bar. A sampling of company records from 1991 and 1992 listed nineteen accidental injuries involving Glocks. There may have been more; these were the ones the company acknowledged. Eleven of the cases by mid-1992 had led to lawsuits.

Some of the cases concerned pistols that allegedly malfunctioned, harming the owner. Others involved shootings in which the gun operated properly but someone pulled the trigger unintentionally. In these latter instances, the victim blamed the Glock's design.

Yet another set of six suits were labeled "container" cases, referring to the padded plastic box in which Glocks were sold. The box resembled a miniature black suitcase. It had a handle for transporting the pistol—say, to a firing range—and, inside, it had room for a spare magazine and ammo. A small post in the box was meant to protrude through the trigger guard and keep the gun in place. The post was the problem.

Some users stored their pistol with a round in the chamber, ready to fire. If the box were jostled, so that the post contacted the trigger, the gun could go off, as it did in the case of Marshall Rosen. "Claimant removed his Glock 17 from its holster, removed the loaded magazine and unloaded same," the file on Rosen states. "He then placed the pistol into the container, and it discharged. Injuries to the left hand (palm). Tendon and severe nerve damage requiring surgery. Permanent disfigurement." Another Glock owner, Mark Herman, similarly shot himself in the left hand, sustaining "permanent disability."

When informed of the box accidents, Gaston Glock "wanted to blame the dumb Americans," according to one former longtime company employee in the United States. "They should know better than to store the gun loaded." Mr. Glock showed little regard for the American business credo of "the customer is always right."

Callous as this might seem, the Austrian manufacturer did have a legitimate point. The user manual that came with each pistol stressed emptying the gun before storing it. The owner was told to remove the magazine and check the chamber to make sure there was not a round left there. Following those instructions would preclude exploding gun boxes.

Still, as a practical matter, some people, especially homeowners who thought of their Glock as protection against intruders, were bound to keep it loaded and ready to fire. Others were careless. The file on Mark Herman noted that he "forgot his Glock 17 was loaded and placed it into the storage container." Such accidents were eminently foreseeable.

A more high-minded company might have announced a

recall in the name of consumer safety, issued an apology, and established a claims process to pay victims' medical bills. That did not happen at Gaston Glock's company; confessions of fallibility were not his style.

Paul Jannuzzo, Glock's corporate counsel, knew the carrying case was poorly designed. Many in the company knew—almost everyone, apparently, except the founder. Fighting the cases in court made no sense, because Glock might lose, piquing the interest of the plaintiffs' bar. Since a recall and apology were out of the question, Jannuzzo moved quietly to put out legal brushfires as they ignited. If injured Glock owners were persistent, they received a settlement—in exchange for which they had to sign binding legal papers promising not to discuss the case or the flawed gun box. Marshall Rosen got $95,000 to drop his suit; Mark Herman, $99,000. Wounded Glock owners who failed to hire a good lawyer received little or nothing for their trouble.

As a result of Glock's efficiently executed policy of settlement-and-silence, some gun owners who might have been alerted sooner to the peril learned about it the hard way. No one knows how many people shot themselves or others before Glock changed the box design in the early 1990s to one where the handgun rested securely in heavy foam, without a post that could contact the trigger.

/ / /

Carrying cases were not the only hazard of owning a Glock, of course. Firearms, like lawn mowers or microwave ovens or motorcycles, occasionally malfunction. The reason could be bad parts, a mistake in assembly, or recklessness by the user. The world is full of imperfections and misfortune. When guns break down—and all brands of firearms suffer glitches from time to time—it's not uncommon for someone to get hurt.

The Glock legal files describe a suit filed by Jeffrey A. Gueno, an Air Force captain who badly injured his right index finger when his Glock 21 .45-caliber "exploded in his hand." Gueno, an experienced firearm user who was practicing at a range, "alleged that Glock placed on the market a product in defective condition which is unsafe for its intended use."

When confronted by such cases, Jannuzzo had one over-riding initial objective, he told me: "Get the gun." The company lawyer made sure that Glock recovered the supposedly substandard pistol for examination and, if the case were to be settled, destruction. He did not want faulty Glocks being passed around, and possibly photographed, to the detriment of the manufacturer's reputation.

The company's inspection of Captain Gueno's Glock attributed the accident to the plaintiff's ammunition, rather than his pistol. "There was no indication of any obstruction having been lodged in the barrel," the file states. "The damage to the pistol was caused by an ammunition failure–related problem."

Ammunition can fail in several ways. A batch of rounds may be poorly fabricated, leading some to disintegrate. Shoddy ammunition may jam as it moves from the magazine to the chamber or from the chamber to the barrel. To save money, some gun owners "reload" ammo, using basement hand-crank machines to insert new lead bullets into spent brass cases they collect at the shooting range. Unless it's done expertly, reloading can lead to problems. Glock explicitly voided its warranty if the customer used reloaded ammunition.

The company's determination in the Gueno case was that the plaintiff's factory-made ammunition was of poor quality and lacked full-metal jacketing or plating. This was often the company's response when confronted with the claim of a malfunctioning pistol. Glock instructed users from the outset to buy top-grade, factory-made, full-jacketed ammunition. Rounds that have exposed lead because they are not fully jacketed, whether those rounds are reloaded or factory-made, are much more likely to produce malfunctions in Glocks than in certain other handguns, as a result of the kind of rifling in Glock barrels.

Rifling refers to the spiraling grooves in a gun barrel that cause the bullet to spin in flight. The rotation stabilizes the bullet, increasing accuracy. Traditional rifling incorporates twisting lands and grooves. With an exposed-lead bullet, the lands actually engrave the projectile's relatively soft metal. Gaston Glock designed his barrel with polygonal flat sides: six or eight, depending on the caliber. Polygonal rifling provides a superior bullet-to-barrel seal when jacketed or plated ammunition is used. "This leads to an increase in velocity over conventional cut rifle barrels of the same length," according to *The Complete Glock Reference Guide*, a volume published independently of the manufacturer. However, the *Guide* continues, "the lack of lands in the polygonal rifled Glock barrel tends to allow a lead bullet to skip down the bore rather than spin, leaving larger lead deposits, while creating buildup and reducing the bore diameter." In a barrel constricted by lead detritus, excessive pressure can accumulate, leading to an explosion, or what the reference book politely calls "a Glock KB (Ka-Boom)." The easiest way to prevent ka-booms is to use jacketed or plated bullets, as Glock admonishes its users to do.

Jeffrey Gueno may or may not have used substandard ammunition. In any event, he was not the sort of plaintiff Jannuzzo wanted to fight in court: a clean-cut Air Force captain who many jurors would assume knew how to handle a gun.

Gueno offered to drop his suit for $24,000, not an extravagant amount. The company legal file suggested that the case "should be settled on economic analysis, i.e., less expensive to settle than defend." Jannuzzo listed an "anticipated expense" of only $14,000, indicating his expectation that Gueno, whose medical bills were paid by the military, would agree to the lower amount. (The file doesn't indicate the company's actual payout.)

As a result, the entire potentially embarrassing episode—labeled a "catastrophic failure" in the Glock records—disappeared from public view. Glock, Inc., obtained the damaged gun and disposed of it. Upon receiving settlement, Gueno swore in writing not to discuss the incident.

In a memo dated December 17, 1992, Jannuzzo urged Gaston Glock to sign off on a joint settlement in which the company would share the costs of a confidential $20,000 payment with the ammunition manufacturer Olin/Winchester. "It is important to note that Olin/Winchester Corporation has approximately 30 damaged Glock pistols at their facility," the attorney wrote. "Should this case be tried, it is safe to assume that those pistols will be presented as evidence, which would have a destructive and widespread effect for Glock Inc." The complaint, brought by a US Customs agent named Wernli, whose .45-caliber Glock 21 had exploded, causing a "crush injury to the distal tip of his right index finger," was resolved out of court. The damaged guns did not surface.

On occasion, Glock employees in Smyrna testing pistols as they arrived from Austria identified mechanical problems before the guns were shipped to users. Senior executives in Austria typically had a short and impatient reaction to any suggestion of a flaw: "Impossible!"

In 1998, Smyrna discovered a batch of .40-caliber Glock 22s

that mysteriously jammed even when loaded with appropriate ammo. "These malfunctions were very difficult to clear and could not be cleared with the normal 'tap, rack' drill," according to a February 12, 1998, memo addressed to Gaston Glock. "Law enforcement officers see this type of stoppage as a serious failure and one which has life-threatening implications."

When executives in Austria brushed off the concern, saying the balky guns merely needed to be "broken in," Jannuzzo followed up with a sharply worded letter to his employer. The notion of having to break in a new handgun, he wrote, "flies in the face of the Glock pistol's reputation as being the best-shooting semiautomatic 'out of the box.'"

There is no evidence that Glock 22 jams were a widespread problem. But neither is there any indication that the company warned its customers, police or civilian, that at least some .40-caliber guns might not work properly. When questions about defects have arisen, Glock has consistently maintained that every single pistol is carefully tested and, if used correctly, functions without flaw.

/ / /

Yet another category of legal complaints about the Glock focused on the negligent or criminal misuse of handguns, sometimes by someone other than the owner. This kind of suit first began cropping up against gun manufacturers in the early 1980s. Under traditional American injury law, the intervention of a third party—the curious child who foolishly shoots a friend, the convenience-store robber who attacks a clerk—was thought to break the chain of liability between the victim and the manufacturer. But since the 1960s, some US judges and law professors had been expanding theories of liability to give injury victims a better chance of finding a defendant with deep pockets. The consumer-protection movement led by Ralph Nader reinforced this trend and helped turn up new evidence that manufacturers often knew more than they liked to admit about hazards associated with their products. Rising crime rates in the 1970s and 1980s added a sense of urgency to the gun-control movement and prompted some activists to turn their attention to the courts, as well as the legislature, as a venue where they might rein in companies that make and sell firearms.

Initially, the targets of these innovative suits were manufacturers and retailers of inexpensive, unreliable "Saturday Night Specials": revolvers and pistols that could be purchased for as little as $29 and were favorites of stickup artists, drug dealers, and cash-strapped residents of inner-city neighborhoods who feared those criminals. Lawyers representing accident and crime victims argued that Saturday Night Specials had no redeeming social value; they couldn't plausibly be marketed for target shooting, hunting, or police work. By their very nature, according to this view, cheap handguns were meant only to kill people and therefore were "unreasonably hazardous."

The plaintiffs' argument had visceral appeal to gun foes, but also significant weaknesses: As a matter of economics and fairness, it didn't address the concerns of people living in violence-ridden neighborhoods who might seek to defend themselves with cut-rate handguns. More broadly, suits seeking to hold gun manufacturers responsible for crime and negligence implicitly demanded that juries look away from the role of the person who pulled the trigger. While suits over individual guns that exploded in the hands of their users sometimes resulted in plaintiffs' verdicts or settlements, most courts were hostile to claims that handgun makers should be liable for the misuse of otherwise lawful articles of commerce. The product, after all, was supposed to fire bullets; that there was risk should have surprised no one. Even in a period of expanding liability theories, there were limits to what judges would tolerate.

Despite the failure of most manufacturer-liability suits stemming from crime and negligence, the litigation continued into the 1990s. Plaintiffs' lawyers thought that if they achieved just a few breakthroughs, gun companies would be intimidated into a series of lucrative settlements. Some of the suits were sponsored by gun-control organizations willing to spend hundreds of thousands of dollars on the litigation, no matter how unlikely the odds, because the mere existence of legal combat drew attention to their cause. In this environment, gun opponents inevitably took aim at Glock, given the Austrian-based company's success and profitability. Maybe its unusual design would make it more vulnerable to legal attack, or so the plaintiffs' attorneys and activists hoped.

Of course, Glock did not make Saturday Night Specials. By the late 1980s, the lowest end of the handgun market was dominated by a group of small interlocking companies based in Southern California. According to police departments, the Austrian pistol had ample social value as a tool to fight crime. It wasn't cheap, and it clearly was suitable as a target pistol or home-defense weapon. What distinguished the Glock from other handguns was that it was easier to fire and it lacked an external safety lever. These differences troubled some people, and not just gun-control advocates.

In May 1988, a team of FBI shooting instructors involved in the federal agency's arduous process of replacing its revolvers issued a skeptical internal evaluation of the Glock. "Unintentional discharges of the first shot lead to safety and liability issues in view of the manner handguns are routinely used by

FBI agents," the report noted. This wasn't the last word on the topic; in fact, other FBI officials came to think highly of the Glock. By the mid-1990s, the agency was arming thousands of agents with the Austrian pistol. But the early FBI evaluation indicated hesitations about the fast-firing firearm.

Herbert Timm, the police chief of the Chicago suburb of Winnetka, lobbied his village board to buy Glocks for his small force, only to embarrass himself with the new pistol. "I was transferring the gun from the holster I was wearing into another holster in the desk drawer, and assumed—which is something that no one should ever do—that it was not loaded," he told the *Chicago Sun-Times*. It was loaded. "I pulled the trigger, and it fired into the wall just below the ceiling." Luckily, no one was hurt. "I've been a policeman for twenty-five years," Timm said, "and never had an accidental discharge of a weapon."

Negligence with guns has occurred as long as there have been guns. Visit any older police station, and you may notice posters and photographs in odd places: very high and very low on the walls. Remove the strangely placed decorations, and behind them you will find bullet holes.

In some places, the arrival of the Glock almost certainly contributed to a surge in unintentional firing. When the Metropolitan Police Department of Washington, DC, switched to the Austrian pistol in 1989, Gary Hankins, chairman of the Fraternal Order of Police labor committee, announced: "We've got the right gun. . . . This is going to make all of us feel better out there on the streets." Almost immediately, however, Washington cops began shooting themselves and each other. The *Washington Post* found that in the decade after the 3,800-person department adopted the Glock, more than 120 accidental discharges occurred, with 19 serious officer injuries. The police mistakenly wounded nine DC citizens and killed one. The skein of accidents resulted in the city government paying out millions of dollars to settle lawsuits.

Looking back, DC officials concluded that the fiasco stemmed from an unhappy coincidence of three factors. The department, responding to generational turnover and rising crime, hired fifteen hundred new officers in just eighteen months. It then failed to train many of the rookies. Recruits often received only three days of firing-range instruction, rather than the goal of ten. "They just rushed through this stuff," said Lowell Duckett, a retired instructor at the DC Police Academy. The final factor was putting an easy-to-fire Glock in the hands of each and every one of the underprepared new officers. The Austrian pistol is an excellent first firearm because it is so simple and light. But without expert guidance, a novice is probably more likely to make a dangerous mistake with a Glock than with another pistol or revolver.

Police departments from Tampa to Tucson reported accidental shootings soon after changing over to the Glock pistol. In November 1990, Richard Johnson, an officer with the Port Huron Police Department in Michigan, "was in his patrol car when he removed the gun from its holster," the Glock legal files note. "As he did so, the gun discharged, shooting him in the left foot." The following year he sued the manufacturer, alleging that the Glock's unusual "trigger safety" was inherently dangerous.

Glock countered that Officer Johnson had handled his firearm too casually. Like Captain Gueno of the Air Force, Johnson sought only modest damages, described in his suit as "in excess of $10,000." In his file, Jannuzzo wrote: "Should be settled for less than it would cost to defend" and added an anticipated outlay of $12,000. Glock settled dozens of suits in this manner, with little or no fanfare.

/ / /

On occasion, plaintiffs and their lawyers held out for bigger payoffs. One such clash occurred in Knoxville, Tennessee, as a result of a disastrous encounter in the early-morning hours of July 9, 1991.

Cheryl Darlene Grant and her husband, Benny, both in their early forties, had driven back to Knoxville after attending a concert. Police said that they noticed the Grants' late-model Camaro speeding. In the ensuing chase, Benny Grant jumped out of the Camaro, while his wife drove off. Eventually cornered, Cheryl Grant rammed a police cruiser and started to run. Patrolman Danny Wagner chased her on foot. The officer said that Grant turned and reached behind her back, as if to draw a weapon. He pulled out his Glock. When the cop finally caught up to Grant, they tussled, causing him to fire accidentally. A single shot smashed into Grant's head, killing her. As he tried to holster his handgun, Wagner fired a second errant round into the pavement. Grant had consumed alcohol and cocaine that evening, but she was not armed.

The city of Knoxville and Wagner jointly settled with the Grant family by paying them $130,000. But the Knoxville PD didn't abandon the Glock as its duty weapon; in fact, it subsequently traded in its nine-millimeter Glock 17s for .40-caliber Glock 22s. (Wagner kept his job on the force.)

Grant's relatives, represented by prominent local plaintiffs' attorneys Bob and Wayne Ritchie, a father-and-son duo, sued Glock for $7.2 million. As with Officer Johnson in Port Huron, the woman's family alleged that the basic design of the Glock 17 was "unreasonably dangerous." The manufacturer knowingly made a risky product, the relatives claimed, and should have foreseen accidents such as the one in Knoxville.

The lawsuit described the Glock 17's key selling points as flaws—specifically, that its trigger pull was too light, that the distance the trigger had to travel was too short, and that the gun's lack of an external safety lever made it a deadly hazard. "Glock Perfection," the company's sales slogan, was shoved back in Gaston Glock's face.

"The very idea that anyone would criticize his invention offended Mr. Glock, let alone that they would sue him," Jannuzzo explained. "When accidents happened, Mr. Glock assumed it was the user's fault, and usually it was. Be that as it may, we were getting sued more and more often all around the country."

Sometimes, Jannuzzo advised that his employer put on a full-dress courtroom defense to send a message to plaintiffs' lawyers that Glock was not a patsy. Seeking a jury verdict against the company would be time-consuming, expensive, and probably not successful. With millions at stake in the Knoxville case, the company didn't even offer to settle.

The plaintiffs' side put Officer Wagner on the witness stand. He testified that he had pulled his Glock as he chased Cheryl Grant because he feared being shot. He regretted the death but suggested that the pistol, not he, was at fault. He told the jury that after the accident, he remained on the beat and now carried what he considered a less dangerous handgun: a nine-millimeter pistol made by Smith & Wesson. (Knoxville allowed its officers to choose from a short list of authorized weapons.) Wagner told the jury that the S&W took a full twelve pounds of pull on the trigger to fire, instead of the five required for the Glock. "I didn't feel that the [Austrian] weapon was safe," he testified.

The jury learned that the Knoxville PD could have bought its Glocks with five-pound or eight-pound trigger weights; the company offered both. Knoxville chose the lighter weight, on the theory that it made shooters more accurate and was more manageable by officers with less hand strength. Wagner testified that the Smith & Wesson also had a much longer "trigger travel": one and a quarter inches, compared to the Glock's half inch.

The plaintiffs' team elicited testimony from a retired FBI agent and forensics consultant, who reinforced Wagner's position on trigger pull and trigger travel. "I think that the [Glock] has a tremendous allure for many police agencies because it is easy to shoot; it is easy to shoot it well," said the ex–FBI man, Donald Bassett. "Those agencies are not aware of the safety deficiencies of trigger design, or they simply ignore those, or consider them inconsequential in favor of ease."

Nonsense, countered Ronald Grimm, the company's locally hired defense lawyer. If you pull the trigger of a Glock, he argued, it will fire. That is what it is supposed to do. Officer Wagner should not have had his index finger on the trigger as he tried to subdue the suspect.

The defense called a Knoxville PD weapons expert to the stand. He testified that Officer Wagner had violated the department's safety rules when he chased Grant with his finger on the trigger of his Glock 17. The Knoxville government essentially sided with the Austrian manufacturer, leaving its police officer to take the fall.

Why would the city blame Wagner but not fire him? Knoxville apparently sought to resolve its liability without acknowledging flaws in its training methods. By keeping Wagner on salary, quickly settling with the victim's family for $130,000, and admitting no wrongdoing, the city dodged the threat of a multimillion-dollar payout.

As his star witness, Grimm summoned Gaston Glock.

Putting the Austrian engineer on the stand was not an obvious call. One reason to do so was that the Knoxville jury would be curious to hear from the man whose invention was at the center of the dispute. When talking about his pistol, Glock came across as self-assured. He spoke slowly, with a certain gravitas. On the other hand, he could also come off as arrogant and supercilious, especially when dealing with Americans.

During a pretrial deposition in November 1993, all of these qualities were evident. "We have such an incredible success," Glock boasted. "It certainly can be said that based upon our economic success, our system functions without a flaw." Would jurors see him as condescending or supremely confident? Questioned sharply by plaintiffs' lawyers in the deposition, he never gave an inch. "With our weapon," Glock said, "it is possible with a lightning-fast move to instinctively fire the weapon."

In the courtroom seven months later, Glock, speaking in German with the aid of a translator, reiterated that his gun was "flawless," stating it always operated exactly as it had been designed to. Asked about the skeptical testimony of the former FBI expert, Bassett, Glock heaped scorn on the witness and the famous agency. "The statement of the FBI is useless," he said.

Glock informed the jurors that his company told all users in its operating manual to keep their fingers outside the trigger guard until they intended to shoot. "The officer knows from his training that when he has taken his finger off the trigger, the gun is absolutely safe," Glock testified. "That is our absolute basic rule," he said. "Keep your finger off the trigger" until prepared to fire.

No longer the self-conscious engineer, too timid to talk to his own bankers, Glock presented a poised public persona. The

Knoxville News Sentinel, which provided daily coverage of the weeklong trial, reported that "Glock testified for three hours to defend his design before a jury of five men and three women, who, at times, appeared mesmerized by his explanation of how his gun operates." Moreover, his German struck the Tennesseans as worldly. He displayed no doubts and deflected unfriendly interrogation with a bemused countenance. "At times," the paper observed, "some [jurors] laughed with Glock at his stylish and light-hearted nature while others smiled at him as he testified."

Sent off to deliberate, the jurors had little difficulty reaching a verdict. After less than ninety minutes, they returned to the courtroom. Their judgment was stark: no liability whatsoever on the company's part—a complete victory for the defense.

"Mr. Glock never considered any compromise in this case," a triumphant Grimm said afterward on the courthouse steps. "The Glock pistols are the safest pistols on the market for police use."

Gaston Glock's calm, assertive performance in the witness chair was a crucial factor. "The jury liked him more than our client," Bob Ritchie conceded to a reporter after the trial. Equally, if not more, important was the fact that the Knoxville policeman had violated his department's safety standards. Ronald Grimm told me: "You don't put the finger on the trigger until you're prepared to destroy something—kill it."

Yet that wasn't the rule all handgun owners followed. The FBI, until it fully changed over to pistols in the 1990s, instructed recruits to keep their index finger on the trigger of their handgun anytime they had it drawn. The idea was that the agent should be ready to shoot. Of course, it was safer to rest your finger on a revolver trigger that provided twelve pounds of resistance. In many places, police trainers taught new cops to cover suspects with their finger on the trigger. Some civilian shooting instructors favored the same approach until at least the early 1990s. It was not until 1995 or so, with the semiautomatic pistol having become the predominant American handgun, that finger-off-the-trigger became gospel.

/ / /

Some civilian shooting experts dissented, at least to an extent, from the majority's unmitigated admiration for the Glock. "The gun factory ads cry, 'Glock Perfection,'" Massad Ayoob wrote in the September 1990 issue of *GUNS* magazine. "But perfection is an amorphous term. I for one don't think it's been achieved yet."

One of the best-known private firearm trainers in the United States—he ran a rural New Hampshire academy called the Lethal Force Institute—Ayoob lauded the Glock as a military weapon and target-shooting gun. He worried, however, about whether it was well suited for civilians to carry for self-protection.

Ayoob's was a voice taken seriously among firearm buffs. The grandson of an Episcopalian immigrant from Damascus, Syria, he did as much as any other single person in the late twentieth century to codify the mind-set of ordinary Americans who felt it wise to go about their business armed. His long list of books includes the seminal *In the Gravest Extreme: The Role of the Firearm in Personal Protection*. He came to firearms naturally, he told me: "There were guns in the house. There were guns in my father's jewelry store, of course. Like there's a telephone for calling people, there is the gun for self-defense."

Ayoob counts himself as the third generation in his family to stave off mortal danger with a handgun. His grandfather, the owner of a bowling alley, once shot and wounded an armed would-be robber. Ayoob's father, the jeweler, was accosted one night on a Boston street. The mugger fired a shot that zipped past his ear; Ayoob's father pulled his own handgun and killed his assailant.

Massad Ayoob himself started carrying a gun as a boy of twelve. Later he served for many years as a part-time police officer in several small towns in New Hampshire. He pointed his service weapon at threatening arrestees a few times but never fired. He became a private instructor and a champion shooter, passing along his skills to his two daughters, one of whom, he told me, once had to use her handgun to scare away a pair of men intent on raping her.

In his *GUNS* magazine piece, Ayoob noted that the Glock "didn't have as many accidental discharges as I'd feared it would when it came into common police use." He speculated that cops and civilians were being extra careful. "Any intelligent person who handles a loaded Glock," he wrote, "handles it gingerly."

But caution wasn't enough. "Two design features of the Glock concern me," he wrote: "the short trigger pull and the lack of a manual safety." Glock's official specifications say that from a resting position to firing, the trigger travels half an inch with resistance of five or five and a half pounds. Ayoob measured the trigger travel as more like three-eighths of an inch. "However," he noted, "with the standard trigger, much of that pull is a light take-up like a military rifle before the firm resistance of the final pressure [is] encountered." By his calculation, "real resistance is only felt in less than a tenth of an inch of trigger pressure. A tenth of an inch is not a lot."

Glock introduced a modification in 1990 called "the New York Trigger." The New York State Police had bought the

Glock 17 on the condition that the manufacturer would replace its regular trigger assembly with one that offered firmer
resistance from the beginning of the pull. The substitute trigger module and spring result in a steady eight pounds of resistance. Having installed the New York Trigger on his own
compact Glock 19, Ayoob wrote: "I feel much more comfortable." He suggested in the article that Glock make the heavier
trigger standard. But the company never did—five to five and
a half pounds remained the norm.

Yet even the New York Trigger wasn't sufficient, in Ayoob's
opinion. He thought the Glock should have an external safety
lever, as well. Glock warned users to keep their index finger off
the trigger until they intended to fire. "But that answer is too
pat, too ignorant of the dynamics that can occur under stress,"
Ayoob wrote. "For a manufacturer to say, 'You don't need a
safety, just keep your finger off the trigger and there'll be no
accidents,' is as if General Motors were to say, 'You don't need
seat belts or air bags. Just avoid collisions and you'll be fine.'
Guns are made to be held with the finger on the trigger. That's
why the Glock shoots so well when you do fire it intentionally,
and because everything from childhood cops n' robbers to television habituates you to hold the gun that way, that's how it's
going to probably happen under stress."

If Glock routinely provided a thumb safety and the New
York Trigger, Ayoob concluded he would "volunteer to be the
Glock Poster Child. Until then, much as I like it as a shooting
gun, I'll still carry it on the street with feelings of reservation."

CHAPTER 13

Pocket Rockets

In June 1995, *Advertising Age* magazine named Gaston Glock one of its "Marketing 100." The Austrian businessman, then sixty-seven, was honored for having taken on "some of the biggest guns in American firearms." "It was a conscious decision to go after the law enforcement market first," Glock told the premier advertising industry periodical (in English so fluent it suggested vigorous polishing by an editor). "In marketing terms," he added, "we assumed that, by pursuing the law enforcement market, we would then receive the benefit of 'after sales' in the commercial market."

"Ten years ago, there wasn't a single Glock pistol in the US," *Ad Age* noted. "Today the company sells more than 20,000 a month at an average cost of $600 apiece," the retail price for civilians. "The lightweight frame, reliability, and easy maintenance quickly made this semi-automatic handgun a favorite with cops."

By the time the advertising industry paid homage to Gaston Glock, more than 500,000 Glock pistols were in use in North America, according to a company brochure. The bulk of sales had shifted from law enforcement to the more lucrative commercial market. Four out of five Glocks produced in 1995 were purchased by civilians, who paid much higher prices than police departments. Retaining law enforcement business and winning new public contracts remained essential, however, for the reasons *Ad Age* suggested: credibility and name recognition. Sam Colt had taught that lesson a century and a half earlier.

Gaston Glock learned it so well that at the time he was named to the Marketing 100, he had taken a hiatus from buying advertising. The factory in Austria could not make pistols fast enough to meet demand, so Glock ceased for a time purchasing space in gun magazines. "They were one step ahead of everyone else in the semiautomatic pistol revolution," said Cameron Hopkins, a former editor of *American Handgunner* magazine.

/ / /

Glock's training sessions in Smyrna, capped off with the Thursday evening bacchanals at the Gold Club, had become legendary among police department shooting instructors. Bills for those outings ranged as high as $10,000 a night; quality champagne and Atlanta's best lap dances did not come cheap.

One Gold Club attendee, a former law enforcement trainer, recounted how he and Karl Walter were admiring a particularly acrobatic pole dancer one Thursday in 1992. The trainer mentioned to Walter that it was his birthday. "Later that night," the retired cop recalled, "I'm just standing there, and someone taps me on the shoulder. I turn around, and it's the pole dancer. . . . And she says, 'Karl Walter told me it's your birthday, and I'm the gift.' That's the kind of guy Karl was, very generous." (The beneficiary insisted the transaction remained entirely lawful.)

One way or another, Glock continued to persuade police

departments to trade their old Smith & Wesson revolvers
for discounts on new nine-millimeter pistols. In 1993, Doug
Kiesler, a major gun wholesaler in Indiana, estimated that po
lice departments nationwide exchanged two hundred thousand
revolvers during the previous year to acquire pistols made by
Glock and rival manufacturers. A *Newsday* survey published in
December 1993 found that of forty-five police departments in
large and mid-sized cities, all but two had converted to semiautomatic pistols, or were doing so. Thirty-six of these agencies
had exchanged or sold their old revolvers in the process, putting the used handguns onto the commercial market.

By 1994, Glock had updated their offer to some cities: Police
could trade in the Glock 17s they had acquired in the late 1980s
for new versions of the same pistol, at no cost. Used Glocks for
fresh Glocks. How could police departments go wrong?

ʹ These deals may seem peculiar. Why would the company
give away valuable merchandise? The Metropolitan Police Department in Washington, DC, agreed in 1994 to exchange
more than five thousand Glock 17s purchased in 1989. The new
Glocks the DC cops received were identical to the old ones except that they had textured, as opposed to smooth, grips—a
minor improvement. Sergeant Joe Gentile, the agency's spokesman, said the new guns, worth an estimated $3 million at
retail, were donated by the manufacturer "as a public service."

The real story was more complicated. The accidental discharges that accompanied Glock's arrival in Washington were
beginning to receive media coverage. While senior department
officials didn't blame the pistol, some street officers were mur-
muring that there had to be something wrong with the Austrian gun. There were also reports that Glocks were jamming.
The malfunctions and mistaken discharges stemmed from
similar causes, although not from mechanical flaws.

As noted earlier, Washington had hired legions of raw recruits around 1990 and then failed to train them adequately to handle firearms. Until late 1994, range time for experienced officers wasn't mandatory, and less than 50 percent bothered to show up. Poor technique can lead not only to accidental shootings, but also malfunctions. For example, if a semiautomatic pistol isn't held with the hand as high as possible on the grip and the wrist firmly locked, unchecked recoil can cause the slide to fail to cycle properly. When that happens, a cartridge can jam as it moves from the magazine to the chamber, or a spent casing can fail to eject. Known as limp-wristing, the dangerous habit is not unusual among insufficiently trained Glock users.

The police leadership in DC defended the Glock. "It is not an unsafe weapon, and it does not have a mechanical problem," Max Krupo, assistant chief for technical services, told the *Washington Times*. But the negative media attention was a source of embarrassment for both the department and the manufacturer. Glock was especially sensitive to its image in the nation's capital. In October 1994, Paul Jannuzzo wrote a letter to Krupo to formalize an offer to exchange the weapons "one-for-one, free of charge." Jannuzzo asserted that "this offer is not being made for any other reason than Glock's dedication to our law-enforcement customer base." The Washington department, he added, "is one of our oldest customers and therefore a flagship of this corporation." Both sides hoped that the exchange would underscore Glock's good faith and reassure Washington's cops and citizens. The department announced separately that it would get serious about firearm training.

If Glock's dedication to law enforcement didn't fully explain the Washington gun exchange, neither did the company's concern about potential harm to its reputation. Glock had an additional motivation. As a part of its trade with the Washington police, Glock received the agency's sixteen thousand used high-capacity clips, as well as its five-thousand-plus older pistols, which could accommodate the big magazines. After 1994, there was a finite supply of "pre-ban" Glock 17s and their seventeen-round clips. The company had filled warehouses with large magazines during the run-up to the assault weapons ban but had to discontinue manufacturing them as of September 13, 1994. Post-ban, this gear gained an astounding cachet among gun owners, and prices jumped accordingly. Trade-in deals in Washington; Hartford, Connecticut; and many other cities allowed Glock to augment its inventory of perfectly legal and hugely profitable pre-ban pistols and magazines. With the porous federal law in place, the secondhand plastic morphed into gold.

Opponents of firearms quickly realized what was happening. "Even for the gun industry, it's amazingly cynical to get the police to help you circumnavigate the assault weapons ban," Josh Sugarmann, head of the anti-handgun Violence Policy Center, told the *Washington City Paper* in April 1995. "Glock has the notorious distinction of being the first to find a way to do that."

Paul Jannuzzo sounded indignant about the allegation that Glock and its wholesalers were undermining the spirit of the ban or behaving in anything other than an entirely upright manner. "It's not a way around the crime bill. It is well within the law," Jannuzzo said. "I'm not sure what the spirit of the crime bill was. I think the whole thing was an absolute piece of nonsense."

An intelligent and politically sophisticated lawyer, Jannuzzo knew very well what the purpose of the ban was. He relished the opportunity to emasculate the law and its liberal backers.

Jannuzzo gloated in an interview with *Gun Week* in January 1995 that he personally had been doing his part to thwart the ban by stockpiling forbidden firearms before the law went into effect. "I've bought more guns than I have ever bought in my life," he said. "My plan always was to buy everything that was on the ban list . . . and I got a bunch of them. And they became more precious this year."

One Glock trade-in episode, involving the New York State Department of Environmental Conservation, showed how insistent the company's marketing of police weapons could get. New York's 260 conservation officers had full police powers and carried handguns. Occasionally they put down a deer injured on the highway or a rabid raccoon. Armed encounters with humans were rare. Nevertheless, in 1990, the conservation department joined the move to greater firepower, trading its Smith & Wesson .357 Magnum revolvers for 325 higher-capacity Glock nine-millimeter pistols. Scarcely three years later, Glock regional sales representative Milton Walsh, a former Massachusetts state trooper, urged the New York environmental cops to make another trade, this time for what he called the "new toy"—the more powerful Glock 22 .40-caliber pistol.

"Glock did whatever it could to curry favor" with department officials, a subsequent state inspector general investigation found. Among other questionable tactics, Walsh arranged for the chief conservation law officer to obtain Glock pistols for his personal collection at a large discount. In 1993, the department allowed the chief and other officers to buy the agency's 325 used Glock 17s, and their magazines, at very low prices. Many of the conservation cops turned around and resold the guns at a profit. The inspector general concluded that after enactment of the federal assault weapons legislation, some of the self-dealing officers benefited from the sharp rise in prices for pre-ban Glock equipment. The department's officers collectively netted more than $60,000 in profits. "Their actions," the IG said, "turned DEC into a veritable weapons supermarket, and individual . . . officers into unlicensed gun dealers."

///

For the gun industry, and especially Glock, the assault weapons ban turned out to be far more notable for its unintended consequences than for its goal of restricting the spread of semiautomatic firearms. Gun-control advocates and their allies in Congress didn't anticipate that rifle manufacturers would adapt to the ban by making cosmetic changes to their military-style long guns, allowing the companies to continue to sell virtually identical models. Likewise, handgun makers responded to the prohibition on large-capacity magazines by channeling their design and marketing energies into a new generation of smaller handguns whose clips accommodated ten or fewer cartridges.

In 1995, Glock introduced the Glock 26 and Glock 27 in nine-millimeter and .40-caliber, respectively. (The eccentric Glock model-numbering system, beginning with the Glock 17, tells one nothing about each gun's characteristics.) The barrel and grip of the new models were an inch shorter than standard Glocks', but the ammunition packed just as much punch. The new products became known as "Pocket Rockets" or "Baby Glocks." They fit in the palm of a hand and could be conveniently tucked into a pocket or a purse. They were "a perfect choice for women," Glock said in a press release. "Those concerned about defending themselves can walk down a dark street with confidence knowing they have the power of a service caliber Glock pistol at their side," the marketing materials added. "The concealability of these pistols will be their main selling point as a self-defense weapon."

And sell they did. The Baby Glocks were almost instantly on a four-month back order. Demand "is hot as hell," Jannuzzo told the company's hometown paper in the States, the *Atlanta Journal-Constitution*. "We can't keep up."

The gun industry collectively reinforced Glock's pitch that small handguns were the perfect response to crime-ridden streets. The prolific Massad Ayoob advised in *Shooting Industry,* a periodical aimed at gun retailers: "Customers come to you every day out of fear. Fear is what they read in the newspaper. Fear of what they watch on the 11 o'clock news. Fear of the terrible acts of violence they see on the street. Your job, in no uncertain terms, is to sell them confidence. . . . An impulse of fear has sent that customer to your shop, so you want a quality product in stock to satisfy the customer's needs and complete the impulse purchase."

Smith & Wesson, Beretta, and other rivals followed suit. Thanos Polyzos, cofounder of Para-Ordnance, a handgun manufacturer now based in North Carolina, recalled years later: "We all rushed to make the smaller packages with larger calibers in direct response to the federal law. What was the point of trying to sell a pistol made for twenty rounds when the law allowed only ten? The law had the opposite effect from what the liberals intended, and Glock, as usual, led the way."

Beyond congressional Democrats and the Clinton White House, Glock had other parties to thank for the liftoff of Pocket Rockets. Spurred by the debate over the assault weapons ban and its enactment in 1994, the NRA stepped up its nationwide campaign supporting state laws that gave civilians the right to carry concealed handguns to shopping malls, Little

League games, and anywhere else they chose. Pocket Rockets were the ideal handgun for suburban concealed carry. Melding their message with that of the industry, the NRA argued that lawfully armed citizens were the first line of defense in stopping crime—a Second Amendment spin on the cliché that there's never a cop around when you need one.

Before 1987, only ten states, including Indiana, New Hampshire, and the Dakotas, had right-to-carry laws. That year, NRA activists in Florida pushed successfully for a statute that obliged authorities to issue a concealed-carry permit to anyone with a clean criminal record who agreed to take a firearm-safety course. The Florida fight for "shall issue" legislation emboldened local gun-rights groups elsewhere to seek similar laws, backed by the NRA. In 1994 and 1995 alone, eleven states enacted right-to-carry statutes, bringing the total to twenty-eight. "The gun industry should send me a basket of fruit," Tanya Metaksa, the NRA's chief lobbyist, told the *Wall Street Journal*. "Our efforts have created a new market."

The firearm press, effectively the marketing arm of the industry, did its part for the Pocket Rocket as well. Glock had benefited from lavish and mostly positive attention in the pages of the "gunzines." With the advent of palm-sized handguns, even those firearm writers who initially expressed hesitations became full-throated Glock fans. The Austrian company had demonstrated staying power. Gun writers eager to ensure future assignments figured it was safer to endorse Glock than to question the company, said Cameron Hopkins, the former editor of *American Handgunner*. "Everyone has to make a living, you know."

In the wake of the buying spree sparked by the 1994 assault weapons ban, the industry overall happened to be going through a sales slump in 1995 and 1996. Many consumers had exhausted their discretionary gun budgets. The firearm media moved to prop up the manufacturers, whose advertising they needed to survive. One *Guns & Ammo* contributor described a Glock demonstration of Pocket Rockets for gunzine writers in 1995: "Soon after, the pistols were passed out, and like a greedy bunch of kids pawing at the candy jar, we all dug in." The not-so-subtle message was that readers ought to dig into their wallets and head to the handgun counter of their local firearm shops.

Taking a broader and more analytical view, Massad Ayoob wrote in January 1996 in *Shooting Industry:* "Two bright rays of sunshine gleam through the dark clouds of the slump in the firearms market. One is the landslide of 'shall issue' concealed-carry reform legislation around the country. The other is the emergence of a new generation of compact handguns. The new [concealed-carry] permits open a new market for people from all walks of life who have need of a truly concealable handgun—since for the first time they have the right to carry one. The new-generation guns also tap a much more familiar market: your current pistol packers who are seeking something small with more power than they could pack in such a small package before."

Several years earlier, Ayoob had identified himself as a Glock skeptic, at least when it came to civilians carrying the handgun. Now his tone had changed. "What of the new Baby Glocks?" he wrote for his retailer readership. "Just try to keep them in stock." Praising various technical specifications, he wrote that the Pocket Rockets "finally make the Austrian brand a true hideout gun that fits ankle and pocket holsters. . . . I've shot them both, and the recoil is amazingly controllable. They're much nicer to shoot than hot-loaded .38 snubbies, let alone the baby Magnums. How many customers do you have who already own at least one Glock? Each of them is a candidate for one of the new shrunken models."

Asked about his evolution into an unabashed Glock enthusiast, Ayoob told me the manufacturer had responded to his earlier criticism by introducing on-request options such as a heavier trigger pull. That the company also began paying him to write promotional material, a gig he shared with other prominent firearm instructors, did not lessen his enthusiasm. But Ayoob emphasized that he did not sell out. "The Glock works for me, as it does for so many others," he said.

His fervor for smaller Glocks was widely shared. One of the first high-volume purchasers of the Glock 27 .40-caliber subcompact, he noted, was the Georgia State Patrol, which ordered eleven hundred to be used as backup guns to the full-sized Glock 22 service pistols the patrol had issued to its troopers.

/ / /

The pocket pistol vogue of the mid-1990s accelerated two related trends in the American small-arms industry: the proportional increase of imports and the relative rise of handgun sales versus long gun sales. The import boom helped propel a shift away from hunting rifles and shotguns and toward pistols made for competitive shooting and self-protection.

At mid-century, according to Tom Diaz, a former Democratic counsel to the House Crime Subcommittee and the author of a critical history of the industry, handguns accounted for less than 13 percent of domestic US firearm production. Shotguns (45 percent) and rifles (43 percent) dominated the market. During the 1960s, the industry was transformed. Gun sales in general soared. Handguns overtook long guns, because of rising domestic production and increased importation of pistols and revolvers. By the 1970s, Diaz wrote, "handguns grew to thirty six percent of the market, whereas rifles and shotguns fell to thirty-two percent each. The mix has never gone back— handgun share of the market has steadily risen, while rifles and shotguns have fallen."

Larger social changes were at work. Hunting continued a gradual decline, as farming communities contracted, exurban subdivisions expanded, and the tradition of stalking deer, duck, and quail began to seem old-fashioned to many younger people. "Grandpa or Dad isn't taking the kid out into the field to teach him how to shoot anymore," Paul Jannuzzo told the *Financial Times* in 1996. Increasingly, the Glock counsel served as a public spokesman for, and an interpreter of, the broader industry. Glock, of course, did not suffer as a result of the slow demise of hunting as a hobby and means of sustenance. To the contrary, Glock and other overseas manufacturers profited from gun owners' desire for something new and different.

In the first half of the twentieth century, imports accounted for less than 5 percent of all firearms purchased in the United States. By the mid-1990s, with the advent of globalization and the enterprise of Glock and other foreign brands, that figure had grown to more than 33 percent. In 1996, Brazilian and Italian manufacturers were bested by their Austrian rival. For the first time, Glock claimed the top spot among handgun importers, shipping 213,000 pistols to the United States.

CHAPTER 14

"My Way"

A corporation does not have a soul. Its character reflects that of the people in charge. Gaston Glock was very much in charge of his company, and he was a man with a complicated soul.

Even those who came to have grievances against Mr. Glock did not dispute his drive and tenacity. Well into middle age, he discovered a reservoir of ambition that fed the design of a truly innovative handgun. He then had the temerity to try to sell his invention in the United States, a country in love with its home-grown firearms. To a remarkable degree, he succeeded, and no one can gainsay that feat.

Was Glock a visionary engineer, covertly sophisticated in his understanding of the American gun market? That is how he and his handlers crafted his image in retrospect. And fair enough: In the 1850s, Sam Colt, too, cultivated a personal my-thology to move his handguns.

A more realistic perspective, though, suggests that Glock was a late-blooming tinkerer whose breakthrough came at ex-actly the right moment. He had the common sense to hire an inspired marketer in Karl Walter, a man willing to do what-ever it took to make a deal. At the beginning, Gaston Glock had no feel at all for the United States, or much of anything outside of Austria. He evolved from a provincial manager of a radiator factory to a world traveling industrialist. He met celebrities, flew on private jets, and had minions at his beck and call. He showed visitors a photograph of him shaking hands with Pope John Paul II at the Vatican, feeding an apocryphal notion that the two were friends. Brushes with Hollywood distorted Glock's sense of his personal status in America. In the mid-1990s, a Los Angeles movie prop master introduced him to Sharon Stone. Glock arranged for the elegant actress to receive one of his pistols as a gift. About a week later, Stone sent a bouquet of flowers to Glock—in all likelihood, a routine thank-you gesture. Glock, then in his mid-sixties, was so pleased by this interaction that on a subsequent trip to Los Angeles, he showed up at Stone's gated home for an unannounced visit, accompanied by one of his West Coast sales representatives. The actress did not make an appearance, and Glock was not invited into her mansion. He eventually got back into his car and left. When word of the embarrassing misadventure filtered back to Smyrna, it became a watercooler favorite among those employees prone to gossip.

The owner's amusing pretensions did not inhibit his company's performance. Glock built a veritable cash machine, with margins in the neighborhood of 70 percent—the kind of performance that would warrant a Harvard Business School case study were Glock not so secretive about his decision making. Few outsiders knew how he had accomplished what he had done.

As often happens in business, the profit imperative over time propelled the company and its owner into morally ambiguous territory. Glock's crafty response to the assault weapons ban provides one example of the manufacturer's deftness at outmaneuvering lawmakers and regulators.

The slogan "Glock Perfection" was not puffery to Gaston Glock. He believed it. His organization projected coolness, certainty, even arrogance. In public, the founder was capable of beguiling charm, as he demonstrated when testifying before the jury in Knoxville. At other times, he struck people as distant and condescending. To his German-speaking aides, he expressed disdain for Glock, Inc.'s, American employees, based on nothing more than their nationality. His all-purpose complaint concerned the prevalence of "crazy people" in the world, by which he meant incompetents, fools, and crooks.

He had an unforgiving management style, which, one day, he summarized for Monika Bereczky, the head of human resources for the American subsidiary. Bereczky, a Romanian native of Hungarian descent, spoke German fluently and for a number of years served informally as a personal assistant to Glock and his wife, Helga. "Every morning," he told her, "you have to slap everyone on the head, just in case they did something wrong."

///

Bereczky first met Gaston Glock in 1995, when she worked days as a hotel concierge in Atlanta and nights as a hostess at an upscale seafood restaurant. The Austrian businessman sometimes stayed at the hotel and ate at the restaurant. He stopped to speak to Bereczky, a slim, attractive young woman with a pale complexion and short dark hair. "He spoke to me in German," she recalled. "He was this kind old man who paid attention to me."

She had left her native Romania in 1989 as the Soviet bloc crumbled. Eventually she followed her divorced mother, a former ballet dancer, to the United States. Mother and daughter lived in a dingy, insect-infested apartment in Atlanta. Monika worked seven days a week from five a.m. until late at night. After several conversations, Glock invited her to visit his gun plant in Smyrna. Monika's suspicious mother told her not to go. The older woman did not trust Glock and assumed he had lecherous intentions.

Monika was torn. In her mid-twenties at the time, she knew nothing about guns or the firearm business and was not particularly interested in learning. But she wanted a better life and sensed that Glock was offering her something. "I didn't know how to say no," she said.

The tour of Glock, Inc., turned into an offer of an administrative job, which Monika accepted. The post evolved into overseeing human resources: hiring and firing lower-level employees and complying with regulatory paperwork. Glock sponsored her work visa, allowing her to remain in the country with her mother, who had become a citizen. The pay was generous compared to hotel and restaurant jobs, and the hours were more reasonable.

At first, Bereczky enjoyed being a favorite of the company's owner. When he was in town, Glock went out of his way to talk with her privately about how other employees conducted themselves in the office. Glock did this with a number of German-speaking underlings, creating resentment among the Americans. "I was awful to the Americans," Bereczky admitted. "This was how Mr. Glock liked it. We spoke in German. The Americans were 'stupid.'"

Her coworkers returned the favor by calling her a spy and

gossiping about her relationship with the boss. Glock encouraged the hostile talk with his tactile manner of showing affection for his slender young employee. "He would come out of a conference room or a meeting with his hand around my waist," she said. "He laughed and let them know he owned me. I was something like a fool. . . . I went along with this to keep my job, keep my visa, and to make the money, which was good." Bereczky said she rebuffed Mr. Glock's more amorous advances and never slept with him. "I hated that the Americans thought I was Mr. Glock's bimbo."

Her duties, meanwhile, progressed in two very different directions: She gained responsibility and influence in the office, while at the same time Glock demanded that she carry out highly personal errands. The Glocks purchased, among other Atlanta real estate, a luxurious home in a wealthy neighborhood called the Vinings. When Glock was in town, it fell to Bereczky to clean the house, stock it with food, make the beds, and place candy on the owner's pillow. He sometimes called her in the middle of the night to bring him toiletries or batteries for the television remote. When she arrived, she said, Glock greeted her on some occasions in his underwear. "I don't know what he thought I would do when I saw him half-naked," she recalled. "I just wanted to get out of there as fast as possible."

Despite Bereczky's resistance to what she saw as his romantic overtures—or perhaps because of her reluctance—Glock expected her to look after other women with whom he socialized. Over the years, according to Bereczky, she took several of these women to lunch and on shopping trips to upscale stores in Atlanta. This occasionally led to awkward scenes. Once, the day after Bereczky accompanied one of her employer's female friends to the local Saks Fifth Avenue, Glock's wife, Helga, arrived in town and asked to visit the same store. Bereczky worried about returning to Saks but could not come up with an excuse to steer Helga Glock elsewhere.

"Welcome back!" a Saks salesperson greeted Bereczky, who signaled desperately for the retailer to stay quiet and play dumb. Mrs. Glock seemed not to notice the exchange, and the shopping trip proceeded without further incident.

/ / /

Gaston Glock traveled in luxury and dropped thousands of dollars on visits to the Gold Club. His female friends had carte blanche at Atlanta's most expensive stores. But he could explode in rage when underlings bought what he considered unnecessary office supplies. On one occasion that lived long in company lore, he became furious that the front-desk receptionist at the executive offices in Smyrna used a $29 headset to answer the phone more efficiently. In Austria, he bellowed, we pick up the telephone the old-fashioned way!

American employees, not surprisingly, came to anticipate his visits with dread. They fretted when the convoy of BMW and Mercedes sedans carrying him and his entourage pulled into the company parking lot: "Mr. Glock is here, Mr. Glock is here."

Patched together on the fly, the company evolved into a prodigious moneymaker powered by excellent product design and a fearful desire not to displease Mr. Glock. And the reserve of the reticent engineer at the helm gradually gave way to capricious grandiosity. "He started out pretty humble and unassuming," said one former American sales manager, who recalled that on his first trip to Austria, Gaston Glock picked him up personally at the Vienna airport. "Then he began believing his news clippings."

///

Karl Walter took tremendous pride in his role as Glock's top executive in the United States and architect of the company's marketing success. Gaston Glock found ways to remind all his employees that they were subordinates, but for a time Walter enjoyed special standing. Most visitors to the Glock factory in Deutsch-Wagram were left to fend for themselves at midday, while Gaston Glock went home to be served lunch by his wife. Walter, by contrast, broke bread with his boss at the Glocks' kitchen table, while Helga laid out the meat, bread, and beer. The Glocks sometimes invited him to the family's villa in Velden and took him along when they went swimming in the large lake nearby. In the late 1980s, before the Glocks knew their way around Atlanta or had bought a house there, they stayed with Walter and his family in their suburban home.

Success, however, eroded this camaraderie. "My contract was signed the day after the [American subsidiary] was incorporated," Walter recounted. "I had a very small salary, like $50,000 a year, plus a small percentage on net revenues." He would not reveal his exact commission, but others familiar with the company speculated that it was 1 percent. "If you came close to $100 million [in company revenue], this small percentage is quite something," Walter said. The "super gun" stood to make him a wealthy man. "Initially," he said, "Mr. Glock had no difficulty. Then some of his coworkers and managers became envious."

Wolfgang Riedl, Glock's Vienna-based marketing chief, recalled the jealousy growing in Austria among other executives, as they questioned why Walter was so much better compensated than they were. "They started to poke Mr. Glock in the side, I believe, and said, 'He is making too much money. I want to make this money,'" Walter said. His colleagues failed to acknowledge, he added, that "whatever money they made, most of it was generated in the United States." And it was largely, Walter thought, because of his sales acumen. "Karl was very sure the Glock organization would not work in the United States without him," Riedl said.

Richard Feldman saw more at issue than money, however. Ego, too, was a factor. The industry operative met Gaston Glock for the first time at the 1992 SHOT Show, held in New Orleans. For the third year running, the Glock booth was mobbed. "Everybody treated Gaston like a celebrity, and he enjoyed being treated that way," Feldman said. He picked up chatter from within the company about Walter's compensation. Feldman also noticed that when the Austrian company received industry awards at the show, it was Walter who went up to the stage to accept them. To Feldman, that was a big mistake. Studying Glock's body language, Feldman could see that Gaston seemed annoyed not to be the one in the spotlight. "Rule number one," said Feldman, "is you always let the guy who pays the bills take all the credit."

In late 1992, during a visit to the Smyrna facility, Glock proposed changing Walter's contract to cut drastically his percentage commission. The owner had no intention of making Walter a millionaire.

Taken aback, Walter refused. He and his wife, Pam, had lived and breathed Glock pistols for seven years. Was this to be his reward for all the sacrifice—to be cheated by the man he had made rich?

Glock remained unmoved. "He gave me an ultimatum," Walter said: "'Accept it, or . . .' I took the 'or.'" Without hesitation, Glock fired Walter, the man widely credited with establishing the company in America.

"I didn't believe he did it," Walter said, "because not only did I put a huge effort into it; I picked some of the best people that I could find in the industry to make it happen."

Walter continued to work in the US gun industry as an executive and consultant, but he never regained the prominence he had at Glock.

Over the next eleven years, Gaston Glock would run through seven US sales managers. Distinguishing oneself within the company became a career-killer, and longtime employees learned to keep their heads down. Wolfgang Riedl realized that his own goal of one day directing the European branch of the company was futile. Herr Glock intended to pass control to his children. Before he could be fired, Riedl left the company for another industry job, eventually becoming a successful independent military arms broker with government clients in Asia.

/ / /

As a fuming Karl Walter departed, another Glock lieutenant was ascending within the company. Charles Marie Joseph Ewert met Gaston Glock in 1985, when the Austrian traveled to Luxembourg to set up a holding company, also known as a shell company, as the partial owner of his manufacturing operation. Luxembourg does not tax holding companies on income or capital gains, making the tiny principality a popular haven for this sort of arrangement. As far as Luxembourg is concerned, shell companies are a legitimate means of sheltering business revenue (or a personal fortune) from taxation. But from the perspective of other jurisdictions, such as the United States, routing revenue generated elsewhere through a Luxembourg shell corporation may constitute fraudulent tax evasion.

Charles Ewert earned his living operating along this murky line. He served as a financial adviser to wealthy individuals and had worked for the Luxembourg stock exchange. Glock told Ewert that he was seeking to expand his firearm corporation while minimizing its tax liability.

"I am your man," Ewert said.

Asked in 1995 during a legal deposition about his relationship with Ewert, Glock explained defensively: "I was not a salesman. I am a technician. I had no experience, no English, so I had to find a partner that helps me to sell the pistol."

Ewert was not really a salesman or a conventional business partner. Rakish and multilingual, he had connections all over the world. He acquired the sobriquet "Panama Charly" in recognition of his activity in Latin America. He was a financial fixer. At Glock's request, Ewert set up a web of paper corporations intended to insulate the gun business from government taxing authorities in the United States and Austria, and from American product-liability lawyers who thought about suing a profitable firearm manufacturer. With Ewert's assistance, Gaston Glock purchased a Panamanian shell called Reofin International. Reofin, in turn, bought Unipatent Holding, a Luxembourg entity that Ewert owned. Unipatent received a 50 percent stake in Glock's unit in the United States, where the company generated the vast majority of its revenue. Half the wealth from American gun sales ended up flowing to Glock's putative co-owner, Unipatent, which, in fact, Glock controlled via the paper company in Panama. The complexity, though seemingly gratuitous, made following Glock's money more difficult.

Ewert also formed shells for Glock in Ireland, Liberia, and Curaçao. These corporate entities issued bills for various "services" to Glock headquarters in Austria and to operating units that were established in Latin America and Hong Kong. One effect of the various arms of Glock owning and billing one another was to decrease the profits that had to be reported in Austria and the United States, which are relatively high-tax jurisdictions. Many companies seek to lessen their tax bills in a similar fashion. Tax attorneys at the most prestigious law firms in Manhattan devote their working lives to corporate tax minimization. Whether all of this is accomplished within the letter and spirit of the relevant laws is sometimes a close question.

Vociferously proud of his pistol and its commercial success, Gaston Glock was shy about publicly discussing the maze of shell companies constructed by Ewert. During the 1990s, he was asked repeatedly in the course of civil lawsuits in the United States about the convoluted ownership structure of his companies. He gave answers that, at best, seem uninformative. On various occasions, he testified that he did not own—or did not know who owned—Unipatent, the shell that theoretically controlled fully half of Glock, Inc. In one case, an injury-liability suit called *Shultz v. Glock,* filed in state court in New Jersey, Gaston Glock was asked in a deposition, "Do you know who owns Glock, Inc.?"

"Glock, Inc., is owned by Glock Austria and Unipatent," he responded.

"Do you know who the principals of Unipatent are, who owns the company?"

"I don't know," Glock said.

"Do you have any ownership interest in that entity?"

"No."

In fact, Reofin International owned Unipatent, and Gaston Glock owned Reofin. Glock either suffered from acute and conveniently timed memory loss, or he did not want to share this information with a plaintiffs' lawyer who might have cause to track down Glock assets. (Since the company rarely suffered a courtroom defeat, the issue was largely academic.)

But Glock did not conceal his relationship with Panama Charly from employees. Executives in Smyrna sometimes addressed corporate correspondence to Ewert as a "director" or "managing director" of Glock GmbH, the Austrian parent company. Ewert occasionally visited the United States to meet with Gaston Glock. At the Smyrna offices, workers referred sneeringly to Ewert behind his back as "the Duke," because of his aristocratic affectations.

Florian Deltgen, who worked briefly for Glock, Inc., as a sales manager in the late 1990s, was well aware of Ewert's reputation. An experienced gun industry executive, Deltgen was born in Luxembourg. His father, decades earlier, had retained Ewert as a consultant but soon fired him. "My father realized this man was cheating him," Deltgen told me. "Everyone in Luxembourg knew Charles Ewert as a thief." Deltgen, who left Glock, Inc., after a falling-out with Gaston Glock, professed to know nothing firsthand about the Glock-Ewert relationship. He did know this: "If you deal with thieves, they may turn on you."

/ / /

As Glock continued to ascend in the American gun industry, the company's rituals grew more elaborate. Sharon Dillon of the Gold Club was eclipsed by the Dallas Cowboys cheerleaders. For a couple of years in the mid-1990s, the National Football League's premier sideline sex symbols performed at the Glock SHOT Show party in midriff-baring tops and supershort white hot pants. Invitation-only guests watched the entertainment as they ate thick steaks or two-pound lobsters. The gun industry had not previously witnessed such razzledazzle. Chipper and athletic, the Cowgirls brought the crowd to its feet as they high-kicked and shimmied through a floor show backed by loud pop music.

"Gaston Glock was the king of that world," Robert Ricker, a former NRA lawyer and industry lobbyist, said in an interview before his death from cancer. "The girls, the guns, the money and liquor—and at the center of it all was this Austrian engineer none of us really knew very well."

In later years, the Glock party took a turn from American heartland-kitsch toward Turkish exotica. Glock imported an Austrian belly dancer as the main attraction at the SHOT Show. The dancer had impressed Glock when he saw her entertain in Vienna. During each of her visits in the late 1990s, she practiced for several days in the basement gym of the Glock residence in the Vinings, which was equipped with a dance bar and wall-length mirror, according to Bereczky.

The Middle Eastern–style diversion drew lusty cheers from the gun crowd. "You've got the Turkish harem music, and the spotlight on this belly dancer," recalled Ricker. "A lot of people didn't know whether it was a joke, or what. But, hey, it was the Glock party, so you went with it."

Ricker for a time worked with Richard Feldman at the ASSC, which was eager to ingratiate itself with Gaston Glock. With Jannuzzo's encouragement, the company agreed to give the trade group $1 for each gun shipped from Smyrna. The

annual Glock donation grew to more than $120,000 a year—
the largest contribution the ASSC received from any single
company, according to Feldman.

Feldman sometimes accompanied Mr. Glock on outings to
the Gold Club, where the usually taciturn Austrian was able to
unwind. Some of the dancers knew the free-spending magnate
by sight, and on a couple of occasions they brought him up on
stage for a round of applause. One evening, Glock received a
varsity-style Gold Club jacket, which the dancers autographed.
On another visit, to celebrate Glock's birthday, the erotic en-
tertainers invited the gun maker to the stage and then playfully
stripped him down to his boxer shorts, dark dress socks, and
black shoes, according to Jannuzzo. Far from resisting, Glock
helped remove his shirt and slacks, grinning broadly the whole
time. He had come a long way from running his radiator factory in suburban Vienna.

/ / /

In Austria, the date of Glock's birth is known to his employees and admirers as "Glockmas." Celebrants mark the event
with the presentation of ice sculptures and toasts of praise.
Champagne and wooden casks of wine accompany a spread of
Wiener schnitzel, sausage wrapped in flaky pastry, and other
traditional Austrian fare. And Glock thanks attendees in the
style of a country baron blessing his peasants.

Glock spent an increasing amount of his time in Velden in
the southern state of Carinthia. A favorite spot for the bour-
geoisie of Austria and Germany, the resort featured water
sports, pricey jewelry stores, restaurants, and boutique hotels.
Here the once-shy engineer carried himself like the mogul he

had become: imperious, proud, demanding of respect. "A person changes when they make a lot of money, and they go to America and see they are famous there," observed Wolfgang Riedl, the former Glock executive. "Suddenly, everyone wants to know what they can do for Mr. Glock. He thinks he is important. In a way, he is."

Glock became a more expansive host. He no longer left guests without so much as a glass of water while he ate lunch alone. He held court at sumptuous dinners and took his senior employees for rides on his boat across the Wöthersee, a large and scenic lake down the hill from his villa. Sometimes the destination was the village's main lakeside casino. Upon the entrance of Glock and his entourage, the casino manager would signal to the conductor of the house jazz band, and the musicians halted whatever they were playing. After a moment's pause, the band would swing into a brassy rendition of Frank Sinatra's "My Way."

"This was the Glock theme: 'I did it my way,'" explained Florian Deltgen. Gaston Glock sat at his reserved table, and one by one, members of the serving staff came by to pay homage.

Glock's three adult children remained in his close orbit but fit awkwardly into his social and business life. The patriarch cast a long and intimidating shadow. Gaston Jr. worked as an engineer for the family company, without enjoying significant executive responsibilities. Introspective and unassuming, the middle child rarely asserted himself. Brigitte, the eldest, had a more outgoing personality, but her father restricted her to low-level administrative tasks within the company. She joked bitterly that he treated her as a personal slave. For a time, she was married to a Glock marketing executive.

Robert, the younger son, had a confident swagger. He wore his jet-black hair slicked back and favored tailored leather jackets. His father dispatched Robert as a front man to trade shows and for a while set him up as the company's top representative in the United States. But eventually Robert was called back to Austria. He never had much real authority in the company. American executives with Glock either laughed at him behind his back or expressed sympathy for the patronizing way his father treated him.

Deltgen recalled that Robert was a reckless driver whose fender benders kept local mechanics busy repairing his sports cars. With a gun, he could be even more of a menace. "On a visit to Deutsch-Wagram, I was with someone else from the US, and Robert was going to demonstrate the latest modifications on the Glock pistol," Deltgen said. "Suddenly the gun goes off, and we're ducking for our lives."

/ / /

A former Socialist Party loyalist, Gaston Glock mixed with the politically powerful of Carinthia, a stronghold of Austria's right-wing Freedom Party. The region was known for its residents' animus toward immigrants and for pockets of nostalgia for the Third Reich. The Freedom Party's charismatic leader, Jörg Haider, who served for many years as the governor of Carinthia, was notorious internationally for making a series of provocative pro-Nazi statements in the 1990s. He praised elite SS troops as "men of character," and he hailed the wisdom of Hitler's "orderly employment policy."

During one visit to Austria, Paul Jannuzzo recalled, Glock told him they would "take a beer" before dinner and meet some local friends. At the restaurant where Glock took him, "there was a bit of an unidentified buzz in the air," Jannuzzo said, "and it reached its crescendo when the star arrived": Jörg Haider. The politician shook hands and exchanged pleasantries with Glock and the others.

"It was the Beer Hall Putsch Redux," Jannuzzo said ruefully. Uncomfortable mixing with the Haider crowd, the American lawyer decided to step outside—"in case the Israelis decided to use this occasion to take out Haider and his group with a cruise missile."

Over the years, Glock vehemently denied Austrian media reports linking him to the Freedom Party. But several employees were aware of his friendliness with Haider.

/ / /

By the late 1990s, the gun business had made Gaston Glock a billionaire. Estimating the size of his fortune was (and is) difficult, because most of it remains tied up in his privately held corporation. The shares of Glock GmbH do not trade on an exchange and therefore do not have a price. Valued conservatively, the company and its offshoots are probably worth $500 million, according to executives and investors familiar with the gun industry. Glock has invested in real estate in Atlanta and southern Austria worth tens of millions of dollars more. He has two corporate jets worth eight figures and a helicopter that ferries him around Austria (probably worth another $3 million or $4 million). He owns expensive show horses. It is impossible to say how much cash he has stashed away.

For all his wealth, though, Glock has spent his money awkwardly, in fits and starts. He has never seemed entirely comfortable living large. His ostentation has been tentative.

When his senior American employees traveled to Velden

for consultations, Glock often had them stay at his villa, an enormous structure decorated in pink-and-white Italian marble, glittering crystal chandeliers, and heavy brocade curtains. The home cost millions to build, but guests wiped their shoes on tacky black-and-silver Glock-branded doormats. Inside the front door were withered houseplants turning shades of yellow and brown. The parlors were filled with expensive white couches and divans, but some were wrapped in transparent plastic, presumably to prevent stains. A garish fake leopard skin was draped across one living room sofa. Guest room beds were made up with slippery silk sheets the color of Pepto-Bismol. Glock did not obsess about thread count.

The master of the mansion spent much of his time in a windowless basement room, according to visitors. From this underground bunker, he could control the villa's security cameras and alarms, as well as the air-conditioning and elevator. He could even set the temperature of the heated tile floors in the many bathrooms upstairs. "He was down there alone for hours," Jannuzzo said.

Glock employed a cleaning staff and a computer technician but no other household servants. He drove his own BMW and never graduated from the $80,000 car to a Rolls-Royce or a Bentley. He frequented pricey restaurants, but typically those popular with tourists, rather than the most exclusive establishments. He insisted on caviar for the whole table and plentiful bottles of Gray Goose vodka, yet he demonstrated unease ordering from an elaborate wine list. One of his favorite spots was Essigbratlein, a dining establishment in Nuremberg, Germany, where Glock traveled for business. Originally a sixteenth-century meeting place for wine merchants, the tiny restaurant is famous for its roast loin of beef. But it is hardly extravagant by the standards of corporate titans or movie stars. A six-course dinner of Franconian cuisine can be had for $120.

When visiting Austria, Glock employees ate all their meals with their hosts. Mr. Glock dominated the conversation, often holding forth on physical fitness and human longevity. On occasion, he discussed his intention to live to the age of 120. The key to his biblical durability, he said, was a substance called megamine, which he consumed daily. Just what he was ingesting is not clear. There are various dietary supplements of dubious value that are marketed under names similar to megamine. A company called NaturalMost sells Megamino Amino Acid Complex "for the satisfactory maintenance of physiological functions." Glock described megamine as a derivative of volcanic ash, which when ground finely and taken orally, could enter human cells and purge them of impurities.

Business meetings with Mr. Glock in his large office in the villa at Velden lasted hours at a time. Typically, executives presented him with a decision—whether to move ahead with a hiring, firing, or scheduling of a promotional event—followed by extended periods of silent rumination. Glock stared out his window at the broad lawn and tall trees surrounding the villa. "One hundred words per hour is probably a high estimate," Jannuzzo said, speaking of Glock's verbal contributions. Another Glock in-house lawyer, Peter Manown, occupied himself by surreptitiously conjugating verbs in German, scribbling on a pad as if he were taking notes about company matters.

Visiting executives were at the Glocks' command twenty-four hours a day. Jannuzzo recalled an autumn Sunday morning in Velden: "At about six thirty a.m., there was a knock at my door, and it was Mrs. Glock: 'Time for swim.'" The villa had a heated indoor pool, but this day's exercise would commence outdoors in the Wöthersee. Wearing a bathrobe, Gaston Glock led the way down to the dock. He signaled for the others to enter the frigid water first, which they did. Upon surfacing and looking back up at the dock, Jannuzzo saw his employer disrobing. "All you could see from the rear was a long skinny body, some semblance of ass, and a ball sack." While Mrs. Glock and the executive were clothed conventionally in swimsuits, Glock himself took his constitutional au naturel.

CHAPTER 15

Glock Culture

Amerrican gun owners express enthusiasm for firearms in distinct and varied ways. Would-be cowboys dress up in Old West costumes, assume the identities of frontier marshals and gunslingers, and collect single-action Colts. They compete in target shoots that feature re-created nineteenth-century saloons and poker games gone bad. The more serious single-action shooters display the intensity of Civil War reenactors.

Sniper-rifle disciples gather in groups of two or three at undecorated rural ranges. They speak softly and peer through high-powered scopes before squeezing off a shot at a plywood bull's-eye six hundred yards away. They assess their accuracy with binoculars and recalibrate for another go. Machine-gun enthusiasts, who must register their automatic weapons with federal and local authorities, gather for a twice-yearly festival at a Kentucky gun club called Knob Creek. Participants fire at abandoned washing machines and refrigerators, although more emphasis is placed on quantity of ammunition expended than on accuracy.

At the more conventional end of the gun-owning spectrum, hunters track everything from gray squirrels to white-tailed deer to grizzly bear. Some use bolt-action rifles based on the 1903 Springfield; others prefer AR-15s with flash suppressors and thirty-round mags that resemble the rifles American troops carry on patrol in Kandahar or Kabul.

No brand of modern firearm commands greater loyalty than Glock. "Glockmeisters" see themselves as rugged, unromantic, and above all, lethally effective—like the gun they love. The website Glock Talk (glocktalk.com) sponsors scores of online forums where Glock "fanboys" (and the occasional interloping "hateboy") dissect a range of topics connected to the pistol. The obsession and vituperation characteristic of the Internet are often evident. Virtual symposia parse the qualities of the Glock, usually in service of proving its superiority over rival handguns. One rambling group discussion in 2010 addressed the similarities between the Glock and the AK-47 semiautomatic rifle. The two firearms share a reputation for reliability in the field, even in the absence of diligent maintenance. The reason? "Loose tolerances and a simple design with few parts," noted a participant from Colorado using the screen name Voyager 4520. "More room for dirt before the friction becomes too much for the slide to cycle," agreed Ambluemax. The AK-47, invented in Russia, does not incorporate polymer, but its lack of delicacy made it a favorite of the militaries of the old Soviet bloc. It can last for decades and rarely jams. Children can be taught to use it, as demonstrated by the youthful ranks of African guerrilla armies. Glock, wrote Vis35 of Alaska, "is the AK-47 of handguns."

Glockmeisters who stray even momentarily from slavish devotion risk ostracism. Dean Speir, the Long Island firearm dealer and gunzine writer who helped break the Suffolk County ban on Glock in the late 1980s, made a habit of pointing out that "Glock Perfection" was a marketing device not to be taken literally. He used his own website, The Gun Zone (thegunzone.com), to compile instances when substandard ammunition, improper shooting technique, or a factory flaw led to Glock malfunctions. Glock Talk regulars pilloried Speir for his apostasy and effectively banished him from their site. "Speir has very little knowledge about firearms; does not tell the truth; lies; prevaricates," ranted WalterGA. "I have from a reliable source that his I.Q. is less than that of an unborn rhinoceros."

In fact, Speir is a meticulous if prickly gadfly—and a loyal Glock owner. "All critical thinking skills are checked at the gate of the Tenifer Temple," he told me. "Polymer is the highest power, and Gaston Glock is the combination prophet-and-deity."

/ / /

Nationally known guardians of the American firearm ethos early on helped define the Glock's everyman (and everywoman) practicality. Marion Hammer, a legendary NRA figure from Florida, told a story in 1989 about why she switched from carrying a Colt revolver in her purse to a Glock. Several years earlier, she said, she had been cornered in a Tallahassee parking garage late one night by no fewer than six men. She brandished her Colt, and, thank goodness, the assailants fled.

"The revolver I was carrying had six shots, and there were six men," Hammer noted. "What if I ran out of shots?" With seventeen rounds in her Glock pistol, she felt more secure. When it comes to ammo, in Hammer's view, more is better, and more is what you get with the Glock.

Glock cultivates devotion to its product with the American

gun industry's most diligent customer-loyalty program. The company-underwritten Glock Shooting Sports Foundation sponsors a series of target competitions limited to owners of the Austrian pistol. For a modest $25 annual fee, GSSF members gain access to events held at ranges around the country. "My whole family and I had a great time at the Beaver State Ballistic Challenge last week," D.W. of Washington State wrote to the *GLOCK Report* in 2010 (correspondents to the newsletter are identified only by initials). "This year my wife, sister, brother-in-law, and son joined us. At eleven years old, it was my son's very first match, and now I can't get him to take his GLOCK cap off. . . . We experienced the same thing when my daughter started shooting at the same age. Very cool!" The letter was accompanied by a photo of a smiling boy in a Glock hat and sound-reducing earmuffs, pointing at a cardboard target punctured by bullet holes.

The gun manufacturer and the vendors that feed off its reputation supply all manner of Glock paraphernalia: clocks, key chains, playing cards, lamps, and custom license plates. Curvaceous pinup model Candy Keane grips a Glock in online lingerie photos. GSSF members submit images to the *GLOCK Report* of Glock-shaped birthday cakes and babies in T-shirts that read FUTURE GLOCK OWNER. A father from Florida submitted a snapshot of his blond daughter at her wedding, raising her gown to reveal a shapely thigh and a Glock 19 tucked snugly in her silk garter. Her kneeling husband stares at the gun, enraptured. "He enjoyed the surprise," the proud dad wrote in 2009, "and he promised to love, honor, and shoot GLOCKs with the princess."

/ / /

I did not grow up with guns, although my father earned a marksmanship award with his M-1 when he served in the army at Fort Dix in the late 1950s. As an adult, I have fired handguns and rifles from time to time as a part of my journalistic work covering the firearm industry. While researching the mechanics and use of the Glock for this book, I took some private lessons and participated in competitions sponsored by the International Defensive Pistol Association. A private organization, the IDPA promotes "combat shooting" skills and has chapters in gun-friendly precincts throughout the United States and abroad. Despite the military-sounding terminology, combat shooting refers to techniques for defending against armed aggressors in a civilian setting. In contrast to stationary target shooting, IDPA teaches its members how to draw and fire in unfolding circumstances of simulated danger.

IDPA is not officially affiliated with Glock, but it might as well be. During my visits to the First Coast IDPA chapter, which meets at a range outside of Jacksonville, roughly 75 percent of the members competed with Glocks, and most of the rest used American- or Croatian-made Glock knockoffs. A few people shot Berettas or Sigs, and a handful of old-timers brought S&W revolvers.

In preparation for my maiden IDPA match, I sought individual instruction from self-defense expert and gun writer Massad Ayoob and his girlfriend, Gail Pepin, a champion shooter in her own right. Ayoob and Pepin live in a one-story house on several verdant acres about ninety minutes west of Jacksonville. Step one was learning to draw. "Everyone has to start somewhere," Gail said charitably.

In an IDPA match, the gun starts in your holster, often covered by a jacket to replicate the experience of carrying a concealed weapon. Florida requires gun owners who obtain carry permits to keep their weapons hidden in public. Concealment is thought to discourage precipitate gunplay. Gail explained that one of the most dangerous parts of shooting is getting the gun out of the holster and clear of your clothing without accidental discharge. This is especially so when using a Glock, she said, because it lacks an external safety switch. It is always "on" and ready to fire.

Rookies tend to grab the weapon too abruptly, putting the index finger immediately on the trigger or tangling themselves in their overgarment. First rule: sweep the jacket back with the shooting hand and grasp the gun with index finger extended *outside* of the trigger guard. "Do not touch that trigger," Gail said, "until you are prepared to destroy something."

Just to be safe, she demonstrated with a hard rubber dummy Glock. She handed the yellow fake to me, and I imitated her deliberate motion, withdrawing the pistol from the plastic holster on my belt and pointing it straight in front of me. We were standing in her kitchen, aiming at an empty Coke can on a couple of telephone books on top of the Formica counter. I held the imitation Glock in the two-handed crush grip, arms locked at eye level. It was amazing how much false muscle memory I had to overcome from decades of television and movies. My instinct was to swing the weapon up at the ceiling as I drew. Actors do that in Hollywood, Gail explained, but it is risky showboating. Point the gun only where you will shoot: directly at the target. The proper movement is economical, almost robotic.

At that moment, Massad shouted some encouragement from the living room. I turned in his direction, unthinkingly sweeping the dummy Glock ninety degrees to my right. "Whoa, partner," Mas said. "You do that, and you'll get kicked off the range before you even start." Another unbreakable rule: put the gun back in the holster before turning away from the target.

"Anything that barrel aims at you should be prepared to destroy," Gail reiterated slowly, as if I were not very bright. "OK, let's do it again."

I drew one hundred times in the cramped kitchen that afternoon. Gail showed me how to draw while backing up toward the refrigerator and stepping sidewise in the direction of the sink. Combining the movements felt like spinning plates on sticks while riding a unicycle. And this was with a harmless imitation weapon.

"If you can't get comfortable with it, you just don't shoot," Gail said. Like many avid gun owners, she demonstrated an obsessive dedication to safety. We all read in the newspaper about people who accidentally shoot themselves or, worse, their child. But as a result of more safety training, better storage practices, and a decline in hunting, the rate of reported gun accidents has fallen 80 percent since 1930.

"Practice tonight in your motel room," Gail told me.

I had three days to figure out how to draw and shoot before firing nine-millimeter rounds at an imaginary hostage taker while darting through a facsimile of a shopping mall. The next day we would go live on the practice range behind Gail's and Massad's house; Friday was the competition in Jacksonville. I was going to have a long night at the motel with the fake yellow Glock.

/ / /

Gail Pepin, at first glance, does not seem particularly threatening, but she would be the wrong five-foot-tall former obstetrical nurse to hassle on a dark street corner. The gun safe she and Ayoob have at home contains more than two dozen weapons. The ammunition shed out back resembles a small military depot. In the supermarket, at Walmart—pretty much everywhere—Pepin carries a handgun concealed in a holster on her hip. She sometimes has another, smaller weapon strapped to her ankle, as a backup. Ayoob also carries, usually a Glock. They see the world as a dangerous place in which it is simply intelligent to be prepared for trouble. Falling crime rates since the mid-1990s do not console them. Like many gun owners who carry, they find last night's local television news report of an armed robbery at the neighborhood 7-Eleven more compelling than the statistically small chance of being the unlucky customer paying for a Slurpee when a bad guy attacks.

Ten years ago, Pepin was living outside her native Chicago, working in a hospital not far from O'Hare Airport. She didn't grow up in a gun family and had never owned one. She thought of herself as fairly liberal. She and a group of friends decided one day on a lark to try shooting handguns. "Let's see what this is all about," Pepin thought.

So they got Illinois gun permits and took a basic NRA safety course. They went shooting at an indoor range. "I got more into it than the rest of the group," Pepin said. "When I went to go shoot, I could think of nothing else but shooting. I had to focus on where my feet were, where my shoulders were, where my hands were, where the gun was: 100 percent focused on shooting. I had a stressful job in the hospital. You know, labor and delivery is number one for lawsuits. . . . Shooting was my stress release . . . like a Zen thing."

But not a laid-back Zen thing. "I've been a student of one thing or another my whole life," Pepin explained. "I'm always trying to learn new things." She's also highly competitive.

Most of the people at the shooting ranges around Chicago were men. "I was the only woman who shot with this group at the time. I had a lot to prove, so I had to just get better and better and better."

The perpetual student, Pepin, then in her early forties, heard about Ayoob as a lecturer. "If you ever thought about taking this class, take it, because it's life-changing," a friend told Pepin. The friend was a Chicago police officer who seemed to know what he was talking about. "When he said that," she recalled, "I said I better find out what this is." Significant eye contact in the classroom led to a date. Pepin came around to carrying a handgun all the time. "It sure was life-changing," she said, smiling. She and Ayoob had a long-distance romance for several years (his first marriage had ended). For the past five years they have lived together in north-central Florida, where gun ownership is common and the weather is conducive to outdoor target practice.

/ / /

Driving in their Ford SUV, Pepin and Ayoob lead a monthly caravan east along US Route I-10 to Jacksonville for the IDPA shoot. According to the rules, competitors must "use practical handguns and holsters that are suitable for self-defense use. No 'competition only' equipment is permitted in IDPA matches." Glocks fit the bill, and both Ayoob and Pepin frequently use one from their collection.

On one of the days I attended, five squads of fifteen competitors each faced a series of imaginary life-threatening scenarios. In one, the participant was wandering a shopping mall when shots rang out. Another put us in the shoes of a pizza-delivery person who encountered potentially fatal circumstances.

Retreat was not offered as an option. We were armed, and we were going to address the situation. The police play no role in these simulations.

At the sound of a buzzer, a competitor drew his or her weapon and began shooting at cardboard and metal cutouts representing an army of bad guys. We each ran the drill individually, with a range officer in a red T-shirt and ball cap standing nearby and watching closely for safety violations. The shooting distances varied from three yards to twenty. Most of the targets were stationary, but a few waggled back and forth on springs or moved on wheels along tracks. Innocent bystanders were indicated by targets with open hands stenciled in Day-Glo colors. There are penalties for hitting an innocent.

Competitors moved in and out of mock buildings and along blind passages constructed from home-insulation material stretched between tall poles. There was a great deal of scampering and ducking for cover. The ammunition was live, and the sound deafening, which is why everyone wore ear protection.

All the shooting was done in one direction, with the bullets piercing the targets (most of the time) and landing in ten-foot-high earthen hills along the back side of the range. Competitors were measured on the amount of time it took them to place two rounds within a designated kill zone on each target. You could fire as often as you liked, but penalty points were added to a competitor's score for errant shots.

Mas Ayoob's turns drew the most attention. He was a national and regional champion in his younger days. Five-ten and sinewy—his chain-smoking retards his appetite—Ayoob, sixty-one, moved nimbly on the balls of his feet. He fired quickly in short bursts. So swiftly did he eject empty magazines from the grip of his Glock and insert fresh ones, I had trouble seeing what he was doing. His raw times were among the lowest, and he collected few penalty seconds for inaccuracy.

Gail Pepin shot at a more deliberate pace, her rounds erupting in a steady cadence. She rarely fired more than twice at each target, because her aim was flawless—every shot a kill. At the end of the four-hour match, she had the best score for accuracy in the entire seventy-five-person competition, men and women combined. This was no great surprise. Although she didn't get serious about shooting until middle age, Pepin was now the IDPA women's champion in Florida and Georgia. "You can run, but you'll just die tired," she likes to say. Fortunately, she has never had the need to shoot a real person.

/ / /

John Davis, who also competed on the Ayoob squad with his wife, Mary, loaned me an old Glock 17 for the morning. I had already trained for hours with Ayoob and Pepin, close friends of the Davises. "This is the best gun for a newbie," Ayoob said of the Glock.

During my preparation for the IDPA match, Ayoob had started me slowly, drawing back the slide and letting it snap forward to load the first round into the firing chamber. I stood in his backyard range about seven yards from a cardboard target with the vague shape of a human but no personal features. My left foot was in front of my right; my arms, straight and locked.

"Keep the wrist firm," Ayoob said. "Put your finger on the trigger now and squeeze smoothly, slowly. No rush." I lined up the single spike of the front sight within the U of the rear sight.

Bam! The Glock fired with a gentle recoil. I lined it up again.

Bam, bam! Even less of a jump now that I had adjusted my right hand to hold the gun as high as possible on the grip, as Ayoob suggested.

"Not bad," he said. I hit the target on all three initial shots. I emptied the ten-round magazine, and Pepin handed me a fresh one. I racked the slide myself, aimed, placed my finger on the trigger, and squeezed. I fired steadily with no difficulty. The Glock is easy to shoot and does not demand great strength. A .38-caliber Smith & Wesson, by contrast, requires a real tug—and rewards you with a firm kick.

When I was through practicing, I took my finger off the trigger, lowered the pistol, removed the magazine, checked the chamber to make sure it was empty, and pointed the weapon downrange. I pulled the trigger again, as instructed, to make *really* sure it was empty.

I had created a circle of holes about three or four inches in diameter, almost all of them in what would be the upper chest of the headless form. My heart was beating quickly. I wanted to go again.

///

Shooting in competition several days later—with the start buzzer going off, time being kept, and the need to move steadily while firing—was a challenge of a different order. I chose to emulate the tortoise rather than the hare and still missed some of the trickier targets altogether.

I did better as the relatively stationary besieged pizza delivery guy than as the passerby moving through the mall where a gunman has taken hostages (one of whom I inadvertently hit, hurting my score). Shooting while maintaining cover was difficult. The Glock's smooth trigger pull and comfortable er-gonomics did not compensate much when I felt off balance.

To my surprise, I did not come in last place. Out of the seventy-five competitors, I finished ahead of two people, one of them a female prison guard. Pepin noted that I was prob-ably the only participant with so little experience. "You did good," she said, "and you didn't shoot yourself, which is always a plus."

CHAPTER 16

Glock Goes to the White House

In October 1997, Washington broiled under an intense autumn sun. Whatever the temperature, the gun executives would have been sweating, for Paul Jannuzzo and Richard Feldman had led them into the enemy's lair. Sitting shoulder-to-shoulder with President Bill Clinton, his attorney general Janet Reno, and other administration notables were senior executives from Smith & Wesson and seven other major American handgun manufacturers. The public affairs network C-SPAN broadcast the ceremony live. At the Northern Virginia headquarters of the NRA, which routinely demonized Clinton as the "most anti-gun president ever," top association officials stared in disbelief at their television screens.

Before the formal Rose Garden announcement started, the industry representatives made nervous small talk in the Oval Office. "I want to thank you, Mr. President," Feldman joked, "for offering to find me a spot in the witness protection program." Clinton laughed, relishing his guests' unease.

The peculiar gathering stemmed from a White House push for federal legislation mandating that firearm manufacturers ship a trigger lock with every handgun. Democrats in Congress had introduced a bill and appeared to have the votes for passage. The NRA was preparing for scorched-earth resistance, even though gun-control proponents seemed to have an attractive argument: that "child safety devices" would deter accidents. Who opposed child safety?

Feldman, with Jannuzzo's support, suggested an alternative idea: Why couldn't gun manufacturers voluntarily provide safety devices? The mechanisms could be as simple as a padlock blocking the trigger or a cable threaded through the gun's barrel. Gun makers could take credit for helping protect the families of their customers. The cost would be modest—$5 to $10 per handgun—and most of that could be passed along to consumers.

A young Clinton aide, Rahm Emanuel, negotiated in secret with Feldman over a mutually beneficial pact: Glock and other gun manufacturers would swallow their pride and chance the NRA's wrath, accepting an invitation to the White House, where they would share credit with Clinton for a common-sense advance in gun safety. In exchange, the proposed legislation mandating locks would be dropped, sidestepping an ugly fight.

"Mr. President, we are all Americans," Feldman said when it was his turn to speak in the Rose Garden. With the red record light of the TV cameras illuminated, he continued: "By being here today, we demonstrate that there are issues on which we can all agree and work together."

"This administration and the gun industry from time to time have stood on different sides of various issues," Clinton told an audience dominated by police officers being honored for their heroism. "But today we stand together and stand with the law enforcement community to do what we all know is right for our children."

Afterward, Jannuzzo defended the deal in a gun industry trade magazine. It would "avoid a train wreck. . . . I'd much rather have something on a voluntary basis where we can make the decision as to what fits mechanically our own products, as opposed to somebody whose real goal is to outlaw firearms deciding how they should be locked up." Glock stood for pragmatism. "If you're only working one side of the aisle, you're bound to get screwed sooner or later, because people will take you for granted," Jannuzzo said. "When the Republicans wake up, they'll realize that what could have been a very contentious issue has been taken off their plate."

A day after the White House photo op, the top official of the NRA, Wayne LaPierre, sent a vitriolic open letter to Jannuzzo and the other executives who'd braved the Rose Garden. The rebuke offered an illustration of how the NRA did not always see eye-to-eye with gun companies like Glock. "Firearms safety—as it's being pressed by the Administration—is a phony," LaPierre wrote. "It is simply a stalking horse for gun bans." Without explaining how providing trigger locks would lead to banning guns, LaPierre added: "You are not selling firearms to Bill Clinton and Janet Reno. And he is not selling firearms safety to the public. He is selling a means to an end. Your end. . . . You have made a grievous error. It is now left to others—your customers, all peaceable gun owners—to keep it from being a fatal error."

Most gun executives maintained stoic public silence in the face of the NRA's condemnation. But Glock did not. In a letter he faxed back to LaPierre, Jannuzzo reproached the gun-rights activist for his extremism, including past comments in which LaPierre had compared federal agents to fascists. "Finally," Jannuzzo concluded, "if you ever again feel the need to speak to me in such a condescending manner, have the spine to do it in person, but be prepared to have your head slapped."

People in the gun industry did not communicate with Wayne LaPierre like that. With a pat on the back or a sharp word, LaPierre could make or break careers. His friendship translated into instant influence. Jannuzzo's temper temporarily outweighed his sense of caution.

The NRA wasn't the only constituency left out. Excluded from the Rose Garden festivities, gun-control activists fumed. "The big winners today are American gun manufacturers, not America's children," said Kristen Rand, the legislative director at Josh Sugarmann's Violence Policy Center.

Nonetheless, the trigger-lock truce received resoundingly positive coverage on television news shows and in the press. As it had in the past, Glock had managed to turn unlikely circumstances to its commercial advantage.

/ / /

The tension between the NRA and Glock actually began several years earlier. The enactment in 1994 of the assault weapons ban, including the magazine-capacity limit that ironically proved such a boon to Glock, became a central Republican campaign issue in the midterm elections that year. Newt Gingrich, the conservative Republican from Georgia, made the rollback of gun control a top priority. With characteristic hyperbole, the NRA paid for advertising campaigns calling the assault weapons ban and the Brady Act "the largest step ever toward the disarmament of American citizens." (Neither provision even hinted at disarming law-abiding gun owners.) Local NRA affiliates mobilized to oust powerful congressional Democrats, including those who traditionally promoted Second Amendment rights, such as House Speaker Tom Foley of

Washington and Judiciary Chairman Jack Brooks of Texas. In November 1994, Foley and Brooks were defeated, and Republicans took over the House of Representatives, elevating Gingrich to Speaker. "The NRA," said a chagrined Bill Clinton, "is the reason the Republicans control the House."

The 1994 election exacerbated paranoia on the fringes of the gun culture. Militia groups, some inspired by the standoffs at Ruby Ridge and Waco, expanded in parts of the Midwest, the Plains states, and the Southwest. Rumors materialized about deployment of unmarked black helicopters and foreign-speaking United Nations troops. Survivalists dug backyard bunkers, storing rifles and ammunition in sealed polyvinyl chloride drainpipes. Computer bulletin boards bristled with alerts about the "Zionist Occupation Government."

The NRA fueled the fear. Its chief lobbyist, Tanya Metaksa, met with members of the Michigan Militia during a trip to Lansing. Neal Knox, one of the organization's more vituperative figures, insinuated in a column in the December 1994 *Shotgun News* that the assassinations of John and Robert Kennedy and Martin Luther King, as well as various mass killings in the United States, reflected a plot to justify private gun confiscation.

In March 1995, the NRA bought full-page advertisements in the *Washington Post* and *USA Today* accusing the US Bureau of Alcohol, Tobacco and Firearms of terrorizing ordinary gun owners. A large photo showed helmeted black-clad federal agents armed with submachine guns breaking into a home. Clinton policies could lead the BATF "to intensify its reign of storm-trooper tactics," the ad stated. During the same period, the NRA's Wayne LaPierre distributed a fund-raising letter claiming that the Clinton administration's "semiauto ban gives jack-booted government thugs more power to take away our

Constitutional rights, break in our doors, seize our guns, destroy our property, and even injure or kill us." As if the point had not been made with sufficient emphasis, LaPierre added: "Not too long ago, it was unthinkable for federal agents wearing Nazi bucket helmets and black storm trooper uniforms to attack law-abiding citizens. Not today."

The NRA's rhetoric seemed even more out of bounds after April 19, 1995. On that day Timothy McVeigh, an antigovernment militant, used a truck bomb to blow up a federal office building in downtown Oklahoma City. The facility housed regional branches of the FBI and the BATF. McVeigh killed 168 people, including many children in the facility's day-care center; he injured more than 800. Former President George H. W. Bush used the occasion to resign his life membership in the NRA. Bush said the association's "broadside against federal agents deeply offends my own sense of decency and honor."

Paul Jannuzzo did not turn in his NRA card. But the NRA's ceaseless cultural warfare struck the Glock executive as counterproductive, especially for a company like his that built its reputation selling guns to police departments. He had a further motivation to steer Glock away from the fanaticism: McVeigh had been arrested in possession of a .45-caliber Glock pistol.

"I agree with most of what the NRA wants to do," Jannuzzo later told me. "I disagree with how they try to do it, and I see through their agenda of constantly provoking political fights for fund-raising purposes. The NRA sees paranoia as good, because paranoia makes gun owners get out the checkbook."

Jannuzzo argued in private that to appeal to a broader swath of the American public, the industry needed to distinguish itself from Wayne LaPierre and talk of jackbooted federal storm troopers. "I want to sell a Glock to a suburban mom concerned about keeping her kids safe," Jannuzzo explained. He had little in common with camouflaged militia members preparing to resist an imaginary United Nations invasion. Jannuzzo played tennis on weekends and rode horses with his children. He enjoyed expensive single-malt Scotch, imported chardonnay, and black market Cuban cigars. "I don't need to be associated with guys playing survivalist games in the woods."

Operating under the aegis of Feldman's trade group, the American Shooting Sports Council, Jannuzzo looked for subtle ways to lower the volume of the gun controversy. Months before the controversial Rose Garden ceremony, he and Feldman had visited Philadelphia mayor Ed Rendell, a prominent gun-control proponent. Rendell, a Democrat, had his staff researching a potential lawsuit that Philadelphia and other cities might file against the gun industry, modeled on the litigation state attorneys general had brought against major tobacco companies. In a meeting in Philadelphia's ornate City Hall, Rendell insisted that firearm manufacturers had to take more responsibility for urban gun violence. He accused Glock and other companies of "flooding the streets" with weapons, fully aware that a substantial portion of them would end up in the wrong hands.

Jannuzzo disagreed with the novel legal theory that Rendell espoused: that the gun companies created a "public nuisance," akin to the pollution emitted by a mismanaged industrial plant. Nuisance suits were rare and difficult to win. The courtroom weapon had never been aimed at an entire industry in anything approaching this fashion. Moreover, the criminal misuse of guns required the intervention of third parties—muggers, murderers, and rapists—whose illegal conduct broke what lawyers call the "chain of causation" between gun manufacturers and victims. Litigation seemed like a long shot.

Rendell, though an attorney by training, was not concerned

with legal niceties. He warned of dozens of suits filed by cities from coast to coast. A barrage of municipally funded legal actions could lead quickly to heavy legal defense expenses. Pretrial discovery could reveal embarrassing corporate documents. Glock and other gun companies historically had fended off product-defect suits filed by injured individuals. But a coordinated assault by government bodies seeking to recover the aggregate cost of police and hospital services related to gun violence presented a far more daunting threat. In light of the tobacco lawsuits, which were on their way to a multibillion-dollar settlement, Jannuzzo concluded that Rendell and the cities had to be taken seriously.

The Glock lawyer also thought that there were modest regulatory and safety steps, such as the concession on trigger locks, that his employer could offer as a way out of prospective suits. Jannuzzo indicated that he would be willing to discuss helping law enforcement agencies take a closer look at customers seeking to buy multiple handguns. Such buyers sometimes turned out to be illicit gun traffickers. If agreeing to restrictions that did not interfere with sales to honest consumers would forestall pricey lawsuits and bad publicity, Glock was open to talking. Rendell expressed interest, and they agreed to stay in touch.

The conciliatory tone in Philadelphia did not last. Other liberal big-city mayors saw the political appeal of taking the gun industry to court. Once Rendell floated the idea, it could not be contained. Gun-control activists hoping to cripple firearm production whispered to any politician who would listen that the tobacco-litigation strategy could be applied to guns.

Backed by a group of wealthy plaintiffs' lawyers who had helped push tobacco suits, Mayor Marc Morial of New Orleans jumped to the front of the line. His city filed suit in October 1998 against Glock and every other major handgun maker.

"Today is a day of atonement," Morial said at a press conference. "This suit is about holding that very successful industry accountable." Two weeks later, Chicago mayor Richard Daley fired off the second such suit, demanding $433 million from the industry to compensate his city for public safety and medical expenditures over the prior five years.

Rendell was incensed that rivals had stolen his thunder, but there was nothing he could do about it. Boston, Los Angeles, Miami, New York, and San Francisco all prepared to join the legal offensive. Others soon followed.

///

Jannuzzo, combative and not averse to publicity, responded to the challenge. In 1998 and 1999, he emerged in the national news media as the industry's most forceful and articulate front man. At the same time, he continued to talk to Rendell and other mayors behind the scenes, probing, negotiating, and gathering intelligence. Jannuzzo once again displayed his knack for the dismissive sound bite. "They don't have a leg to stand on, as far as the law is concerned," he told the *New York Times*. "Cigarettes were supposed to be enjoyable, relaxing, and they turned out to be lethal. But guns are designed to be lethal. That's why people buy them." He waved off the notion that firearms were defective because they lacked adequate safety mechanisms, a theory that New Orleans and some other cities argued in conjunction with the public nuisance allegation. "What we have," he said, "is a bunch of frustrated big-city executives who have lost control of the crime problem, and they are looking to blame someone else."

Playing the family values card, Jannuzzo argued that the best way to prevent juvenile accidents with firearms was to instruct children how to use guns properly. "My wife is having our fifth child in January," he wrote in a letter to the editor of the New Orleans *Times-Picayune.* "Three of the other four have been taught firearms safety based on the [NRA's] Eddie Eagle program. . . . They would no more pick up a firearm without adult supervision than they would put their hand in a moving chainsaw or step in front of a moving car."

On ABC's *World News Tonight,* he answered Morial's contention that the industry should be held liable for failing to invent a "smart" gun, meaning one that integrated a microchip or a fingerprint reader that would make it impossible for anyone except the rightful owner to pull the trigger. Such gadgetry may sound appealing, and it had been researched. But Jannuzzo noted, correctly, that engineers within and outside the industry had not been able to make "personalized" guns work reliably. Tiny electronic circuitry tended to malfunction when placed in proximity to gunfire. "I don't know what they can mandate that we can put on guns," Jannuzzo told ABC. "The greatest fallacy with Mayor Morial's suit is that [electronic smart-gun technology] simply doesn't exist."

In the most memorable public airing of the municipal litigation, Jannuzzo faced off against Morial on NBC's *Today* show. The confrontation in late January 1999 seemed stacked in favor of the politician from New Orleans. He spoke of innocent young victims of gun violence and a profitable industry's indifference. New Orleans, he said, was taking the bad guys to court in the name of justice.

Jannuzzo, cast as the corporate heavy, had come prepared. He turned toward Morial and said: "You have to put the suit in an incredible context. The City of New Orleans is the biggest distributor of used guns in the state of Louisiana."

Morial looked stricken. He recognized where Jannuzzo was

headed. In an attempt to save money, New Orleans had quietly done business with Glock in a way that had put thousands
of handguns on the street. Ten months before suing firearm
manufacturers for gross negligence, New Orleans had agreed
to give Glock 7,200 old service pistols and confiscated weapons in exchange for 1,700 new Austrian .40-caliber handguns.
This was one of dozens of such trades Glock had made with
police departments around the country.

"I only approved that deal on the condition that none of the
guns were sold in Louisiana," Morial said. New Orleans, in
other words, had done exactly what it accused the industry of
doing: sought financial benefit from dumping guns indiscrimi-
nately on the street. On top of that, Morial had tried to foist
the weapons on other communities, as if that would absolve
him of any connection to subsequent misuse of the older guns.

Jannuzzo succeeded in upending the televised morality play,
exposing his foe's blatant double standard. The details that
came to light after the *Today* episode made New Orleans look
even worse. The guns the city traded went to a wholesaler in Indiana to be resold. Included were confiscated TEC-9s and AK-
47s prohibited two years earlier by the federal assault weapons
ban. Rafael Goyeneche, president of the Metropolitan Crime
Commission of New Orleans, a private watchdog group, was
livid: "To learn that the city has exported 7,000 guns seized
from street criminals to other parts of the country is really
mind boggling and the height of hypocrisy."

Morial's attempt to keep the used guns out of his backyard
proved feckless. Two months after the exchange, a New Orleans pawnshop ran a newspaper advertisement for Beretta
nine-millimeter pistols that were part of the Glock deal: "Own
a piece of New Orleans history," the ad said. "Guns formerly

belonged to members of the police department. All are stamped NOPD and come equipped with two 15-round 'pre-ban' clips."

"The people of the city were under the impression they were doing away with these guns," said Linda McDonald, head of the New Orleans chapter of the nonprofit Parents of Murdered Children. "There's no assurance these guns will not come back here, and even if they don't, they will be used to kill people in other areas."

Nationally, the BATF had already noticed thousands of former police weapons among crime-scene guns that it traced. In 1998 alone, the federal agency identified at least 1,100 former police guns among the 193,000 traces it conducted. In one case in August 1999, neo-Nazi Buford Furrow used a compact Glock 26 pistol in a shooting rampage at a Los Angeles Jewish community center. He injured five people at the center and then killed a mailman of Filipino descent. The Glock 26 had been exchanged for a new, larger Glock by the police department of Cosmopolis, Washington. The compact pistol changed hands a couple of times and turned up at a retail gun show before Buford acquired it.

By aggressively fostering gun exchanges, Glock, in effect, had set a trap for municipalities, implicating them in the mass redistribution of firearms and muddying the waters over responsibility for the profusion of guns on urban streets. The gun company had not planned its marketing strategy as a legal defense, but that is how it worked out. And it was not just New Orleans and tiny Cosmopolis that were tarnished. Jannuzzo's Today ambush led to media investigations and official confessions in Boston, Detroit, Oakland, and other large cities suing the gun industry. As a practical matter, the municipal litigation was deeply compromised before it even got off the ground.

///

Beyond the cloud of doubt created by municipal gun exchanges, the city and county lawsuits quickly ran into technical legal hurdles. By early 2000, thirty local governments had jumped on the litigation bandwagon. But in some jurisdictions, judges rejected what they saw as an inappropriate effort to shift the gun-control debate from the legislative arena to the judicial. Dismissing a suit filed by the city of Cincinnati, an Ohio judge in October 1999 called the litigation "an improper attempt to have this court substitute its judgment for that of the legislature, something this court is neither inclined nor empowered to do. Only the legislature has the power to engage in the type of regulation which is being sought by the city here." In Louisiana and other states, lawmakers passed statutes blocking the courts from entertaining municipal suits against the gun industry: in essence, shielding gun makers from this type of legal threat.

As their suits hit obstacles, lawyers for some cities privately communicated to Jannuzzo and other industry executives that they would be willing to drop the litigation, with no damages paid, if gun makers would agree to a list of concessions. These ranged from limiting customers to buying a maximum of one gun per month—a deterrent to illegal trafficking—to spending a small portion of revenue to develop high-tech smart guns.

In tactical terms, the settlement overtures communicated weakness and uncertainty on the part of the municipalities. The NRA sensed this lack of resolve and pressured gun companies not to give ground. The moderation exemplified by the industry's visit to the Rose Garden in 1997 eroded. Feldman, the advocate of compromise, lost the support of major companies other than Glock. With the NRA's encouragement, the industry summarily fired him in early 1999 from his job as executive director of the ASSC. Soon thereafter, his conciliatory trade group was abolished. Jannuzzo lacked the muscle to protect his friend; he tried to mitigate the dismissal by quietly hiring Feldman to do consulting work for Glock. Most other gun makers migrated back to the NRA fold, unwilling to risk the ire of the lobbying group, in no small part because of its ability to influence consumer attitudes toward their products.

The Clinton administration tried to salvage the stalling anti-gun litigation by threatening in December 1999 to organize a class-action suit to be brought on behalf of more than three thousand federally subsidized public housing authorities across the country. Andrew Cuomo, Clinton's secretary of housing and urban development, said he would lead this audacious litigation unless gun makers came to the negotiating table. Cuomo tried to force the manufacturers to talk by simultaneously forming a coalition of local, state, and federal law enforcement agencies that vowed to buy guns only from companies that signed a code of conduct restricting manufacturing and marketing practices.

Jannuzzo reacted nimbly to the administration's intimidation. He jabbed and feinted, coordinating courtroom efforts to get the municipal suits dismissed while quietly talking to emissaries from the cities and Washington. Glock and Smith & Wesson, more than other manufacturers, depended on the patronage of government customers buying their handguns. Both Glock and S&W also had foreign owners hesitant to antagonize the White House. Tomkins, the British conglomerate that had acquired Smith & Wesson in 1987, was particularly keen to resolve the liability issues because it wanted to sell the struggling Massachusetts-based company. Jannuzzo suspected that S&W's American CEO, Ed Shultz, might try to cut a deal with the Clinton administration in exchange for government contracts. Keeping an eye on Shultz, Jannuzzo attended a number of secret settlement talks with administration lawyers in Washington, including sessions held in an unoccupied wing of the United States Mint.

As a legal-affairs reporter at the *Wall Street Journal*, I tried to decipher the increasingly puzzling gun litigation and backroom negotiation. I spoke frequently with Jannuzzo, Shultz, and their government contacts as they maneuvered for advantage. For public consumption, Jannuzzo sounded patient and open to a deal. "There are undoubtedly . . . commonsense solutions that take a crime-fighting approach without affecting law-abiding citizens," he told me at the time. "We are still weighing the idea of bleeding to death with legal bills versus the cost of complying with government demands," he said on CNN. Privately, the Glock lawyer worried about offending the NRA and being seen as appeasing Clinton, Cuomo, and Democratic big-city mayors.

The covert negotiations culminated on March 17, 2000, when Smith & Wesson's Shultz met with Cuomo in a Hartford, Connecticut, hotel room to sign a twenty-five-page agreement. Smith & Wesson would obtain immunity from government suits at all levels, in exchange for agreeing to a long list of restrictions, well beyond what the law mandated. The company committed to designing all of its guns so that small children could not operate them—for example, increasing trigger-pull resistance to at least ten pounds. Smith & Wesson also promised to stop making guns that could accommodate magazines with more than ten rounds. And S&W was to allocate 2 percent of its annual revenue to R&D on smart-gun technology. In a move viewed as even more far-reaching, the gun maker said it would impose a series of requirements on its distributors and retailers. These included limits on customers seeking to buy more than one gun at a time and new obligations for keeping computerized records and locking up inventory every night to prevent theft. For the first time in history, a gun manufacturer—in fact, the largest maker of handguns—agreed to serve as a quasi-regulator of the entire supply chain, from factory to distributor to retail store.

Cuomo told Shultz that he was confident he could persuade Jannuzzo to sign the pact on behalf of Glock—if for no other reason than that the Austrian company would fear Smith & Wesson becoming the favorite with American government. "We thought that there would be two names on that agreement—Ed's and Paul's," Cuomo said in a later interview.

But Cuomo miscalculated. While the Clinton administration trumpeted its breakthrough with Smith & Wesson, the media provided saturation coverage, and gun-control groups celebrated, Glock headed in the other direction. Jannuzzo denounced the agreement, giving the impression that he had never seriously considered signing. At his direction, Glock employees did a quick straw poll of all customers who called the company for any reason in the days after the S&W settlement was announced. The reaction was overwhelmingly negative. Gun owners thought Smith & Wesson had sold out to political forces hostile to firearms and the Second Amendment.

The NRA, meanwhile, signaled to its four million members that they should boycott the traitor. "Smith & Wesson, a British-owned company, recently became the first to run up the white flag of surrender and run behind the Clinton-Gore lines," the NRA declared in one of a salvo of Internet alerts and mass faxes. Gun enthusiasts got the point, and many obeyed, swearing off Smith & Wesson.

Glock Talk and other websites buzzed with condemnation

of Smith & Wesson. L. Neil Smith, a science-fiction author popular in gun-owner circles, wrote a widely distributed e-mail that repeated thirteen times "Smith & Wesson must die." The switchboard at S&W headquarters in Springfield nearly melted down. CEO Ed Shultz, a former army sergeant and firearm-rights advocate, received death threats. Gun shops in many states canceled purchase orders and sent S&W inventory back to the factory. The company announced a monthlong employee furlough in July 2000, and sales dropped 50 percent for the year. Some in the industry wondered whether Smith & Wesson would survive.

Watching his strategy backfire, Cuomo personally called Glock, Inc., headquarters in Smyrna. "What percentage of Glock's business is derived from law enforcement?" the cabinet secretary asked Jannuzzo.

"About 30 percent," Jannuzzo answered.

"You know, Paul," Cuomo continued, "I have a lot of push with the big-city mayors. Your business is likely to suffer unless Glock agrees to the terms of the March 17 agreement."

"The decision has already been made," Jannuzzo said.

Cuomo did not give up. He telephoned again to let Jannuzzo know that he was going to arrange for the American ambassador in Vienna to speak directly with Gaston Glock.

"Fine," said Jannuzzo. "I didn't know the ambassador corps answers to HUD, but I guess they do in this administration."

Kathryn Walt Hall, the US emissary to Austria, did take a message to Gaston Glock, inviting the industrialist to meet with Secretary Cuomo. Glock was polite but noncommittal, saying perhaps they could arrange something the next time he was in the United States. That meeting never happened.

Further undercutting Cuomo's credibility, police chiefs across the United States did not abandon their Glocks and buy

Smith & Wessons. And as S&W sales to civilians plummeted, Glock gained market share. "This will probably be our best year in history," Jannuzzo told the *Hartford Courant* in June. "Guns sales go up, dramatically, as soon as gun owners feel threatened by gun control." While this was true for Glock, it was decidedly not true for Smith & Wesson.

A particularly painful rebuke to the Clinton administration came from the Inspector General's Office of Cuomo's own department. The IG at Housing and Urban Development was scheduled to buy seventy new pistols for its investigators in mid-2000. Rather than switch the purchase to Smith & Wesson, the HUD IG went ahead with a preexisting deal to buy the guns from Glock. In the future, Michael Zerega, a spokesman for the IG, told the *Wall Street Journal*, "We will probably continue to purchase Glocks." The Austrian pistol was simply the better gun for the money.

By flirting with a settlement and then pulling back at the last moment, Glock had isolated S&W and further entrenched itself as the dominant pistol maker in America. And it was largely Jannuzzo's doing. The attorney had played a risky game of firearm poker and won.

Lost in the process was a unique opportunity for an industry, or at least some industry leaders, to agree to police their conduct more vigorously. Although not a panacea for gun violence, the Smith & Wesson settlement contained a number of constructive elements. As the company retreated in the face of NRA and consumer attacks, the concessions it had made became irrelevant. In September 2000, Ed Shultz resigned as CEO. Tomkins soon thereafter sold Smith & Wesson to a group of American investors, who formally renounced the pact with the Clinton administration.

"The firearms industry is a family," said S&W's new

president, Robert Scott. "We need to be part of that family." The NRA, in turn, heaped honors on Scott, letting it be known that Smith & Wesson was absolved of its sins. Gun shops began selling the company's products again. The yearlong boycott ended.

After the 2000 presidential election finally ended in victory for George W. Bush, Andrew Cuomo left Washington to prepare to run for office in his home state of New York. The new resident of the White House made it clear that the litigation war against the gun industry was over. As governor of Texas, Bush had signed a state statute barring municipal lawsuits against gun companies. In his second term in the White House, he signed a similar law passed by Congress. The federal measure marked the official end of the city suits. Those that had not already been dismissed by judges were extinguished by the federal statue. Apart from keeping a lot of lawyers busy, the campaign to restrict gun manufacturing and marketing via the courts had accomplished nothing.

CHAPTER 17

An Assassin's Attack

Gaston Glock arrived in Luxembourg in July 1999 for an urgent talk with the shell company artist Charles Ewert. In ordering the meeting, Glock had told Ewert he wanted to discuss company finances—matters best addressed in person. Glock did not sound pleased.

For fifteen years, Ewert had served as a director of Glock GmbH and a corporate trustee. Ewert sometimes suggested to others—out of Glock's presence—that he was the Austrian's partner in the firearm business. Glock saw Ewert as more of an adviser and international representative. Hearing the stern tone of Glock's voice, the Luxembourger had to worry about what was on the company owner's mind.

Ewert picked up his guest personally at the airport. Before proceeding to their meeting, he suggested that Glock take a look at a new sports car he had just acquired. It was parked in a garage on the Boulevard Prince Henri. Glock agreed.

At the car park, Ewert guided Glock to the third underground level, where they found themselves alone. Ewert pointed out the snazzy roadster, and Glock approached on foot to take a closer look.

Suddenly, a tall man stepped out of the shadows, lunging at Glock. The Austrian raised his arms defensively. The attacker, his face obscured by a stocking mask, swung a large rubber mallet of the sort normally used to install bathroom tile. With a vicious overhand motion, he struck Glock on the top and side of the head.

Rather than intervene to help Glock, Ewert turned and ran for the stairwell. "I am a coward," he would explain later.

Glock, meanwhile, was fighting for his life. The gun maker, who usually carried a pistol, lacked one on this day. With no other option, Glock fought with his hands. He swung his large fist into his attacker's eye and mouth. Though seventy, the industrialist put up a stout defense. His frequent swims in the frigid lake near his villa in Velden had helped him maintain a younger man's stamina. Glock drew blood and knocked out several of his attacker's teeth. Despite the hammer blows to his skull, he gained the advantage.

Apparently summoned by Ewert, the police soon arrived. They found a bizarre scene, according to John Paul Frising, Luxembourg's deputy attorney general: The bloodied aggressor lay collapsed on top of Glock, "with his arms outstretched like Jesus." The bleeding victim was pinned to the ground but not mortally wounded. Glock's attacker was unconscious.

The mallet-wielding assassin was identified as Jacques Pecheur, a sixty-seven-year-old former professional wrestler and member of the French Foreign Legion, whose nickname was Spartacus. With credentials like his, and with the benefit of surprise, one might have expected a more effective performance from Pecheur. The police assumed that the attacker had not been prepared for the fight Glock put up.

Whatever the reasons for Pecheur's failure, the real question was "For whom was he acting?" noted the local newspaper *Luxemburger Land*, and "for what reason?"

/ / /

Glock had suffered a total of seven hammer blows to the head, along with other cuts and abrasions, and he lost a liter of blood. At the hospital, though, he was strikingly composed. He posed for a police photographer with a placid expression on his face. Before doctors finished patching him up, he summoned his personal bankers from UBS and Banque Ferrier Lullin. Those two institutions held $70 million of his cash in accounts to which Ewert had access. Within three hours of the attack, Glock had moved $40 million to a secret Swiss account.

Ewert was busy too. He blocked the other $30 million from being transferred, Glock would later learn. Clearly, all was not well between the two men.

Ewert had established Glock affiliates in Switzerland, France, Hong Kong, and Uruguay, among other locations. Gaston Glock had approved of the proliferating corporate structure and told his family and Austrian executives that if anything ever happened to him, they should rely on Ewert in deciding what to do with the company. "I was considered the eldest son," Ewert bragged.

Earlier that spring, Glock had received a telephone call from a former employee of his company's Geneva office. The former employee said Ewert had been stealing from Glock. The Luxembourg financial adviser had siphoned funds from the company to buy a house in Switzerland, according to the informant.

Gaston Glock didn't believe the accusation at first. He was concerned enough, though, to ask Ewert to meet in Luxembourg, leading to the fateful attack in the underground parking lot.

Police investigators found Ewert's business card in Pecheur's car, a strange mistake for a putative hit man to commit. The investigators discovered that the two had become acquainted at a gun range in Paris in 1998. The detectives concluded that Ewert, realizing Glock had discovered his embezzlement in Switzerland, had hired Pecheur to kill the old man. The use of the rubber hammer, as opposed to a gun or a knife, suggested that Ewert and Pecheur planned to make the killing look like an innocent accident: that Glock had fallen and hit his head.

That the plotters thought repeated mallet blows would be mistaken for a tumble down a stairwell was one of several odd aspects of the plot. Another was Ewert's presence at the scene of the attack. Someone who goes to the trouble of hiring a retired French Foreign Legionnaire to kill a prominent businessman would ostensibly want to fabricate an alibi. Any experienced police detective will tell you that many criminals are surprisingly dumb, but this had to be one of the least competent high-profile contract murders ever attempted.

After he recovered, Gaston Glock told the authorities that he had discovered that Ewert had set up numerous additional offshore companies without his permission. Glock's lawyers alleged that Ewert had stolen not just money to buy a Swiss chalet, but some $100 million of Glock funds. The embezzled cash had been channeled into the secret shell companies. The Glock lawyers claimed that Ewert had attempted to take control of Unipatent, the main Glock holding company in Luxembourg, and its chief asset: a 50 percent stake in Glock, Inc., the American operating subsidiary that generated the vast majority of Glock revenue. In due course, the Luxembourg prosecutor, Frising, charged Ewert and Pecheur with attempted murder.

Ewert's attorneys claimed he had nothing to do with the

attack. Ewert insisted he was framed and that he did not know Pecheur. But he could not explain how his business card ended up in the attacker's car. The defense team insisted on behalf of their client that Glock had approved of all of Ewert's corporate activities, including Ewert's takeover of Unipatent. There had been no secrets between the two men, Ewert maintained. Glock had retained Ewert specifically to set up the network of paper corporate entities around the world as a tax dodge. In return, Ewert was to receive certain ownership interests in the Glock affiliates he created.

In an interview years later, Ewert contended: "Glock says I have less than five percent of Unipatent? Glock is a nut!" As for the murder attempt, he blamed unnamed Glock associates who he alleged wanted to gain control of the gun-manufacturing empire. His presence in the underground parking garage was part of a diabolical conspiracy, he said: "They needed me out of the way so they could grab everything."

Pecheur, faced with the sticky problem of having been arrested at the scene of the attack, had no coherent explanation of his actions beyond a vague contention that it was he who was the victim of an unexplained assault by Glock. Unlike Ewert, Pecheur seemed resigned to a prison term.

In March 2003, Ewert and Pecheur were found guilty after a three-week nonjury trial in Luxembourg. Ewert was sentenced to twenty years, the maximum penalty for attempted murder. Pecheur received seventeen years as the would-be hit man. In the courtroom, Ewert didn't react to the verdict, sitting motionless. Pecheur sighed but said nothing.

"It is a good day," Glock said afterward. He added ambiguously, "It is one step in a war." In 2003, in a rare interview, with *Forbes,* he explained: "The attack is the best thing that happened to me. Otherwise I would have gone on trusting Ewert."

Pecheur served seven years of his seventeen-year sentence and was released on good behavior. Ewert remains behind bars at a maximum-security prison in rural Luxembourg, continuing to insist on his innocence.

/ / /

The investigation and prosecution of Charles Ewert resulted in more than his conviction. It also brought to light a trove of documents describing the intricate financial structure of the Glock companies. This information received little attention outside of certain legal circles in Luxembourg—until two colleagues and I reviewed it while researching an article about internal intrigue at Glock, which was published in *BusinessWeek* in September 2009.

Gaston Glock's attorneys aided the Luxembourg investigation with the explicit goal of demonstrating that Ewert had created an international daisy chain of fraudulent Glock affiliates. The Glock legal team argued that Gaston Glock retained ownership of the interrelated companies—or at least those that had any real economic value. While trying to establish that Ewert had made false claims to owning parts of the gun-making kingdom, the Glock attorneys were not shy about conceding that one original purpose of establishing a complicated corporate structure was to shelter portions of the profits from taxation in the United States and Austria.

For example, the Glock lawyers submitted documents to the court in Luxembourg showing that in 1987, Ewert, acting on Glock's behalf, transferred ownership of the valuable 50 percent stake in the American unit of Glock to Unipatent, the

Luxembourg holding company. "The purpose of this holding company was to appear externally as a partner of Glock and hold approximately 50 percent of the shares of its subsidiaries," according to an April 3, 2000, document entitled "Establishment of the Glock Group," which the Glock attorneys filed with the court. In other words, Ewert helped Gaston Glock create an essentially fictional co-owner, making it more difficult to trace company earnings generated in the United States.

Other shells established in Ireland, Liberia, and Curaçao were fabricated to issue bills for various "services" to Glock headquarters in Austria and to operating units in Latin America and Hong Kong, the documents show. But these service firms "had no economic substance and were motivated by tax reasons," according to a confidential ninety-two-page analysis of the Glock companies conducted by Pricewaterhouse-Coopers. The Luxembourg court had appointed a provisional administrator to sort out who owned Unipatent, and that administrator hired the giant auditing firm to do the arduous forensic accounting. Pricewaterhouse found that the Glock service companies' role appeared to be the shielding of company profits from potential taxation in Austria, Latin America, and Hong Kong. The Latin American and Asian operating units, in turn, appeared to be used to extract profits from the US subsidiary, Pricewaterhouse alleged.

The point of the paper shuffle, as noted, was to reduce Glock's tax liabilities. This was accomplished by having pistols manufactured in Austria sold first to the Latin American and Hong Kong units and then resold for higher prices to Glock, Inc., in Smyrna. By inflating costs to the American subsidiary, this practice decreased the profits the subsidiary was required to report to the US Internal Revenue Service.

The court in Luxembourg did not show any interest in

enforcing the tax laws of other countries—hardly surprising, given that Luxembourg's economy rests on its reputation as a tax haven. The court was trying to sort out whether Ewert had a legitimate claim to Unipatent and half of Glock's lucrative US unit. Once the Luxembourg judiciary concluded that, on the contrary, Ewert was an embezzler and failed murderer, it left the propriety of Glock's tax-minimization strategies to others.

/ / /

As part of his effort to clarify ownership of his companies, Glock hired a team of American investigators based in Atlanta. The lead private eye, James R. Harper III, had served as a federal prosecutor and was active politically in Republican circles in Georgia. Harper retained a quartet of former cops and US government agents to help with his work for Glock. Their locked workspace on the Glock grounds in Smyrna was off-limits to regular company employees. Before long, the Harper group was traveling around the world, looking for evidence of Ewert's wrongdoing. Referring to themselves as the "A-Team," the secretive private detectives reported only to Paul Jannuzzo and, sometimes, directly to Gaston Glock.

Jannuzzo, who had risen to chief operating officer of Glock, Inc., and was the company's most senior executive in the United States, seemed a little baffled by the mysterious Harper group. "A lot of the time," he told me, "no one knew what these guys, the so-called A-Team, were even up to."

Harper, a captain in the Marine reserves with a bulldog head and demeanor to match, traced the peripatetic Ewert to far-flung locations and connected him to unsavory characters. Harper amassed enormous files of corporate documents, witness interview transcripts, and PowerPoint flowcharts. The A-Team discovered that Unipatent was once owned by Hakki Yaman Namli, a controversial Turkish financier with a reputation for doing business in North Cyprus, a well-known center for money laundering and other financial fraud. The Glock-affiliated Panamanian company Reofin also had a tie to Namli, Harper determined. In 1995, Reofin and Namli co-founded Unibank Offshore, a bank in North Cyprus.

Harper warned Glock and Jannuzzo that by associating Glock with Unipatent, Reofin, and Unibank Offshore, Ewert had created a seeming link between the Glock companies and Namli. In a memo dated November 1, 2000, Harper wrote that Gaston Glock was "in danger of being flagged as an international money launderer because by all appearances . . . Ewert was working at [Gaston] Glock's direction up until the time of the assault" on Glock. "Even a rumor in the press about the Glock connection to Cypriot money laundering," Harper added, "could have significant if not devastating effects on Glock sales, especially to law enforcement." The private investigator concluded: "Mr. Glock doesn't understand the breadth of the problems or the potential disaster that could befall him."

/ / /

Nonetheless, Gaston Glock seemed unfazed. A mere five months after fending off the retired French Foreign Legionnaire, he issued his "Annual Message from the President" in a glossy promotional magazine called *Glock Autopistols*, which the company gave away at trade shows and in gun shops. "Another year has come and gone," Glock observed, "and I am proud to say that our successes have far outweighed our shortcomings, and the company is continuing to grow and aggressively take on all challenges with which it is faced." The January 2000 message continued in a triumphal vein, without reference to the bloody attack in Luxembourg. The company carried on outwardly as if all were normal.

In commercial terms, Glock's assessment was accurate. The pistols kept selling. The FBI concluded its long search for a replacement for the Smith & Wesson revolver, bypassing American manufacturers to choose the .40-caliber Glock. The DEA piggybacked on the FBI's procurement contract. Thousands of agents for the agencies—like their brethren in Customs, the Marshals Service, the Border Patrol, and state and local police forces—were issued Austrian pistols as duty weapons. Glock, Inc.'s, annual revenue hit $100 million in the late 1990s, according to former executives.

Success in the marketplace did not, however, cause Gaston Glock to forget or forgive betrayal. His clash with Ewert spawned suspicion that Panama Charly was not the only subordinate attempting to rob the gun maker. Glock was determined to identify and punish the others, as well.

CHAPTER 18

"Monopoly Money"

Gun manufacturers thrive on turmoil. For Glock, the American military response to 9/11 proved a bonanza. At the Pentagon, Beretta retained the main contract to provide handguns to the army, but elite US military units with the authority to choose their own small arms gravitated to the Glock.

Jim Smith, a veteran of Delta Force, the army's premier special-operations unit, explained that highly trained commandos considered the Austrian-made gun more dependable. Most commandos carry handguns as well as rifles; conventional infantry fighters usually are issued only rifles. Smith spoke of the Glock with clipped reverence. "We put it in the sand, in water, extreme heat, fired thousands of rounds," he said. "Pull the trigger, it fires. Reliable."

I met Smith at a small arms trade show in Germany. After retiring from Delta Force, he started a consulting business in Texas where he tutored corporate executives, police SWAT officers, and even some Army Rangers. The Rangers were frustrated that their unit, though elite, was still issued Berettas, he said. They wanted what the secretive Delta Force carried.

After the invasions of Afghanistan and Iraq, US authorities outfitting local security forces turned primarily to the Glock. The American government bought more than 200,000 of the

Austrian pistols for distribution to Afghan and Iraqi police, national guardsmen, and soldiers. Spread over several years, those sales came on top of the company's routine cash flow from police and commercial business.

The rush to award contracts and ship pistols caught American manufacturers unprepared. When they learned that Glock had cornered the post-9/11 market in the Middle East, some objected angrily. "As a US taxpayer and a US manufacturer, I am greatly offended that my tax dollars are being used to buy foreign weapons for the Iraqis when there were US companies that could have supplied that product," Robert Scott, Smith & Wesson's president, protested. Three members of Congress announced investigations of Glock's procurement coup. The indignation drew media attention but had no substantive effect.

On the ground in Iraq, US military officers praised the Glock. "My personal opinion is that the Iraqi people respect power, and power is an AK-47 or a Glock nine-millimeter gun," Captain Kevin Hanrahan of the Eighty-ninth Military Police Brigade told the *Los Angeles Times.* Hanrahan oversaw Baghdad police stations west of the Tigris River. Some Iraqi officers had abandoned their posts, he added, because they "were outgunned and outmanned" by insurgents. He sounded like an American police chief in the late 1980s.

Whether or not they instilled confidence in the Iraqi authorities, US-supplied Glocks definitely became hot items on the Baghdad black market. "The Americans gave us Glocks without registering the serial numbers and without receipts," a former policeman named Yasser told Agence France-Presse. When Yasser quit his unit, he sold the Glock he had been given to "a friend" for $800. The American military eventually lost track of some 190,000 small arms in Iraq, including 80,000 pistols—mostly Glocks, according to US congressional investigators. Insurgents appreciated a reliable weapon as much as anyone else, and the Glock became standard among Sunni militants who attacked Americans

The story was much the same in Afghanistan. Large numbers of Glocks furnished to local army units simply vanished. Whoever ended up with its pistols, Glock prospered from the Bush administration's global war on terror, just as it had from the earlier domestic war on drugs.

/ / /

But Glock's impressive sales figures were accompanied by intensifying disarray within its corporate ranks. It was almost as if selling pistols no longer required the close attention of the company's top executives. The Glock sold itself.

In February 2003, Paul Jannuzzo once again collided with the NRA, this time as a result of an appearance on *60 Minutes.* The CBS newsmagazine broadcast a segment on "ballistic fingerprinting," a digital technology that allows investigators to link bullet casings from shootings to suspected crime guns. NRA leader Wayne LaPierre told *60 Minutes* that the method, which matches the unique marks guns make on spent casings, was unreliable and would facilitate confiscation of weapons from law-abiding owners.

Less hasty to dismiss ballistic fingerprinting, Jannuzzo said in a separate interview that Glock had a pilot program under way with the government. "It has been expensive," he said. "It slows production. To make certain that we're getting the right cases to the right serial number, at this point, we now go through test-firing the guns twice." Still, Glock would consider contributing information to a national database to aid police, if one were put together. "The people who right now are saying there is no use for it," Jannuzzo said, "that it's an intrusion upon our freedom, have arbitrarily drawn a line too soon."

Characteristically, Jannuzzo positioned Glock as an independent-minded friend of law enforcement—but without making any concrete concessions to new regulation. His ambiguity did not mollify activist gun owners. Glock was inundated with demands for Jannuzzo's head. Perceived apostasy against NRA gospel required excommunication. And sure enough, within the space of a few weeks, Jannuzzo announced that, after twelve years at Glock, Inc., he would step down as chief operating officer, general counsel, and, for all practical purposes, the US gun industry's best-known executive.

Second Amendment websites lit up in celebration. "Glock Exec Resigns Because of Us!!!" proclaimed one contributor to a gun discussion group on TheHighRoad.org. "We got pissed, we made calls and wrote letters, the guy resigned," agreed a colleague. "A message was sent here. And someone heard it loud and clear. Sell us out, and sell your last handgun."

In fact, Jannuzzo's departure involved even more drama than the online rabble-rousers assumed. Since the July 1999 attack on Gaston Glock, executives throughout the company had been looking over their shoulder—and with good reason. Private eyes hired by Glock combed company documents, scanned e-mail, and even conducted physical surveillance, ferreting out evidence of financial misbehavior.

As if this did not create sufficient tension, romantic jealousy heightened apprehension in the American subsidiary. Jannuzzo had split with his second wife and become involved with Monika Bereczky, Glock's human resources manager. Bereczky, the former hotel concierge, had remained an object of the owner's affection. Unaware of Jannuzzo's relationship with her, or, more likely, indifferent to it, Glock continued to flirt with the much younger Bereczky. He routinely put his arm around her waist in public, she said, or suggestively grabbed her thigh while she was chauffeuring him to appointments. Jannuzzo, who had a temper to start with, took offense when his employer treated Bereczky as a plaything and, in Jannuzzo's view, implicitly encouraged others to gossip about her sex life. On one occasion, when an Austrian-based Glock executive referred to Bereczky as a loose woman in Jannuzzo's presence, the combustible American jammed a lit cigar into the visitor's forehead. A bigger blowup seemed inevitable.

In the wake of the *60 Minutes* episode, and with personal antagonism mounting, the explosion finally came. One morning, Jannuzzo drove to Gaston Glock's residence in Atlanta. He had decided to get out. With no preliminaries, Jannuzzo announced to his employer that he was quitting. Bereczky was leaving with him, Jannuzzo added. At that moment, she was cleaning out her office in Smyrna.

Jannuzzo had brought an armful of corporate files with him to the Glock home. He dropped these on the kitchen table and threatened that unless he received a sizable severance payment—something in the millions—he would expose the company's unflattering secrets. By this time, Jannuzzo knew quite a lot about Charles Ewert and the network of shell companies constructed to lessen Glock's tax liabilities. He also knew about the A-Team's investigation, which had turned up evidence linking Ewert and the Glock affiliate in Panama with the notorious Turkish financier Namli. Did Glock want this dirty laundry hung out for the world to see?

Gaston Glock was not used to being threatened. "Why are you doing this to me?" he demanded.

Jannuzzo said he was through being pushed around. He had been running the company in the United States, where Glock,

Inc., made most of its money, and now he wanted his rightful share of the profits.

At this point, Glock stood up and left the room. Remaining with Jannuzzo in the kitchen was Peter Manown, the German-speaking American lawyer who handled Glock's personal business in the United States. The next thing Jannuzzo and Manown heard was the racking of the slide of a semiautomatic handgun. Gaston Glock had loaded a round into the chamber.

"Paul, did you hear that?" asked a rattled Manown.

Jannuzzo didn't seem scared. He patted his ankle, allowing Manown to see that he had a holster there and a pistol of his own. It might have been a scene out of a bad thriller, if not for the fact that the guns and the clashing egos were real.

Gaston Glock returned to the kitchen with a black plastic pistol grip protruding above his belt. "I didn't know if we were going to have a shootout at the O.K. Corral, or what," Manown said later.

There was more shouting and some finger-pointing, but in the end, neither man pulled his gun. Jannuzzo scooped up his files and left, bellowing at Glock: "You're history!"

Word of the row in Gaston Glock's kitchen naturally spread through the gun industry. Jannuzzo's friend Richard Feldman heard about it directly from Gaston Glock. The Austrian called Feldman, a Glock consultant. "Richard, Paul has gone crazy!" Glock said. "What is wrong with Paul?"

"I was like, 'Oy,'" Feldman recalled. "It was really about Monika more than anything else."

/ / /

Amorous rivalry doubtless played a role. Feldman also suggested that his friend Jannuzzo's behavior in general had become erratic. On several occasions over the years, Jannuzzo had gotten drunk and passed out during trade shows or other industry gatherings. Once, hotel security found him late at night asleep under a banquet room table, his suit jacket and slacks folded neatly beside him, Feldman said. Another time, Jannuzzo blacked out in a hotel elevator and was discovered with the elevator doors bouncing against his outstretched legs. "As a result of this problem, I guess you'd call it, I don't think he was always thinking at his best," Feldman commented.

And perhaps also weighing on Jannuzzo's mind in 2003 was his anxiety over his role in some unconventional internal company financial dealings. He and Manown, it turned out, had been taking advantage of Glock's sales success to supplement their paychecks beyond officially agreed-upon salaries and bonuses. While they were less ambitious in this regard than Ewert, the two Glock lawyers for some time had used a variety of accounting tricks to siphon company cash into their pockets.

Asked years later during sworn testimony to explain his misdeeds, Manown offered this candid if illogical rationalization: "Glock is not Snow White. He's got a lot of skeletons. He's done, in my mind, a lot of things that are much worse than what Jannuzzo and I did. He makes roughly $200,000 a day—he personally. He spends money on mistresses, on houses, on sex, on cars. He bribes people. He's just a bad guy. And with all this money laying around, he needed it like a hole in the head, and we just, you know, we let our greed and our ethical standards slip." To underscore the point, he added: "It wasn't like we were stealing from Mother Teresa."

At the time he quit, Jannuzzo was hoping he could walk away without negative consequences. His attempt to squeeze his employer for a fat severance payment in exchange for keeping his mouth shut illustrated just how cocky Jannuzzo had become.

Manown was a far less confident individual. He learned in fall 2003 that Glock suspected his lawyers in America of impropriety. Seized with fear and guilt, Manown descended into a paralyzing state of depression. Then he decided to come clean. Manown flew to Austria and confessed everything to Gaston Glock, begging not to be sent to prison. He admitted that he and Jannuzzo had skimmed money from company real estate transactions. They pilfered other funds, he said, by having Glock, Inc., pay phony insurance premiums to a bogus liability carrier they themselves created in the Cayman Islands. They routed tens of thousands of dollars that was not theirs to personal accounts. They did it because they thought no one would notice. "There was so much money flying around in this company," Manown later said. "It was like Monopoly money."

Glock certainly did not absolve Manown, but he suggested a deal. In exchange for a degree of lenience, the lawyer would tell all, repay what he could to the company, and help ensnare Jannuzzo. Manown agreed.

Gaston Glock had his outside lawyers bring Manown's tale of fraud to the authorities in Cobb County, Georgia, where Glock, Inc., was a prominent corporate citizen. Local prosecutors debriefed a chagrined Manown, and eventually he was permitted to plead guilty to low-level embezzlement charges. He received a notably light sentence: no time behind bars, ten years probation, and surrender of his law license. He turned over $650,000 to Glock in restitution. There was no press conference, sparing Manown public embarrassment.

/ / /

As with the investigation of Ewert, the Cobb County probe of Manown shed light on matters that Gaston Glock could not have wanted anyone to know about. For one thing, Manown told prosecutors, Glock, Inc., had arranged illegal political campaign contributions—with the approval of Gaston Glock.

Manown told the district attorney's office that he and Jannuzzo had withdrawn tens of thousands of dollars from corporate bank accounts and distributed it to fellow employees and spouses with the understanding that the recipients would make individual donations to candidates favored by the company. As described, this activity, undertaken over a decade, would have been illegal for two reasons. Federal law prohibited Glock, Inc., as a foreign-owned entity, from making any direct contributions to US political campaigns. Using employees as fronts did not make the donations legal. Indeed, disguising corporate contributions by breaking them up and funneling them through third parties constituted a separate crime.

The contribution conspiracy was not a rogue operation, Manown told prosecutors under oath. "This was all done . . . with Mr. Glock's blessing." He detailed how he withdrew money from a Glock account in increments of $9,000, "so it would stay under the reporting radar of the bank," referring to the federal anti–money laundering rule that requires banks to report to the US Treasury any cash withdrawal of $10,000 or more. Purposely evading the cap is yet another federal crime.

Federal campaign donation records show that from 1991 through 2004, Glock employees made more than one hundred individual contributions to congressional candidates, worth a total of at least $80,000. Manown kept a handwritten ledger enumerating some of these transactions. A November 1, 2000, entry shows $60,000 designated for "Bush election campaign per GG and PJ 4 RF." It appears that "GG" stood for Gaston Glock, "PJ" for Paul Jannuzzo, and "RF" for Richard Feldman, the company consultant. It is not clear what happened to that $60,000. (Feldman said he knows nothing about it.)

Among the congressional recipients of Glock employee donations were Representatives Bob Barr and Phil Gingrey and Senator Saxby Chambliss—all Georgia Republicans. Those three beneficiaries of Glock largesse said that they were unaware of unlawful contributions, if any had been made. Chambliss's office said in 2009 that, just to be on the safe side, it would return all Glock-affiliated donations from that period.

/ / /

The Glock Monopoly money flowed in other, even less likely, directions. One was the promotion of Jörg Haider, the right-wing anti-immigrant Austrian politician from Carinthia. Having earned a reputation for pro-Nazi sympathies, based on his comments praising Hitler and SS officers, Haider traveled in the United States during this period, seeking to repair his public standing. Glock introduced the politician to Richard Feldman over dinner at Canoe, a fashionable Atlanta restaurant. At Glock's behest, and with Glock money, Feldman arranged transportation and hotel accommodations for Haider in New York in 1999 and 2000. "Glock urged me to help Haider overcome some of the [image] problems," Feldman told me.

In Austria, Glock continued to deny that he backed Haider. The industrialist sued both an Austrian newspaper and a politician there for describing him as a supporter of Haider, and the litigation had the desired effect: The Glock-Haider relationship thereafter received little attention in Austria or anywhere else.

The following January, Feldman arranged for Haider to attend a banquet in New York that marked Martin Luther King's birthday. The Austrian sat on the ballroom dais with other dignitaries. Various Republican notables also attended the King dinner, including New York mayor Rudolph Giuliani, then running against Hillary Clinton for an open seat in the US Senate. When she learned that Giuliani had shared the dais with Haider, Clinton used the juxtaposition to condemn her opponent. "Mr. Haider's record of intolerance, extremism, and anti-Semitism should be a concern to all of us," she wrote in an open letter to the World Jewish Congress. Haider, she noted, had "spoken positively" of Hitler's employment policies, referring to former "Waffen SS members as 'men of character' and concentration camps as 'punishment camps.'" The New York media eagerly amplified Clinton's message. Giuliani, who ultimately dropped his Senate bid, complained that he had been blindsided and did not know who Haider was.

/ / /

Even with Peter Manown's confession, Gaston Glock did not immediately go after Jannuzzo for embezzlement. After quitting the company and marrying Monika Bereczy, Jannuzzo spent several years spiraling downward without Glock's help. His drinking got worse. His driver's license was suspended for a DUI bust. Business ventures did not pan out. And his temper turned violent.

Shortly after midnight on August 26, 2007, the Atlanta police received a 911 hang-up call from the Jannuzzo-Bereczy residence in the upscale Prado neighborhood. Officers dispatched to the scene found Bereczy, who had made the abortive 911 call, outside the house with "a large gash on the left side of her forehead, cuts on her left ear, and bruises on her face, hands, upper and lower arms, neck, and both legs." Bereczy said she and Jannuzzo had fought, that he was inside, and he had "many weapons." When Jannuzzo opened the front door, he insisted everything was fine. "Mr. Jannuzzo was bleeding from a large gash on the back of his head, was slurring his speech, and had an odor of alcoholic beverage emanating from his person," the incident report stated. Police handcuffed and arrested him.

Bereczy said an argument had escalated and that her husband had "punched her in the forehead, opening a wound from a previous beating, and pushed her in her chest, causing her to fall backwards and hit her head on the armoire." She threw a lamp at him. In the ambulance, Bereczy told emergency workers: "He is going to kill me for this. I am a dead woman."

Police found seventeen guns in the house, including an AR-15 semiautomatic rifle and a Remington shotgun. Jannuzzo's ex-wife, Karen Dixon, "stated that when she was married to him, he was very violent. She also stated that it was only a matter of time before this happened," the police report said.

Despite the harrowing bloodshed, Bereczy did not press charges. Jannuzzo, soon released from custody, was never prosecuted for the attack. As happens surprisingly often after domestic abuse, the couple stayed together. But Jannuzzo's troubles with the law were not over.

In late January 2008, police returned to Jannuzzo's home and arrested him again, this time for stealing from Glock. Acting through his American attorneys, the gun maker had urged Cobb County authorities to use Peter Manown's confession, combined with company documents, to prosecute Jannuzzo. "The implications were that approximately $5,000,000 had been embezzled from the Glock Group by Mr. Manown, Paul Jannuzzo, and others," according to a Smyrna Police

Department investigative report. The formal indictment of Jannuzzo, filed in May 2008, referred to the theft of far smaller amounts, but sums that could not be written off as incidental withdrawals from the petty cash drawer.

Prosecutors claimed, for instance, that Jannuzzo and Manown had pocketed $177,000 in payments to the phony Cayman Islands insurance company they created. The pair allegedly skimmed another $98,633.80 from a company bank account in Atlanta. And in September 2001, Jannuzzo had a law firm holding Glock funds pay a $16,000 bill for custom cabinetry installed in his home, according to the indictment. All told, prosecutors accused Jannuzzo of having a hand in the theft of more than $300,000. For good measure, the indictment said that Jannuzzo stole a single handgun from his former employer. The pistol—not a Glock—was among the weapons confiscated from Jannuzzo's house the evening he was arrested for beating his wife.

///

I caught up with Jannuzzo in June 2009. He had been released on bail, pending trial, as the wheels of criminal justice were turning slowly in Cobb County. He was not in good shape. He had gained weight, and his face looked puffy. Rather than the neat business suits I recalled when he was flying high with Glock, he wore rumpled trousers and a Hawaiian-style short-sleeved shirt. His wife, Monika, had moved to Holland to take a job there, he said. He was traveling back and forth to Europe, but now was short on money. His car was in the shop, and he could not afford to pay the repair bill.

We met at a noisy downtown restaurant in Atlanta, along with my *BusinessWeek* colleague Brian Grow, who lived in the city. Echoing Manown's "Monopoly money" theme, Jannuzzo described financial practices within the company as unorthodox in the extreme. He said he and Glock first discussed reimbursing company employees for political contributions as early as 1993. "He would say, 'How are we doing? What do the candidates look like? Do we need to make some contributions?'" Glock, he added, knew "100 percent" that disguising donations in this manner violated US law.

He admitted that he and Manown had routed corporate funds to themselves. Some of that money flowed with Glock's approval into the shadow political contributions, Jannuzzo said. He blamed Manown for devising other stratagems, such as the payments to the fake liability insurance company in the Caymans. Jannuzzo insisted that if it appeared that he, too, had embezzled, that was only because he had followed Manown's lead. "Take care of this for me," he quoted Manown as telling him, implying that he had been more of a passive player.

Jannuzzo offered a plausible description of how Gaston Glock, with Charles Ewert's assistance, had set up the system of shell companies to shelter Glock, Inc., profits from taxation in the United States. He handed us a copy of a whistle-blower filing he had submitted to the Internal Revenue Service. "Gaston Glock owns 100% of Glock Inc., a firearms manufacturer in Smyrna, Georgia, through various subsidiaries," the filing began. "He has organized an elaborate scheme to both skim money from gross sales and to launder those funds through various foreign entities. The skim is approximately $20.00 per firearm sold." Multiplied by hundreds of thousands of guns a year, according to Jannuzzo, the amount insulated from US taxes came to $9 million or $10 million annually.

As far as Jannuzzo was concerned, he was being persecuted by his former employer. If Glock wanted to play rough,

Jannuzzo planned to fight back. Exposing Glock's practices in *BusinessWeek* was part of the fight.

It was a compelling story: the murder attempt in Luxembourg, the shell companies, the salvos of fraud allegations, and, all the while, Glock's overwhelming commercial success. In September 2009, my editors at the magazine put the feature on Glock on the cover with the headline GLOCK'S SECRET PATH TO PROFITS. A sub-headline elaborated, "It's the largest supplier of handguns to law enforcement in the US. But behind its success lies a troubling tale of business intrigue." The IRS was investigating Jannuzzo's allegations, the article reported, and had interviewed the wayward lawyer.

/ / /

Glock, Inc., responded with indignation to Jannuzzo's accusations. Company executives refused to sit for interviews and said that Gaston Glock would not talk. But in response to written questions, Carlos Guevara, Jannuzzo's successor as in-house counsel, stated the company's position in a letter. "GLOCK has acted lawfully and properly throughout its history," Guevara said, noting that he had been authorized to speak on behalf of Glock, Inc., and Gaston Glock personally. On the one hand, Guevara argued, "the GLOCK companies are exceptionally well-run and managed." On the other hand, he added, Ewert, Jannuzzo, and Manown, three of Gaston Glock's top lieutenants, were enmeshed in civil and criminal proceedings accusing them of major fraud, deception, and, in Ewert's case, murderous violence.

If that is "exceptional management," one shudders to imagine what shoddy management looks like. Guevara did not acknowledge any inconsistency. "GLOCK," he wrote, using the

all-capital-letter style the company favors, "was able to withstand the damage inflicted by a few bad apples years ago.

"GLOCK's tax filings and reporting are accurate," he continued. "GLOCK underwent a series of comprehensive gov-
ernmental audits going back to 1988, the last being in 2005 in
Austria and 2006 in the United States. . . . No audit has ever
resulted in findings of tax fraud in any jurisdiction." I asked
about the concerns raised by the company's own internal investigation about the connection between Reofin International,
the Panamanian Glock affiliate, and the Turkish financier
Namli. "To the extent your questions imply that GLOCK has,
or is, involved with a banking institution in Turkey or Turkish
Republic of Northern Cyprus, GLOCK has never had such a
relationship." The question, of course, had been whether Reofin, which was owned by Gaston Glock, had ever had such a
relationship.

On the topic of political contributions, Guevara asserted:
"GLOCK has never authorized (and would never authorize)
any act that would violate United States campaign finance
laws. Manown and Jannuzzo stole over $500,000 of GLOCK
money for themselves and then labeled it as political contributions to hide their crimes. In any event, we conducted our
own due diligence, which revealed that Manown's . . . statement that GLOCK money was spread to employees to make
political contributions is entirely false (except as to Manown
and Jannuzzo). . . . With respect to the allegation that GLOCK
contributed $60,000 to the 2000 presidential political cam-
paign, the evidence shows that Manown stole this money from
GLOCK and transferred it to Cayman Island accounts controlled by Manown and Jannuzzo."

Guevara concluded by questioning the origins and trust-
worthiness of the facts in my article. "GLOCK believes that

you have been provided false information by some unreliable sources, including convicted felons," he wrote.

Putting it charitably, the company and its counsel appeared to miss the point. On the central events that made life within Glock so colorful, there was little dispute: Someone tried to kill Gaston Glock. His top financial lieutenant, Ewert, was convicted of having hired the hit man. Glock endorsed this theory of the crime, and it was Glock who accused Ewert of trying to take control of his company. In the United States, Glock's senior executive, Jannuzzo, and a longtime lawyer, Manown, were implicated in stealing from the company—again, with much of the evidence coming from Glock itself. Other evidence came from Manown, who provided prosecutors with a detailed confession.

The important thing is not precisely how much money Jannuzzo and Manown devoted to illegal political donations versus how much they allegedly hid in the Cayman Islands or simply stuffed into their wallets. What is remarkable is that the company operated at all amid such bedlam and that its vital American subsidiary continued to produce healthy profits under such dubious stewardship. That the polymer pistols still managed to flow from the factory and sell throughout the United States and the world—despite the executive chaos— was one of the greatest tributes to the intrinsic quality of Gaston Glock's creation.

CHAPTER 19

The Impact of the Austrian Pistol: Good for America?

The city of Charlotte, North Carolina, is friendly territory for gun owners. When the NRA comes to town, a Second Amendment celebration breaks out. Add Sarah Palin to the mix, and you get a glimpse of Tea Party heaven. "The most famous moose-hunting mom in America," the master of ceremonies called Palin at the May 2010 annual meeting of the NRA in Charlotte. The keynote speaker, surrounded by enormous video images of her gleaming smile and chestnut hair, brought an audience of ten thousand at the Time Warner Cable Arena to its feet. "It is so great to be here with you *bitter clingers*," Palin declared, making a sly dig at President Obama. During a 2008 campaign fund-raising event, he had foolishly disparaged "bitter" conservatives who "cling" to guns and religion. The NRA would never let him forget it.

Wearing a flattering black dress and a large jade crucifix, Palin reminded even dispassionate listeners how effectively she can deliver a prepared speech. "No need to load up the teleprompter," she said, reading from a teleprompter. "I've got everything I need written on the palm of my hand." The "lamestream media," she continued, "are trying to portray us Tea Party Americans as being violent or racist or rednecks." She waited a beat before adding: "Well, I don't really have a problem with the redneck part of it!"

When not faced with pesky media questions, Palin makes the Red State case pithily. "Gun ownership is at an all-time high; violent crime is near a thirty-year low," she noted. "The anti-gun groups, they don't deal in common sense." The crowd in Charlotte signaled agreement with one standing ovation after another.

///

A few blocks away from where the nighttime political rallies were held, tens of thousands of NRA members patrolled a vast exposition floor populated by marketers of rifles, revolvers, pistols, shotguns, muskets, flintlocks, and ammunition of every conceivable caliber; bowie knives, binoculars, bullet-casing art, body armor, blood-clotting gauze, and freeze-dried bison burgers; crossbows, slingshots, paintball launchers, paper targets (human-shaped and abstract); pup tents, deer blinds, duck lures, bear whistles, varmint guns, and vacuum-packed ostrich jerky; Civil War regalia, Nazi medals, survivalist literature, earplugs, hearing aids, trigger locks, and liability insurance.

Out of the scores of promotional booths, only one—the black-and-silver walk-in display for Glock—had a line fifty strong waiting to take pictures with its spokesperson. The days of gun shop owners ogling buxom Sharon Dillon were long gone. Glock years earlier had begun hiring R. Lee Ermey, a Marine drill instructor turned actor, to draw attention at public events. Best known for his bravura performance as a sadistic sergeant in the movie *Full Metal Jacket* (1987), Ermey more recently has hosted *Lock 'N Load*, a cable-television show devoted to weapons. Now in his sixties, he presents an ideal-ized picture of a brush-cut retired marine: leathery, trim, and ramrod straight. Hour after hour, "Gunny," as everyone calls him, shook hands with men, gave chaste kisses to their wives, and patted children on the head. The annual NRA conclave draws more couples and families than the uninitiated might guess.

Several young soldiers mentioned that they had just re-turned from service overseas.

"Hoorah!" Gunny responded.

"Glock rocks!" exclaimed one skinny fellow in hunting camouflage.

"Damn right, son," Gunny answered.

The Glock sales staff, wearing pressed chinos and black-and-silver company shirts, looked on with obvious satisfaction.

/ / /

I walked the expo floor with Cameron Hopkins, the former editor of *American Handgunner* and a paid blogger for the NRA website. A compact man whose hobby is hunting ante-lope and buffalo in Africa, Hopkins has marketed guns and ammo professionally for nearly four decades. "You could say that Glock changed the entire market," he commented. "Every major manufacturer in handguns you see here has its version of the Glock—XD, Smith & Wesson, Taurus, the smaller ones—all of them. It's a Glock world when it comes to handguns in America."

Over the years, the look-alikes had come up in quality, Hopkins said. Other companies now offered variations in er-gonomics and trigger mechanics that made their guns slightly different from the Austrian pistol. And some manufacturers, such as Smith & Wesson, sold a wider array of handguns, including updated versions of the traditional revolver. But when it came to modern high-capacity pistols, they were all still following Glock's lead.

We circled back to the throngs at the Glock booth. "What's amazing is that they keep the excitement level high," Hopkins observed. "People flock to it. There's some kind of allure, even though Glock is selling a gun that isn't much different from the gun it sold ten years ago or twenty years ago."

I asked why.

"I think being on television and in the movies so much helps explain that," Hopkins said. Image counts—from Sharon Dillon to R. Lee "Gunny" Ermey, from Tupac Shakur to Bruce Willis to Arnold Schwarzenegger.

/ / /

Several months earlier, I had visited the main European small-arms trade show in Nuremberg, Germany. There, the Glock installation had a Vienna café ambience, with small circular tables and silver plates of delicate butter cookies. Young women dressed in black blouses and slacks served espresso, cappuccino, and mineral water. The European show had a more upper-crust feel than the NRA event in Charlotte. Some attendees wore forest-green hunting jackets woven from hemp and were accompanied by well-behaved spaniels.

I stopped by the display of Steyr, the manufacturer Glock eclipsed during the competition in the early 1980s to supply the Austrian Army with new pistols. Steyr continues to make high-quality law enforcement rifles, and, over the years, it has designed respectable pistols, as well. But its handguns never caught on in the United States.

A Steyr rep named Gundaccar Wurmbrand-Stuppach demonstrated the features of his company's latest nine-millimeter. "This has many advantages over the Glock," he said, snapping back the slide. "Our pistol rests more naturally in the hand— you see?"

I hefted the unloaded Steyr, which was considerably heavier than a Glock. It felt no more "natural" in my grasp. I asked whether Steyr was selling many pistols in the States.

No, not that many, Wurmbrand-Stuppach acknowledged. He seemed deflated by the question and dropped his sales pitch. "Glock got there first a long time ago," he said. "Now it is hopeless, it seems. The Glock is the U.S.A. pistol."

/ / /

Is it a good thing that the Glock is the "U.S.A. pistol"? How has the company used its leadership position as the market changed over from the revolver to the semiautomatic?

Glock's predominance has not been good for Steyr, obviously, or for Smith & Wesson, Colt, or any other handgun manufacturer that covets Glock's revenue stream. The flip side of competitors' frustration is that for Americans inclined to buy a pistol, Glock has offered a dependable, reasonably priced product. This goes for police departments, the FBI, security-minded homeowners, and weekend target-shooters. Viewed strictly through a commercial lens, Glock is a winner in the globalized economy: a foreign raider that caught American manufacturers snoozing.

Gun-control advocates condemn this success. "Glock changed the industry—and not in a good way," Josh Sugarmann told me. Beginning in the late 1980s, the pioneering Glock 17 nine-millimeter helped spread enthusiasm in the

United States for semiautomatic pistols. The move from revolvers to pistols brought with it the prevalence of large-capacity magazines: seventeen rounds instead of six, in the case of the exchange of a Smith & Wesson .38 for a Glock 17. Then, in the 1990s, Glock persuaded many Americans to switch to larger calibers with more "stopping power." The .40-caliber Glock, equivalent to a ten-millimeter, became the standard sidearm for many beat cops and also a popular item in Main Street gun shops. During the same period, the Austrian manufacturer led the way in introducing more compact models in calibers ranging from the nine-millimeter to the .45. The marketing of these Pocket Rockets was aided by the NRA's push for more permissive concealed-carry laws and, inadvertently, by the passage of the 1994 assault weapons ban, which included the ten-round limit on magazines.

"The gun industry has deliberately enhanced its profits by increasing the lethality—the killing power—of its products," according to Tom Diaz, Sugarmann's longtime colleague at the Violence Policy Center in Washington. Elaborating in his book *Every Handgun Is Aimed at You: The Case for Banning Handguns* (2001), Sugarmann asserts: "Three specific design features enhance killing power: the 'three deadly C's' of concealability, capacity, and caliber." Glock has been a pioneer in all three categories.

/ / /

In assessing whether the gun controllers' indictment holds water, it is necessary to address a few aspects of gun ownership and use in American society that go beyond the story of Glock. Still, what follows is not a comprehensive survey of the gun-control debate, a sprawling conflict polluted by polemics and cherry-picked statistics. As a practical matter, it is a debate that, at least since the 2000 presidential election, when NRA activism helped defeat Al Gore even in his home state of Tennessee, the Democrats have abandoned. Gun rights have expanded steadily for more than a decade, and nothing will alter that tendency in the foreseeable future. It is not necessary to mourn or cheer these developments to evaluate Glock's role in the United States. Instead, this analysis assumes that guns are good *and* bad—like gasoline-powered cars that take people to work while degrading the environment and being involved in fatal accidents; like tasty steaks loaded with cholesterol and calories; like an Internet that purveys vital information, idiotic conspiracy theories, and vile child pornography. Barring repeal of the Second Amendment and a profound shift in the collective psyche of a large portion of our population—neither likely—guns are here to stay.

/ / /

One hard truth of civilized life, George Orwell noted, is that we rely on strong, bold people with weapons to protect us from those who might kill us for our possessions or politics or religious beliefs or real estate. Accepting this reality, we give the police and the military weapons to do the job of protection. The Glock, though not without imperfections, gets the job done.

"It is the gun you want to have if you get in trouble," Eamon Clifford, a former Washington, DC, cop told me. Clifford was in two shootouts in the early 1990s; in both cases, his conduct was deemed justified. Now a trade union organizer, he acknowledged that the Glock's light trigger pull can lead to accidents: "You can fire a Glock pretty easy if you're not real careful." Then he added: "Being careful is what you should be with guns, you know what I mean?"

In the law enforcement context, the issues of caliber and ease of concealment that so concern gun-control advocates seem, on close inspection, mostly theoretical. Uniformed cops wear their guns openly on a utility belt. If detectives and federal agents who work in plain clothes prefer a smaller firearm that is easier to hide beneath a jacket, that choice seems reasonable. In any event, an old-fashioned snub-nose .38 Smith & Wesson was also relatively easy to conceal. Criminals who wish to hide handguns can do so regardless of brand. The wisdom of permissive concealed-carry laws is also a separate issue.

Debates about appropriate bullet caliber (diameter) descend quickly into nuance that can create confusion as much as add clarity. With an equivalent design and propellant charge, a larger-caliber bullet will do more tissue damage than a smaller round. As a result, the stopping power of a single larger round should be greater. Assuming the cops are shooting at the right people—bad guys threatening violence—the goal is for police rounds to knock down targets with the minimum number of shots. That protects the safety of both officers and bystanders. Replacing the .38 revolver with the nine-millimeter pistol had no significant effect in this regard; bullet diameter did not change meaningfully.

Glock's marketing of the .40-caliber in the 1990s presumably increased stopping power for departments that traded up. The gun exchanges may not have been absolutely necessary. They certainly generated a large supply of used police guns that were resold to civilians. New Orleans and many other cities were ultimately embarrassed by their eager participation in Glock's crafty trade-in program. But the .40-caliber pistol seems like a sensible tool in the hands of a carefully trained police officer.

Firearm calibers do not have inherent moral qualities. It's worth recalling that in contrast to some police agencies, the US military traded *down* in the 1980s, exchanging its .45-caliber Colt 1911 pistols for nine-millimeter Berettas. The Pentagon decided that on the battlefield, it was smarter to carry more rounds, even if they were smaller. The generals also hoped that less experienced shooters would be more accurate with a lighter, lower-recoil handgun. It is difficult to say whether these choices made a significant difference. In any case, they do not seem irrational. A couple of well-placed bullets of any standard caliber will do grievous harm.

A more troubling question about the Glock is whether its large capacity and ease of use can exacerbate the occasional incident in which cops fire what seems like an excessive number of rounds. The barrage of forty-one bullets sprayed at Amadou Diallo by four NYPD officers in February 1999 underscored this danger. Approached after midnight in the vestibule of his apartment building in the Bronx, Diallo reached for his wallet. The officers, who thought he resembled a crime suspect, fatally compounded their error by confusing his wallet for a gun. The unarmed twenty-two-year-old immigrant from Guinea was hit nineteen times and killed. All four of the officers carried nine-millimeter semiautomatic pistols. One was a Glock, two were Sig Sauer models, and one was a Smith & Wesson. Those are the three brands authorized by the NYPD. Despite the statistical underrepresentation of Glock in this tiny sample, it is fair to say that New York, like most other American cities, was converted to large-capacity pistols by the Austrian manufacturer.

Media coverage of the Diallo killing, as well as community reaction, understandably focused on the disturbing death of an innocent young black man at the hands of white officers. Beyond this persistent and disquieting subtext of urban law enforcement, there was the question of whether use of the Glock and other semiautomatic pistols encouraged "contagious shooting"—the perceived tendency of jittery policemen to pull the trigger reflexively because fellow officers are doing so. It seems likely that the Diallo affair would have involved fewer rounds fired if the more aggressive shooters had had to reload six-shot revolvers. Fewer rounds could have led to fewer hits. Still, officers who panic with semiautomatics probably would panic with revolvers, too. "It's much more about training, accountability, and protocol than it is about the weapon," Paul Chevigny, a law professor at New York University, observed in an interview after the 1999 incident. "I don't want to sound cold-hearted; Mr. Diallo might be alive if they hadn't had automatic weapons, but I don't think it makes that much difference." The four officers in the Diallo shooting were prosecuted criminally and acquitted of all charges.

Doubts about police use of semiautomatics resurface every several years. In New York, the November 2006 police killing of Sean Bell, a twenty-three-year-old black man, sparked controversy because officers fired fifty shots into the victim's parked car. Police incorrectly thought Bell and several friends had a gun. In a confused confrontation, Bell tried to ram an undercover NYPD van, police said. Once the late-night shooting was over, it appeared that police had not been in mortal danger from Bell's party. Three officers were charged criminally and acquitted.

In rare circumstances, such as the Diallo and Bell shootings, police officers who rightly or wrongly believe they are threatened do seem to incite one another into a flurry of disproportionate shooting. Glocks and other large-capacity semiautomatics facilitate the tendency. On the other hand, there is not any solid social science that documents the frequency of contagious shooting, let alone identifies it as a common occurrence. "As a result, it is not possible to determine the extent of reflexive shootings and whether the phenomenon is increasing or decreasing over time," the Rand Center on Quality Policing concluded in a study released in 2007.

Statistics on the number of rounds individual police officers fire when they use their guns are equally challenging to interpret. As a general matter, cops do not shoot very often. Even in big cities with dangerous neighborhoods, most officers never pull the trigger other than in training. That said, studies of gun discharge rates show that since pistols have become more popular, there has been a substantial escalation from the historic norm of two to three shots per incident with revolvers.

Complicating matters, though, as use of semiautomatics became more common in the late 1990s and 2000s, violent crime rates were falling. In New York, the annual number of police gunfights and the total number of rounds fired have fallen off strikingly. By these latter measures, police are more restrained today than they were when crime rates were rising three and four decades ago.

The rate of fatal shootings by the police in New York had fallen to 0.48 per 1,000 officers in the calendar year before Diallo was killed. That was the lowest pace since 1985. Moreover, the number of NYPD shootings and the shots fired per incident fell as the crime rate dropped during the 1990s, according to city records. In 1995, there were 344 police shootings, with an average of five rounds fired per incident. In 1998, there were 249 shootings, with an average of 3.4 rounds fired. Over the subsequent decade, the number of rounds per incident fell to as low as 3.1 in 2004 and then rose to 5.2 in 2007, the year after the Bell shooting. There is no consensus explanation for the year-to-year changes in this pattern. If, for purposes of a highly cautious back-of-the-envelope estimate, one said that the per-incident rate increased from about three rounds in the 1980s to about four rounds in the 2000s, that constitutes a 33 percent rise, probably attributable to the switch to semiautomatics. You could call that the Glock phenomenon.

To be clear, it would not be fair to blame Glock alone if the police in New York or elsewhere, when they point their guns, are now prone to pull the trigger one or two times more often than they did thirty years ago. Other gun manufacturers have sold plenty of semiautomatics. Glock, though, was the pioneer. It is also important to reiterate that in the aggregate, fewer police bullets are flying today than before Glock and other companies armed American law enforcement with pistols. In 2009, NYPD officers fired a total of 296 rounds, including unintentional discharges. In 1971, the figure was 2,113. The trend is not unique to New York. In many American cities, "we've seen fairly substantial declines across the board in police shootings," said Professor Michael D. White, a former deputy sheriff in Pennsylvania who teaches at John Jay College of Criminal Justice in Manhattan. That promising development is almost certainly linked to the diminished intensity of crime and to better police training—both of which are more important factors than the choice of handgun.

/ / /

The calculus for civilian ownership of the Glock begins with some of the same questions about the gun's suitability and then branches out to encompass whether the Glock has worsened crime in the United States in a distinctive way.

Handguns of all sorts became bigger sellers compared to rifles and shotguns in the 1980s and 1990s. During those decades, firearm makers and the NRA helped persuade many homeowners that rising rates of burglary, assault, and homicide warranted purchasing a handgun for self-protection. Criminologists and public health scholars have engaged in an intriguing and prolific debate over whether the benefits of "defensive gun use"—the justified brandishing or firing of a weapon to deter crime—outweigh potential dangers associated with keeping a gun in the home. It is not necessary to sort out that heated disagreement to observe that Glock helped spark the handgun surge and wider demand for big magazines that make pistols more potent. In its 2010 catalog, the manufacturer boasted that while the Glock 19 is "comparable in size and weight to the small .38 revolvers it has replaced," the pistol "is significantly more powerful with greater firepower and is much easier to shoot fast and true."

Gun-control advocates deplore Glock's marketing strategy. "The rise of handguns to dominance in the marketplace has corresponded with an increase in their efficiency as killing machines," Sugarmann writes. "The human toll in death and suffering exacted by this process has been immense."

This tough rhetoric appeals to many liberal citizens and scholars. But when drained of emotion and set against firearm realities and crime trends, it loses force.

As in the law enforcement context, the gun controllers' objection to the ease of concealing compact Glocks (and other semiautomatics) and the stopping power of larger-caliber models seems like a distraction. Smith & Wesson and Colt both sold small handguns and large-caliber weapons long before Gaston Glock turned his attention from curtain rods to pistols. Shot for shot, either a .45-caliber Colt 1911 or a .44 Smith & Wesson revolver will do more damage than a Glock nine-millimeter.

Still, a Glock, or another large-capacity semiautomatic, can make a very bad situation even worse. During a mass shooting, such as the Luby's massacre in 1991, a deft gunman can fire more rounds and reload more quickly with a modern pistol equipped with hefty magazines. When Seung-Hui Cho slaughtered thirty-two classmates and professors at Virginia Tech in April 2007, he used two pistols: a nine-millimeter Glock 19 and a smaller .22-caliber Walther. Considerable media attention focused on the fifteen-round compact Glock and the fact that it enabled Cho to unleash a greater volume of rounds in less time. Whether his choice of the Austrian brand raised the horrific body count remains a matter of speculation. It probably did.

There is no question that Jared Lee Loughner created more carnage in January 2011 because he brought a newly purchased Glock 19 to a political gathering in a shopping mall in suburban Tucson, Arizona. On a sunny Saturday morning, Loughner, a deranged twenty-two-year-old, opened fire at a constituent meet-and-greet hosted in front of a Safeway supermarket by his congresswoman, Gabrielle Giffords. In just minutes, the gunman sprayed thirty-three rounds, killing six people and wounding thirteen others, including Giffords, who suffered severe brain damage from a point-blank shot that passed through her head. Among the dead were a federal judge and a nine-year-old girl who served on her elementary school student council and wanted to shake hands with the vivacious politician. Loughner used a special oversized magazine, making it possible for him to do much more damage in a matter of minutes than he otherwise might have. He did not stop firing until he had to pause to reload and attendees at the event tackled him.

Since the expiration in 2004 of the ten-round ammunition cap, Glock has led the charge back into the large-capacity magazine business. Sportsman's Warehouse, the Tucson store where Loughner bought his Glock, advertises on its website that "compact and subcompact Glock pistol model magazines can be loaded with a convincing number of rounds—i.e. . . . up to 33 rounds."

The scale of the bloodshed in Tucson, like that at Virginia Tech and Luby's, presents the strongest possible evidence that a restriction on magazine size makes sense. Such a limit would not stop a Loughner or Cho from attacking, but it could reduce the number of victims. Only six states—California, Hawaii, Maryland, Massachusetts, New Jersey, and New York—have their own limits on large magazines. A national ten-round cap seems like a logical compromise that lawful gun owners could easily tolerate. The NRA has concluded otherwise—and pushed the issue off the legislative table.

A problem confronting proponents of magazine restrictions, and critics of the Glock-inspired pistol craze since the late 1980s, is that one cannot correlate the number of guns in the United States, or the popularity of semiautomatics, with overall crime rates. If seventeen-round Glock magazines provide criminals with more efficient killing machines, to use Sugarmann's evocative phrase, the numbers do not prove that ordinary bad guys, as a group, have taken advantage of this edge.

Starting in the early 1960s, crime levels began increasing after a long period of stability. Criminologists generally attribute this trend to a combination of demography (rebellious baby boomers hitting prime crime-committing years), sociology (waves of heroin- and, later, cocaine-related criminality), and racially tinged history (urban riots in the late 1960s, followed by years of decay in inner cities). In the 1960s and 1970s, as crime proliferated, US prison capacity was shrinking and tens of thousands of patients in state mental hospitals were "deinstitutionalized" without adequate arrangements made for their supervision. Some big-city police departments threw up their hands and stopped enforcing minor infractions, aggravating a sense of lawlessness in less-well-off neighborhoods.

Then, after rising from roughly 1963 through 1993, crime began to drop off. In 1993, there were 9.5 murders and non-negligent manslaughters per 100,000 inhabitants, according to the FBI's annual report, *Crime in the United States*. By 2009, the most recent full year for which statistics were available as of this writing, that rate had fallen 47 percent, to 5 per 100,000. As a large subset of violent crime, offenses committed with firearms also fell sharply. Cities, in short, became safer. The reasons are a matter of dispute. Possible factors include a sharp rise in the rate of incarceration, improved policing methods, the burning out of crack-gang rivalries, changes in public housing policy that disperse the poor, and superior emergency medicine protocols that save gunshot victims who in an earlier era would have died.

Pro-gun campaigners posit an additional factor: that expanded rights to carry firearms enacted since the 1990s have deterred criminals, who now must consider whether potential victims will shoot back. The NRA can cite studies to back this up. But the best nonpartisan scholarship on the effect of more permissive carry laws concludes that there is sparse evidence that the statutory changes have had much impact one way or the other.

Liberal advocates such as Dennis Henigan of the Brady Center to Prevent Gun Violence (formerly known as Handgun

Control, Inc.) attribute some of the easing of crime levels in the 1990s to enactment of point-of-purchase background checks and the assault weapons ban. Once again, the activists can point selectively to numbers to buttress their aspirations. But the better social science does not strengthen the gun-control position. More rigorous studies show that the passage of the background check and assault weapons laws actually had negligible effects on crime, according to Mark A. R. Kleiman, a professor of public policy at UCLA and one of the country's most incisive and independent-minded criminologists. By the same token, the expiration of the assault weapons ban in 2004 also has had a trifling effect. Polls show consistently that even most people who support stricter gun control do not believe such laws reduce violent crime. "At some basic level," Henigan writes with palpable regret, "the public is convinced that 'When guns are outlawed, only outlaws will have guns.' This belief cannot help but diminish the intensity of public support for further gun restrictions."

A dirty little secret of the criminological profession is that the experts cannot account for why murder and rape have waned to the degree they have. "If I could predict the crime rate, I would become a stock broker," Barry Krisberg, the president of the National Council on Crime and Delinquency, admitted in 2009. The diversity and volume of potential variables have defied scholars' explanatory capacity.

Sarah Palin got at least one important point right at the 2010 NRA convention: The total number of guns in private hands in the United States is at an all-time high, yet violent crime is back down to where it was in the early 1970s, before most of the modern spike. The murder rate is even lower—at the level of the early 1960s. Anti-gun groups, to their discredit, tend to paper over this good, if difficult-to-explain, news. It makes their fund-raising and lobbying more challenging. Indeed, falling crime rates help explain why these advocates have failed to enact any meaningful new federal gun-control legislation since 1994. Even a series of sensational school shootings in 1999 did not lead to additional national restrictions. Voters and politicians lose interest in alarm about guns during periods when overall crime is down.

Arguing that the Glock and other semiautomatic handguns cannot be held neatly responsible for variations in American crime rates is not the same, however, as saying that there is no relationship at all between gun prevalence and violent crime. Compared to other industrialized Western democracies, the United States does not have an especially high level of crime, or even of violent crime. What it has, Kleiman writes in *When Brute Force Fails: How to Have Less Crime and Less Punishment* (2009), is "a startlingly high level—about five times the Western European/Canadian/Australian average—of homicide. It also has an astoundingly high level of private gun—especially handgun—ownership." The difference in gun homicide rates is linked to differences in the greater lethality in the United States of robbery, residential burglary, and aggravated assault. And that greater lethality accounts for much of the difference in overall homicide rates.

Guns, in other words, make American criminals deadlier. If the prevalence of gun-carrying among criminals in the States resembled that of British or Canadian offenders, the American homicide rate would be closer to the preferable British or Canadian rates. One reason so many criminals in the United States are armed, Kleiman notes, is that so many Americans generally are armed. There just are a lot of guns around. The

United States has about one firearm per adult, not counting those in the hands of cops and soldiers. What is more, decently made guns last for generations.

Would reducing the sheer number of handguns in private hands by some fraction produce an equivalent reduction in homicide? Not necessarily. Most handguns are owned by law-abiding people who would not dream of sticking up a convenience store or robbing a crack dealer. Social scientists have done studies that allow them to assess the effects of hypothetical policy changes. A law that reduced overall handgun possession by 10 percent could shrink the number of homicides by a maximum of 3 percent, with no measurable effect on other crimes, according to UCLA's Kleiman. Taking the far more dramatic step of reducing gun prevalence to Western European or Canadian levels, of course, would have a much larger impact on the homicide rate.

Enacting such sweeping policies, though, is a pipe dream given the Second Amendment and the fact that Democrats have dropped the gun-control cause. President Obama made noises about stiffening restrictions during the 2008 campaign but has done absolutely nothing on the issue since taking office, much to the consternation of the gun-control lobby. For the first time, in 2008, the US Supreme Court stated clearly that the Second Amendment protects an individual right to private possession of handguns in the home, as opposed to a right related to the maintenance of a civil militia or other armed force. The court by a 5–4 vote struck down a Washington, DC, law that effectively prohibited private handgun ownership. In 2010, the high court extended its ruling to other municipalities and states, invalidating a similar law in Chicago. In coming years, jurisdictions with stringent limits on legal handgun ownership will likely either relax those curbs voluntarily or face NRA-inspired court orders to do so.

/ / /

Accepting that there are between 200 million and 300 million guns in private hands in the United States, one can still imagine policy alterations that might put a further modest dent in armed crime. Such adjustments would make it harder for people who should not be trusted with guns to obtain them and make it riskier for those people to carry guns if they do obtain them. One major limit on the efficacy of the background-check law is the loophole that remains for private gun transactions. The Brady instant record check is supposed to screen out categories barred by the Gun Control Act of 1968: children, felons, people under indictment, illegal aliens, and the insane. But the Brady law applies only to regulated gun dealers. An estimated 40 percent of handguns are acquired by private transaction, for which no background check—no paperwork at all—is necessary. That makes no sense. Closing the gaping private-sale loophole and adding more prohibited categories, such as people convicted of more than one violent misdemeanor and those with records of violent crime as juveniles, seem like modest steps that would make it more difficult for the wrong people to get guns. The NRA, of course, opposes these ideas. An initiative that even the NRA might hesitate to dispute would address the failure of many states to transmit to the federal background-check database all existing records of people who have been officially deemed mentally unstable.

Stepping up the use of ballistic fingerprinting—the technique that digitally matches spent shell casings from crime scenes to guns—is another good idea. It would require liberating federal investigators from a variety of existing legislative limits on compiling a national database for tracing weapons to criminals. And this brings us back to the Glock. Modest as current tracing capabilities may be, they have revealed that the discrepancy persists between the Glock's image as a leading crime gun and reality on the streets. Although glamorized as the gun preferred by gangsters and thugs, it has not become one of the guns most commonly traced to crimes.

Large numbers of crime-gun traces are thought to suggest makes and models that criminals prefer. The NRA objects to this use of gun traces, but it is accepted by many criminologists. One of the unfortunate constraints Congress has imposed on gun tracing since 2003 bars the BATF from releasing data on which guns are traced most frequently. Before the restriction was enacted, the agency from time to time disclosed rankings. In 2002, *Time* obtained a BATF study of 88,570 guns recovered from crime scenes in forty-six cities in 2000. Number one on the top ten list was the Smith & Wesson .38-caliber revolver. The next four were pistols manufactured by Ruger, Lorcin, and Raven Arms and a Mossberg twelve-gauge shotgun. Glock did not appear on the list at all.

///

Glock, then, is not a particular villain within the fraternity of firearms. Nor is it a hero—regardless of what Hollywood tells us on both scores. As a weapon, a means of self-defense, and a source of recreation, the Austrian pistol has many positive attributes. It also has aspects now shared by many brands, such as large ammunition capacity, that can be problematic, even fatal.

Gaston Glock is one of the giants in handgun history, deserving of mention alongside Colt, Browning, Smith, and Wesson. Glock executives exploited the frequently ill-conceived attacks of anti-gun activists, turning the imported pistol into an object of Second Amendment enthusiasm. Throughout their history, the company and the gun have enjoyed tremendous good luck and uncanny timing.

As an organization, Glock has not been propelled by high-mindedness, but rather by profits—nothing unusual there; that is the way of capitalism. Given opportunities to help lead its industry toward compromise with its political antagonists in the United States, Glock flirted with moderation—*feigned* moderation might be a more accurate description—and then consistently acted in its own interest. It is a company created to do one thing: manufacture and sell pistols. And this Gaston Glock has done extraordinarily well.

CHAPTER 20

Epilogue

On April 11, 2011, the FBI held a ceremony in North Miami Beach to honor the agents whose deaths and injuries a quarter century earlier marked one of the Bureau's darkest hours and helped usher in the era of the Glock pistol. The folklore of the Miami Shootout has only gotten more inaccurate over time. In its report on the memorial, the Associated Press recounted a fierce battle in which the criminals "didn't go down easily, outgunning the agents' revolvers with machine guns." Of course, the bank robbers did not have fully automatic machine guns; they had a semiautomatic rifle and a shotgun. And some of the FBI agents did have large-capacity semiautomatic pistols and their own shotguns. No matter. In the wake of the shootout, Gaston Glock responded to a perceived need among law enforcement agencies for greater firepower, and the rest is mythology.

The Glock's hold on the American imagination remains as powerful as ever. As the FBI recalled its fallen agents, HBO was entertaining viewers with *Cop Out*, a buddy flick starring Bruce Willis, the actor who first introduced the Glock to Hollywood audiences in 1990. Appearing for the umpteenth time as a cynical cop with a heart of gold, Willis jokes his way with costar Tracy Morgan through the action comedy about a pair of NYPD detectives whose search for a valuable rare baseball card leads to violent shenanigans. Rick Washburn, still the premier East Coast weapons prop man, supplied the guns for *Cop Out*, which first appeared in theaters in 2010. He gave Morgan, who had never held a gun before, a standard Glock 19 for most of his scenes. Warner Bros. promoted the picture in print and Internet advertisements with the slogan "Rock Out with Your Glock Out."

/ / /

As a marketing operation, Glock rarely catches a bad break. In 2011, the company introduced several modest updates for what it calls its Gen 4 models: A "rough textured frame surface" offers a more secure grip. Replaceable "back straps" allow the user to adjust the size of the handle. A redesigned dual spring assembly reduces recoil. The reviews were uniformly warm. "We ran about 200 rounds through the gun and experienced nothing even close to a malfunction," said *Guns & Ammo.* "The enhancements have done nothing more than improve its shootability," added *Handguns.* The conservative political publication *Human Events* included three Glock models in its December 2010 list of the "Top Ten Concealed Carry Guns," more than any other manufacturer's.

Although characteristically secretive about specific financial results, Glock, Inc., announced it had enjoyed "record sales" for fiscal 2010, and growth in both profits and market share. The company now manufactures some of its pistols in Smyrna, as opposed to just assembling them there. It unveiled plans to build four new buildings on eighteen acres in the

Atlanta suburb. Local authorities heralded the expansion as a source of one hundred new jobs, on top of the two hundred people already working for Glock's US subsidiary.

Law enforcement remains the company's key customer. In late 2010 and early 2011, it delivered Gen 4 pistols to the Hillsborough County Sheriff's Office in Florida; the police department in Charleston, West Virginia; and the Madison County Sheriff's Office in Illinois. In Washington, the BATF ordered new Glocks under a $40 million contract, and the FBI signed another order worth $148 million over a period of years. Glock also won an Army contract valued at $70 million.

Public events continue to favor the company. With relentless lobbying and grassroots activism, the NRA has expanded even further the right to carry handguns in public places. At last count, forty-nine states allow concealed carry (Illinois is the sole exception), and only ten of those require applicants to provide a reason. Arizona, Alaska, Vermont, and Wyoming do not demand any kind of permit at all. This is all good news for a manufacturer known for its concealed-carry weapons.

The Tucson shooting in January 2011 drew some negative media attention to the killer's Glock 19, but gun store managers in Arizona knew better and prepared for a sales rush. Sure enough, in the days after the massacre, they could not keep the Austrian brand in stock. "We're doing double our normal volume," Gregg Wolff, owner of the Glockmeister shop in Phoenix, told Bloomberg News. "When something like this happens, people get worried that the government is going to ban stuff."

It was the same old story: a demonstration of the Glock's potency, even in the hands of a mass murderer, immediately sent firearm buffs out to buy another one. Gun-control advocates called for new restrictions, confirming fears of a crackdown. But then President Obama did not get behind the idea, and it swiftly disappeared in the swirl of Capitol Hill debate about the budget, taxes, and deficit reduction. The ability of Glock, and its industry, to turn even a nebulous threat of new legislative limits to their advantage remains undiminished.

/ / /

Gaston Glock's health faltered in his early eighties, raising questions about his oft-stated intention to live to 120. The future leadership of the company appears uncertain as a result. The founder has not lost his lust for life, however. He and Helga have divorced, and shortly after his eighty-second birthday in July 2011, Herr Glock remarried. His new wife is Katherine Tschikof, the thirty-one-year-old director of the Glock Horse Performance Center, an equestrian academy the gun maker sponsors.

Brigitte Glock, Gaston's daughter, now shares the title of chief executive officer of Glock GmbH with Reinhold Hirschheiter, the company's longtime technical supervisor. Presumably the long-suffering Brigitte no longer feels as if she serves as her father's personal slave. Her ascension to co-CEO sparked rumors that perhaps the Glock family would sell the company, so the founder's three middle-aged children could inherit their millions and walk away from the burdens of overseeing an international corporation. But by mid-2011 there was no sign of a takeover, and the gossip faded. "Most people assume that as long as Gaston is alive, no one is going to buy that company," said Cameron Hopkins, the NRA blogger and longtime marketing consultant.

Jörg Haider, the right-wing politician whom Glock supported financially but denied being friends with, died in a car crash not far from the Glock estate in 2008.

Few of the Americans who as company employees helped make Glock what it is today have shared in its success or wealth:

Karl Walter, the standout salesman, after his falling-out with Gaston Glock never regained the stature he had enjoyed in the industry. He has worked for other gun companies and now serves as a broker, helping arrange deals among manufacturers looking to dispose of or acquire assets. Badly injured years ago in a car accident that almost killed him, a stooped Walter appears fleetingly at trade shows. He looks older than his years and not at all like the free-spending host of hedonistic assemblies at the Gold Club. The FBI, as it happens, shut down Atlanta's infamous adult entertainment establishment after busting its operators for racketeering.

Sharon Dillon, the blond stripper who for a time Walter transformed into the face of Glock, has exchanged her fame for anonymity; she could not be located.

Sherry Collins, the feisty advertising and public relations executive who made her name at Smith & Wesson and then jumped to its more successful Austrian challenger, enjoyed being with a winner but never felt entirely comfortable in Smyrna. She was eventually fired after clashes with Peter Manown, the Glock lawyer who was ousted himself after admitting that he had embezzled from the company. "The whole time I was at Glock I always had a feeling there were wheels within wheels," Collins told me. "They had a very strict but unspoken 'don't need to know' policy. Mostly the people who worked there didn't need to know what was going on in Austria."

Richard Feldman, the durable industry operative who advised Glock for many years, now runs a bed-and-breakfast in New Hampshire with his wife, Jackie, a college administrator. From his rural base, Feldman is trying to organize a politically moderate gun owners' association as an alternative to the NRA. So far, he has not had much luck with the project.

Paul Jannuzzo, Feldman's pal and once Glock's top executive in the United States, remains in limbo as of this writing—behind bars. Not long after *BusinessWeek* published its look at the behind-the-scenes intrigue at Glock in September 2009, Jannuzzo failed to appear for a routine hearing in his prosecution in Cobb County, Georgia, for defrauding the gun manufacturer. Several months later, he was arrested in the Netherlands at the request of the FBI. He had gone to Holland to be with his wife, Monika, the former Glock human relations manager. Jannuzzo fought extradition to the United States for more than a year, but in the spring of 2011, he was finally shipped back to Georgia to face trial. His contention that he had been unfairly accused of impropriety by a resentful former employer was now undermined by his having left the country while under indictment. Also undercut by his conduct were Jannuzzo's claims to the IRS about Glock having evaded US taxes by playing invoicing games involving various shell companies in Europe, Asia, and Latin America. The revenue agency could hardly go after Glock for complicated alleged infractions when the putative main witness allegedly had run away from justice himself.

Jannuzzo's tax allegations seemed plausible, if uncorroborated. He had access to the sort of information that would have allowed him to understand Glock's internal financial convolutions. Indeed, he might have been able to negotiate leniency in a plea bargain if he had admitted to personal wrongdoing, provided detailed and accurate information to the government, and declared himself a chastened man. Instead he made the strange and self-incriminating choice of departing for Europe. His trial in Cobb County was expected to commence in late 2011.

The biggest potential danger Glock faced in the United States—a sophisticated former insider who said he knew damaging secrets—was effectively eliminated. The company claimed vindication, crowed about its healthy sales, and continued to ship its black plastic pistols.

Acknowledgments

Many people who have worked for Glock and elsewhere in the gun industry provided information for this book. Some were willing to be named, others not. I thank them all.

Stuart Krichevsky did his usual exemplary job fine-tuning ideas and finding an excellent publisher. At Crown, Roger Scholl, an outstanding editor, saw what I was trying to accomplish and helped me do it. Rick Willett did careful copyediting. Julie Cohen and Laurence Barrett improved early drafts.

Parts of this book began as articles in what is now *Bloomberg Businessweek*. My former colleagues Brian Grow and Jack Ewing collaborated on a cover story in 2009 that got the process started. Steve Adler and Ellen Pollock oversaw early reporting and gave moral support. At Bloomberg, Norman Pearlstine and Josh Tyrangiel indulged my fascination with the gun industry and in 2011 published another cover story on Glock. Talented comrades and benevolent bosses make all the difference to a journalist.

I would get nothing worthwhile done without my wife, the lovely and brilliant filmmaker Julie Cohen. I owe her everything. Beau, our dachshund, sleeps on my lap when I write.

Selected Bibliography

Ayoob, Massad F. *The Ayoob Files: The Book.* Concord, N.H.: Police Bookshelf, 1995.

————. *The Gun Digest Book of Combat Handgunnery.* Iola, WI: Gun Digest Books, 2007.

————. *In the Gravest Extreme: The Role of the Firearm in Personal Protection.* Concord, N.H.: Police Bookshelf, 1980.

Bascunan, Rodrigo, and Christian Pearce. *Enter the Babylon System: Unpacking Gun Culture from Samuel Colt to 50 Cent.* Toronto: Random House Canada, 2007.

Boatman, Robert H. *Living with Glocks: The Complete Guide to the New Standard in Combat Handguns.* Boulder, Colo.: Paladin Press, 2002.

Brown, Peter Harry, and Daniel G. Abel. *Outgunned: Up Against the NRA.* New York: The Free Press, 2003.

Bush, Jacklyn. *The Gold Club: The Jacklyn "Diva" Bush Story.* Duluth, Ga.: Milligan Books, 2003.

Cooper, Jeff. *To Ride, Shoot Straight, and Speak the Truth.* Boulder, Colo.: Paladin Press, 1998.

Diaz, Tom. *Making a Killing: The Business of Guns in America.* New York: New Press, 1999.

Dizard, Jan E., Robert Merrill Muth, and Stephen P. Andrews, Jr., eds. *Guns in America: A Reader.* New York: New York University Press, 1999.

Feldman, Richard. *Ricochet: Confessions of a Gun Lobbyist.* Hoboken, N.J.: Wiley & Sons, 2008.

Hemenway, David. *Private Guns, Public Health.* Ann Arbor, Mich.: University of Michigan Press, 2004.

Henigan, Dennis A. *Lethal Logic: Exploding the Myths That Paralyze American Gun Policy.* Washington, D.C.: Potomac Books, 2009.

Hofstadter, Richard, and Michael Wallace, eds. *American Violence: A Documentary History.* New York: Random House, 1970.

Horwitz, Joshua, and Casey Anderson. *Guns, Democracy, and the Insurrectionist Idea.* Ann Arbor: University of Michigan Press, 2009.

Kairys, David. *Philadelphia Freedom: Memoir of a Civil Rights Lawyer.* Ann Arbor: University of Michigan Press, 2008.

Kasler, Peter Alan. *Glock: The New Wave in Combat Handguns.* Boulder, Colo.: Paladin Press, 1992.

Kleck, Gary. *Point Blank: Guns and Violence in America.* New York: Aldine De Gruyther, 1991.

Kleck, Gary, and Don B. Kates. *Armed: New Perspectives on Gun Control.* Amherst, NY: Prometheus Books, 2001.

Kohn, Abigail A. *Shooters: Myths and Realities of America's Gun Culture.* Oxford: Oxford University Press, 2004.

Lytton, Timothy D., ed. *Suing the Gun Industry: A Battle at the Crossroads of Gun Control & Mass Torts.* Ann Arbor: University of Michigan Press, 2006.

Sugarmann, Josh. *Every Handgun Is Aimed at You: The Case for Banning Handguns.* New York: New Press, 2001.

Sweeney, Patrick. *The Gun Digest Book of the Glock.* Iola, WI: Gun Digest Books, 2008.

Tonso, William R. *Gun and Society: The Social and Existential Roots of the American Attachment to Firearms.* Washington, DC: University Press of America, 1982.

Viscusi, Kip, ed. *Regulation Through Litigation.* Washington, DC: AEI-Brookings Joint Center for Regulatory Studies, 2002.

Wills, Chuck. *The Illustrated History of Weaponry.* New York: Fall River Press, 2006.

Wills, Garry. *A Necessary Evil: A History of American Distrust of Government.* New York: Simon & Schuster, 1999.

Source Notes

CHAPTER 1

For my description of the 1986 Miami Shootout, I drew from FBI files available online under the title "Shooting Incident 4/11/86 MIAMI, FL," as well as local newspaper coverage from April 1986 in the *Miami Herald*, the *Palm Beach Post*, and the *Sun-Sentinel*. These retrospective articles were also helpful: Will Lester, "One Year Later, Vivid Memories of FBI's Bloodiest Shootout Linger," Associated Press, April 10, 1987, and "FBI Developing New Semiautomatic Weapon for Agents," *Sunday Oklahoman*, December 10, 1989. Massad Ayoob's *The Ayoob Files* provides a forensic analysis of the gunfight on pp. 195–223.

CHAPTER 2

The opening chapters of Peter Alan Kasler's *Glock: The New Wave in Combat Handguns* offer a company-authorized account of Glock's early years. Walter Rauch, "Glock: Gun of the Future," *Glock Autopistols* (2002), pp. 76–79, provides another concise history as the company would have it told. Peter G. Kokalis's article "Plastic Perfection," *Soldier of Fortune*, October 1984, helped introduce Glock to American gun buyers. These reference books also have useful background, although some of it is technical: Patrick Sweeney, *The Gun Digest Book of the Glock* and *The Complete Glock Reference Guide* (Ptooma Productions, 3d edition, 2006). I have drawn on a helpful (and rare) interview of Gaston Glock published by *Forbes* on March 31, 2003, entitled "Top Gun," by Dyan Machan.

CHAPTER 3

For background on the history of firearms in the United States, I recommend *Guns in America: A Reader*, especially pp. 1–8 and all of the other explanatory passages written by the editors, Jan E. Dizard, Robert Merril Muth, and Stephen P. Andrews Jr. Another accessible reference work is Chuck Wills (in association with the Berman Museum), *The Illustrated History of Weaponry*, especially pp. 152–155, 178–179, and 194–197. One of my favorite writers about guns in America is the essayist and critic Henry Allen—for example, "The Mystique of Guns: From Daniel Boone to Dirty Harry, America's Fascination with Firearms," *Washington Post*, April 19, 1989.

CHAPTER 4

As noted in the text, I drew heavily from the October 1984 *Soldier of Fortune* piece by Kokalis, "Plastic Perfection." I also relied on Sweeney's *Gun Digest Book of the Glock,* especially pp. 78–83, and on Wills's *Illustrated History of Weaponry,* p. 153.

CHAPTER 5

The plastic-pistol controversy was ignited by syndicated columns by Jack Anderson and Dale Van Atta, including "Qaddafi Buying Austrian Plastic Pistols," *Washington Post,* January 15, 1986; "Lawmaker Seeks to Ban Plastic Pistols," *Washington Post,* March 14, 1986; and "Concern Growing Over Plastic Pistol," *Washington Post,* April 18, 1986. Other important coverage of the affair included editorials such as "Hijacker's Special?," *New York Times,* February 9, 1986, and "Pass Laws to Ban Plastic Handguns," *USA Today,* February 27, 1986. I also relied on the following articles: Josh Sugarmann, "Progress Gives Us Great New Handgun: Hijacker Special," *Los Angeles Times,* March 24, 1986; Gayle White, "Partly Plastic Gun Comes Under Fire: Critics Say Pistol Would Help Terrorists Evade Metal Detectors," *Atlanta Journal-Constitution,* May 1, 1986; Robert J. Mrazek, "The Deadly Truth About Plastic Guns," *Washington Post,* May 15, 1986; "Lincoln Mayor Sponsors Resolution: Call for Ban on Plastic Guns Triggers Response by NRA," Associated Press, June 17, 1986; and Wayne King and Warren Weaver Jr., "Washington Talk: Gun-Control Struggle," *New York Times,* December 7, 1986.

CHAPTER 6

Helpful coverage of American police departments' adoption of the Glock includes: "Miami Police Get New Firepower," United Press International, July 19, 1987; Kevin Diaz, "Faster Pistol for Police Is Gaining Acceptance: Semiautomatics Replace Revolver," *Minneapolis Star-Tribune,* September 7, 1987; Gerald Volgenau, "Police Being Outgunned by Lawbreakers," Knight Ridder, July 3, 1988; Veronica Jennings, "Union Chief Seeks New Police Guns; More Firepower Needed, Officer Says," *Washington Post,* September 15, 1988; "Top Cop Wards Off Ban on Super Gun," *New York Post,* September 29, 1988; "Police Lift Ban on Gun Ward Carries, a Glock," *New York Times,* September 30, 1988; Karla Jennings, "New Gun 'Ugly,' But Effective, Police Say," *Atlanta Journal-Constitution,* October 13, 1988; Mitch Gelman, "Automatic Guns for NY Narcs," *Newsday,* November 28, 1988; Andrew H. Malcolm, "Many Police Forces Rearm to Counter Criminals' Guns," *New York Times,* September 4, 1990; James C. McKinley Jr., "Subway Police to Get New Pistols," *New York Times,* December 21, 1990; and William Bratton, "Don't Knock the Glock," *Newsday,* September 25, 1991. The killing of NYPD Officer Scott Gadell was described by Robert D. McFadden in "Wide Hunt for Killer of Officer," *New York Times,* June 30, 1986, and "Memory of a Fallen Officer," *New York Times,* May 31, 1992. For background on Samuel Colt, see, e.g., William Hosley, "Gun, Gun Culture, and the Peddling of Dreams," in Dizard, Muth, and Andrews, eds., *Guns in America: A Reader,* pp. 47–85, and Wills's *The Illustrated History of Weaponry,* pp. 130–133.

CHAPTER 7

As noted in the text, Rodrigo Bascunan and Christian Pearce provide colorful background about Glock and the hip-hop world in *Enter the Babylon System: Unpacking Gun Culture from Samuel Colt to 50 Cent*. Dean Speir's website, The Gun Zone (thegunzone.com), has a useful section on Glock.

CHAPTER 8

For this chapter I again relied on Allen's April 19, 1989, *Washington Post* essay "The Mystique of Guns: From Daniel Boone to Dirty Harry," as well as historian Richard Hofstadter's "America as a Gun Culture," *American Heritage* 21, no. 6 (1970), and "Reflections on Violence in the United States," in Hofstadter and Michael Wallace, eds., *American Violence: A Documentary History* (New York: Knopf, 1970). The Billy Bathgate passage is, of course, from E. L. Doctorow's 1989 novel *Billy Bathgate* (New York: Random House).

CHAPTER 9

On the decline of the American gun industry in the 1980s, see Resa W. King, "US Gunmakers: The Casualties Pile Up—Depressed Sales, Costly Insurance, and Foreign Competition Keep Claiming Victims," *BusinessWeek*, May 19, 1986; Kirk Johnson, "Gun Valley Tries to Adapt to the Winds of Change," *New York Times*, March 21, 1989; and Henry Allen, "Uncle Sam Can't Shoot Straight: Our Crooks Use Uzis, Our Cops Glocks—Even the Ammo's Imported," *Washington Post*, March 25, 1990. For my discussion of Smith & Wesson, I relied on "Appointments: Smith & Wesson Corp.," *Financial Times*, December 10, 1987; Robert W. Hunnicutt, "SHOT Show 1990," *American Rifleman*, March, 1990; Charles E. Petty, "Smith & Wesson: In-Store Promotions," *Shooting Industry*, May 1, 1991; Greg Cox, "A Call to Arms: Facing Tough Competition, Smith & Wesson's New CEO Presses Ahead with Sweeping Changes," *BusinessWeek*, November 1, 1992; and William Freebairn, "Smith & Wesson at 150: Springfield Gunmaker Defined by Controversy, Innovation," *Springfield Union-News*, August 4, 2002. For this chapter I again referred to Dyan Machan's March 31, 2003, *Forbes* interview, "Top Gun," and to Wills's *Illustrated History of Weaponry*, pp. 134–137.

CHAPTER 10

I relied on a number of accounts of the Killeen massacre and the tracing of Hennard's Glock, including Kathy Jackson, "Gunman's 9mm Pistol Is Type Often Used by Police: Weapon's Accuracy Credited for Its Popularity," *Dallas Morning News*, October 17, 1991; Tara Parker Pope, "Massacre in Killeen: Nevada County's Tough Gun Laws Failed to Stop Killer," *Houston Chronicle*, October 19, 1991; Nick Ravo, "Gun Used in Slayings Has Lethal Reputation," *New York Times*, October 17, 1991; Linda Rehkopf, "Gun Came from Smyrna: Mother Likely Bought It," *Atlanta Journal-Constitution*, October 18, 1991; and Allan Turner, "Bloodbath in Killeen: 'Ugly' Gun Can Fire 16–20 Shots," *Houston Chronicle*, October 17, 1991. For background on the assault weapons debate in Congress, I read Holly Idelson, "House Members Duel on Crime: Assault-Gun Ban Is Rejected," *Congressional Quarterly Weekly Report*, October 19, 1991, and Matt Yancy, "House Rejects Ban on Assault Rifles, Large Clips," Associated

Press, October 17, 1991. Also of use in writing this chapter were "Of What Legal and Practical Use Is a Glock 9mm Semiautomatic Pistol?" *Atlanta Journal-Constitution*, October 18, 1991; "Gun Ownership Has New Champion: Killeen Massacre Survivor," *Shooting Industry*, June 1, 1992; Mark McDonald, "Under the Gun: As Crime Comes Closer and Closer, More and More City Dwellers Consider Owning and Learning to Use Firearms," *Dallas Morning News*, December 12, 1991; and "Top 18 Handguns Used by Criminals," *USA Today*, June 3, 1992.

CHAPTER 11
To describe the unintended consequences of gun control, I relied on, among other sources: "Brady Bill Triggers Local Run on Guns," Associated Press, December 20, 1993; Michael Arena, "Packing Heat in a Hurry," *Newsday*, December 20, 1993; Robert Davis, "Gun Ban Triggers Sales Rush: President 'Finest Gun Salesman in History,'" *USA Today*, May 10, 1994; Jeannette Regalado and Tina Daunt, "Possible Ban Ignites Rush on Area Gun Shops," *Los Angeles Times*, May 12, 1994; Scott Shane, "Curbs on Guns Are Growing, But So Are Sales," *Baltimore Sun*, May 15, 1994; and Bob von Sternberg, "NRA," *Minneapolis Star-Tribune*, May 25, 1994.

CHAPTER 12
Reports about early problems with accidental discharges include: Gilbert Jimenez, "Police Chief Red Faced After Gun Discharges," *Chicago Sun-Times*, December 20, 1989; Kathleen Ovack, "Gun's 'Hair Trigger' Under Fire," *St. Petersburg Times*, February 19, 1990; Dan Huff, "Accidents Happen, But All Too Often with the Glock 19," *Arizona Daily Star*, November 20, 1990; and "Glock Pistol Under Fire in S.C.: Is It Simple and Safe or a Dangerous Hair-Trigger," Associated Press, December 13, 1994. Washington's transition to the Glock is described in Rene Sanchez, "D.C. Officers Get 9mm Pistols for 'Parity with Drug Dealers,'" *Washington Post*, March 4, 1989; Elsa Walsh, "D.C. Police Pistol Gets Poor Safety Marks," *Washington Post*, April 8, 1989; Jeff Leen, Jo Craven, David Jackson, and Sari Horwitz, "D.C. Police Lead Nation in Shootings: Lack of Training, Supervision Implicated as Key Factors," *Washington Post*, November 15, 1998; and Jeff Leen and Sari Horwitz, "Armed and Unready: City Pays for Failure to Train Officers with Sophisticated Weapon," *Washington Post*, November 18, 1998. To describe the Grant suit in Knoxville, I relied on daily coverage by the *Knoxville News Sentinel*, June 13 through June 21, 1994. Massad Ayoob discussed the Glock in "The Glock Pistol: Perspective from the Field" and "Glock's Perfection Questioned on the Street: Enter the New York Trigger," *GUNS*, September 1990.

CHAPTER 13
Among the articles I relied on to write about the advent of Pocket Rockets were Bill Torpy, "Laws Trigger Newfound Market for Small Guns: Easy to Conceal, They're Being Toted by More Women," *Atlanta Journal-Constitution*, December 16, 1995; "Glock's New Pocket Rockets!" *Guns & Ammo*, January 1996; Massad Ayoob, "Building a Big Market with Small Handguns," *Shooting Industry*, January 1996, and "Presentation Guns Make Ideal Gifts While Increasing

Sales," *Shooting Industry*, February 1996; and Alix M. Freedman, "Tinier, Dead-lier Pocket Pistols Are in Vogue," *Wall Street Journal*, September 12, 1996. For this chapter, I also found useful Massad Ayoob, "'Trend Crimes' and the Gun Dealer," *Shooting Industry*, March 1993; "Headache Cure #2000," *Shooting Sports Retailer*, January 1997; and Tom Diaz, *Making a Killing: The Business of Guns in America*, pp. 69–92.

CHAPTER 14

For this chapter, I drew some material from Dyan Machan's interview, "Top Gun," *Forbes*, March 31, 2003.

CHAPTER 15

The Marion Hammer anecdote comes from David Olinger, Tim Nickens, and Kati Kairies, "Gun-Control Opponents Have Their Hopes Up for This Year," *St. Petersburg Times*, March 12, 1989. For this chapter I also immersed myself in two gun-buff websites: Glock Talk (glocktalk.com) and The Gun Zone (thegun zone.com).

CHAPTER 16

Two first-person accounts of municipal gun politics and litigation were highly valuable for this chapter: Peter Harry Brown and Daniel G. Abel, *Outgunned: Up Against the NRA*, especially pp. 7–67 and 171–234, and Richard Feldman, *Rico-chet: Confessions of a Gun Lobbyist*, especially pp. 232–256. Other helpful sources include "Gun Makers Visit Clinton to Announce Safety Locks," Knight-Ridder, October 10, 1997; Curtis Howell, "Hot as a Pistol: Increasingly Prominent Gun Trade Group Wins Praise for Conciliatory Attitude Behind Safety-Lock Agreement," *Dallas Morning News*, October 25 1997; Terrence Hunt, "Gun Makers Agree to Provide Childproof Locks on Handguns," Associated Press, October 10, 1997; Jim Schneider, "Clinton Applauds Gun Makers at Historical Ceremony," *Shooting Industry*, December 1, 1997; Paul M. Barrett, "Courting Trouble? As Lawsuits Loom, Gun Industry Presents a Fragmented Front— Widening Legal Threat Finds Makers, Sellers Are Split on Issues and Tactics," *Wall Street Journal*, December 9, 1998; Roberto Suro, "Cities Plan Legal As-sault on Makers of Handguns: Tobacco Lawsuits Viewed as Models," *Washing-ton Post*, December 23, 1998; Fox Butterfield, "Results in Tobacco Litigation Spur Cities to File Gun Suits," *New York Times*, December 24, 1998; Alan Sayre, "Watchdog Group: Guns Swap Could Leave City Open for Lawsuit," Associ-ated Press, January 29, 1999; Will Anderson, "Gun Maker Takes Aim at Cities' Lawsuits; Smyrna Glock Plant Chief Sees No Ties Between Anti-Smoking Law-suits and Challenges Against Arms Industry Manufacturers," *Atlanta Journal-Constitution*, February 14, 1999; Paul M. Barrett, "Gun Interests, Philadelphia Mayor to Talk Today," *Wall Street Journal*, June 9, 1999; Paul M. Barrett and Jeffrey Taylor, "Focus of Gun-Control Fight Shifts to Cities, States," *Wall Street Journal*, July 8, 1999; Vanessa O'Connell and Paul M. Barrett, "Ricochet: Cities Suing Gun Firms Have a Weak Spot: They're Suppliers, Too—Police Trade-ins Cut Costs, but Many of the Weapons Land in the Wrong Hands," *Wall Street Journal*, August 16, 1999; Matt Bai, "Clouds Over Gun Valley," *Newsweek*, Au-gust 23, 1999; Paul M. Barrett and Vanessa O'Connell, "White House and Gun

Industry May Discover Some Talking Points to Reach Deal on Lawsuit," *Wall Street Journal*, December 13, 1999; Brigitte Greenberg, "Some NRA Allies Renounce Comments from Group's Leaders," Associated Press, March 21, 2000; "Glock Rejects Gun Control Agreement," Associated Press, March 22, 2000; Russ Thurmon, "Smith & Wesson Agreement Draws Fire," *Shooting Industry*, May 1, 2000; Matt Bai, "A Gun Maker's Agony: Inside Smith & Wesson's Fight to Survive the Crossfire," *Newsweek*, May 22, 2000; Rinker Buck, "Agreement Backfires on Smith & Wesson," *Hartford Courant*, June 14, 2000; Gary Fields, "For Smith & Wesson, Blanks Instead of a Magic Bullet—Nation's No. 1 Gun Maker Signed a Deal to Promote Safety, but Is Still a Legal Target," *Wall Street Journal*, August 24, 2000; and Matt Bai, "A Gun Deal's Fatal Wound: As a Landmark Pact to Control Guns Falls Apart, Smith & Wesson Takes the Hit," *Newsweek*, February 5, 2001.

CHAPTER 17

To describe the attempt on Gaston Glock's life and its aftermath, I relied on Veonique Poujol, "Don't Shoot the Pianist," *Luxemburger Land*, January 18, 2002; Gaenor Lipson, "Hard Lesson for Plasticity Tycoon," *Sunday Times (South Africa)*, November 24, 2002; "Luxembourg Holds Suspected Mastermind of Bid to Kill Gunmaker Glock," Reuters, March 12, 2003; Dyan Machan, "Top Gun," *Forbes*, March 31, 2003; "Court Re-convicts Two in Gun-Maker Murder Trial," Reuters, January 11, 2005, and Paul M. Barrett, Brian Grow, and Jack Ewing, "Glock's Secret Path to Profits," *BusinessWeek*, September 21, 2009.

CHAPTER 18

For background on Haider and his activities in the United States, I relied on Frank Litsky, "From One Marathon to Another for Victors," *New York Times*, November 9, 1999; Alison Smale, "A Rightist Leader Stirs Tepid Dissent, and Assent," *New York Times*, December 6, 1999; Clyde Haberman, "Top Honoree at King Event Is Surprising," *New York Times*, January 6, 2000; Rick Brand, "Hillary Slams Austrian Leader," *Newsday*, January 29, 2000; David Herszenhorn, "Giuliani Outlines Some Foreign Policy Views from Austria to the West Bank," *New York Times*, February 2, 2000; Susan Crabtree, "Hatch, RNC Chairman Drawn into Giuliani Controversy," *Roll Call*, February 3, 2000; Nicholas Kulish, "Jorge Haider, Austrian Rightist, Is Dead at 58," *New York Times*, October 12, 2008; and Paul M. Barrett, Brian Grow, and Jack Ewing, "Glock's Secret Path to Profits," *BusinessWeek*, September 21, 2009.

CHAPTER 19

For my discussion of semiautomatics and gun control, I relied on Mark A. R. Kleiman's excellent *When Brute Force Fails: How to Have Less Crime and Less Punishment* (Princeton, N.J.: Princeton University Press, 2009), especially pp. 8–15 and 136–148. For the gun-control perspective, I read Tom Diaz's *Making a Killing: The Business of Guns in America*, especially pp. 1–16 and 83–84; Dennis A. Henigan's *Lethal Logic: Exploding the Myths That Paralyze American Gun Policy*, especially pp. 1–12 and 37–73; and Josh Sugarmann, *Every Handgun Is Aimed at You: The Case for Banning Handguns*, especially pp. ix–xvii and 1–11. Criminologists' difficulty in explaining crime rates is discussed trenchantly in Shaila

Dewan, "The Real Murder Mystery? It's the Low Crime Rate," *New York Times,*
August 2, 2009. Background on the Virginia Tech killings can be found in Bill
McKelway and Peter Bacque, "Killer Bought Handgun, Ammo Last Month:
Roanoke Shop Owner Says Sales to Cho Didn't Raise Any Suspicions," *Rich-
mond Times Dispatch,* April 18, 2007; Jerry Markon and Sari Horowitz, "Va.
Tech Killer's Motives Pursued: Some Actions During Rampage Still a Mystery,"
Washington Post, April 26, 2007; and Jerry Adler, "Story of a Gun: It's Sleek,
Light, and Frighteningly Lethal. How the 9mm Became the Weapon of Choice
for Cops and Criminals, Civilians and Soldiers—and a Very Sick Young Man
in Virginia," *Newsweek,* April 30, 2007. For background on the Diallo shoot-
ing, I relied on Jodi Wilgoren, "Fatal Police Barrage Renews Debate Over Safety
of Semiautomatics," *New York Times,* February 7, 1999, and Jane Fritsch, "The
Diallo Verdict: The Overview—4 Officers in Diallo Shooting Are Acquitted of
All Charges," *New York Times,* February 26, 2000. On the Sean Bell case, I read
Michael Wilson, "50 Shots Fired, and the Experts Offer a Theory," *New York
Times,* November 27, 2006; Clyde Haberman, "Yes, There's a Trial, but There
Are Also Broader Statistics," *New York Times,* February 29, 2008; and Michael
Wilson, "Police Guns Make Jarring Evidence at Detectives' Trial," *New York
Times,* March 6, 2008. Contagious shooting is addressed by Ray Rivera and Al
Baker in "Bystander Injured in Harlem Episode Cites 'Contagious Shooting' in
Plan to Sue," *New York Times,* August 11, 2010. The *Time* piece on ATF crime
gun traces is Elaine Shannon, "America's Most Wanted Guns," which ran on
July 12, 2002.

CHAPTER 20
The FBI's twenty-five-year memorial is described in Ari Odzer and Brian Ham-
acher, "Memorial for FBI Agents Killed in Miami," Associated Press, April 11,
2011. The positive reviews of Glock's new guns are from Payton Miller, "Glock
17 Gen 4," *Guns & Ammo,* January 2011; Dave Spaulding, "A Handier New
Glock," *Handguns,* December 2010/January 2011; and Mark Walters, "Top 10
Concealed Carry Guns," *Human Events,* December 7, 2010. Gun sales in Arizona after the Tucson shooting are described in Michael Riley, "Arizona Shootings Trigger Surge in Glock Sales Amid Fear of Ban," Bloomberg (Bloomberg.
com), January 12, 2011.

Index

About the Author

Paul M. Barrett, a journalist for twenty-five years, writes feature articles for *Bloomberg Businessweek*, where parts of this book originated. He is the author of two earlier books: *American Islam: The Struggle for the Soul of a Religion* (2007) and *The Good Black: A True Story of Race in America* (1999).